Lecture Notes in Computer Science　　12297

More information about this series at http://www.springer.com/series/7408

Marc Zeller · Kai Höfig (Eds.)

Model-Based Safety and Assessment

7th International Symposium, IMBSA 2020
Lisbon, Portugal, September 14–16, 2020
Proceedings

 Springer

Editors
Marc Zeller 🆔
Siemens AG
Munich, Bayern, Germany

Kai Höfig 🆔
University of Applied Sciences Rosenheim
Rosenheim, Germany

ISSN 0302-9743   ISSN 1611-3349   (electronic)
Lecture Notes in Computer Science
ISBN 978-3-030-58919-6   ISBN 978-3-030-58920-2   (eBook)
https://doi.org/10.1007/978-3-030-58920-2

LNCS Sublibrary: SL2 – Programming and Software Engineering

This Springer imprint is published by the registered company Springer Nature Switzerland AG
The registered company address is: Gewerbestrasse 11, 6330 Cham, Switzerland

Preface

This volume contains the papers presented the 7th International Symposium on Model-Based Safety and Assessment (IMBSA 2020), held during September 14–16, 2020. Due to COVID-19 the conference could not take place as planned in Lisbon, Portugal. Instead IMBSA 2020 took place as a virtual conference.

IMBSA focuses on model-based and automated ways of assessing safety and other attributes of dependability of complex computer systems. Since the first edition in Toulouse (2011), the workshop has evolved to a forum where brand new ideas from academia, leading-edge technology, and industrial experiences are brought together. The objectives are to present experiences and tools, to share ideas, and to federate the community.

To foster academic and industrial collaboration, in addition to more traditional talks reporting on novel advances on hot research topics, the program featured a demo session, where speakers had the opportunity to present industrial experiences, and demonstrate their tool interactively.

We believe that a mixture of conventional talks about the newest achievements, the presentation of practical experiences, and interactive learning facilitates fruitful discussions, the exchange of information, as well as future cooperation. Therefore, following the previous edition of IMBSA in Thessaloniki, Greece (2019), an important focus of this year's edition was placed on tool tutorials and demonstrations. Nevertheless, the main scientific and industrial contributions were presented in traditional talks and are collected in this volume of LNCS.

For IMBSA 2020, we received 30 submissions from authors of 17 countries. Following rigorous review, the best 19 of these papers (15 full research papers and 4 tool demo descriptions) were selected by an International Program Committee to be published in this volume. As organizers, we want to extend a very warm thank you to all 40 members of the International Program Committee. Each submission was reviewed by at least three Program Committee members. The comprehensive review guaranteed the high quality of the accepted papers. We also want to thank the organization team, and our fellow members of the Steering Committee: Marco Bozzano, Leila Kloul, Yiannis Papadopoulos, Antoine Rauzy, and Christel Seguin.

Finally, we wish you a pleasant reading of the articles in this volume. On behalf of everyone involved in IMBSA 2020, we hope you will be joining us at next year's edition.

September 2020

Kai Höfig
Marc Zeller

Organization

General Chairs

Kai Höfig — Rosenheim Technical University of Applied Sciences, Germany

Marc Zeller — Siemens, Germany

Program Committee Chairs

Leila Kloul — Université de Versailles, France

Frank Ortmeier — Otto von Guericke University Magdeburg, Germany

Tools and Tutorials Chair

Yiannis Papadopoulos — University of Hull, UK

Industrial Chair

Kai Höfig — Rosenheim Technical University of Applied Sciences, Germany

Organizing Committee

Koorosh Aslansefat — University of Hull, UK

Kai Höfig — Rosenheim Technical University of Applied Sciences, Germany

Marc Zeller — Siemens, Germany

Program Committee

Jose Aizpurua Unanue — Mondragon University, Spain

Eric Armengaud — AVL, Austria

Koorosh Aslansefat — University of Hull, UK

Ezio Bartocci — Technische Universität Wien, Austria

Stylianos Basagiannis — United Technologies Research Centre, Ireland

Saddek Bensalem — Universirsité Grenoble Alpes, France

Lorenzo Bitetti — Thales Alenia Space, France

Marc Bouissou — EDF, France

Marco Bozzano — FBK, Italy

Jean-Charles Chaudemar — ISAE, France

Marielle Doche-Petit — Systerel, France

Jose Luis de la Vara — University of Castilla-La Mancha, Spain

Jana Dittmann	Otto von Guericke University Magdeburg, Germany
Francesco Flammini	University of Naples, Italy
Lars Grunske	Humboldt University Berlin, Germany
Matthias Güdemann	Input Output, Hong Kong
Ibrahim Habil	University of York, UK
Kai Höfig	Rosenheim Technical University of Applied Sciences, Germany
Michaela Huhn	Ostfalia, Germany
Panagiotis Katsaros	Aristotle University of Thessaloniki, Greece
Leila Kloul	Université de Versailles, France
Agnes Lanusse	CEA LIST, France
Till Mossakowski	Otto von Guericke University Magdeburg, Germany
Jürgen Mottok	University of Regensburg, Germany
Peter Munk	Bosch, Germany
Thomas Noll	RWTH Aachen University, Germany
Arne Nordman	Bosch, Germany
Frank Ortmeier	Otto von Guericke University Magdeburg, Germany
Yiannis Papadopoulos	University of Hull, UK
Antoine Rauzy	Norwegian University of Science and Technology, Norway
Wolfgang Reif	Augsburg University, Germany
Alejandra Ruiz	Tecnalica, Spain
Daniel Schneider	Fraunhofer IESE, Germany
Christel Seguin	ONERA, France
Ioannis Sokoros	University of Hull, UK
Ramin Tavakoli Kolagari	Technische Hochschule Nürnberg, Germany
Pascal Traverse	AIRBUS, France
Elena A. Troubitsyna	KTH, Sweden
Marcel Verhoef	European Space Agency, The Netherlands
Marc Zeller	Siemens, Germany

Steering Committee

Marco Bozzano	FBK, Italy
Leila Kloul	Université de Versailles, France
Frank Ortmeier	Otto von Guericke University Magdeburg, Germany
Yiannis Papadopoulos	University of Hull, UK
Antoine Rauzy	Norwegian University of Science and Technology, Norway
Christel Seguin	ONERA, France

Additional Reviewers

| Roberto Nardone | Mediterranean University of Reggio Calabria, Italy |
| David Mailland Dit Baron | Thales Alenia Space, Italy |

Contents

Safety Models and Languages

A Visual Notation for the Representation of Assurance Cases Using SACM

Nungki Selviandro[1,2(✉)], Richard Hawkins[1], and Ibrahim Habli[1]

[1] Department of Computer Science, University of York, York YO10 5DD, UK
{ns1162,richard.hawkins,ibrahim.habli}@york.ac.uk
[2] School of Computing, Telkom University, Bandung 40257, Indonesia

Abstract. The Structured Assurance Case Metamodel (SACM) is a standard specified by the Object Management Group (OMG) that defines a metamodel for representing structured assurance cases. It is developed to support standardisation and interoperability in assurance case development. SACM provides a richer set of features than existing assurance case frameworks. By providing a standardised metamodel for assurance cases, SACM also provides a foundation for model-based assurance case development. For example, model merging can be used to bind packages in complex assurance cases and model validation can be used to check well-formedness of assurance cases. The uptake in the use of SACM has however been slow. The lack of a visual notation for representing SACM arguments has been a major factor in this. As part of the updates for version 2.1 of the SACM standard, we developed a graphical notation that addresses this need. Additionally, there are very few publicly available examples of how SACM may be used in practice, with the SACM standard providing only very limited examples. Moreover, there exists little literature that discusses the potential benefits that using SACM can bring for assurance cases. This paper provides, for the first time, an explanation and worked examples of how to use the SACM notation. The paper also discusses the potential benefits of using SACM for assurance case development and review and the need for empirically evaluating these benefits.

Keywords: Structured Assurance Case Metamodel · Model-based assurance case · Assurance case notations · SACM notation

1 Introduction

An assurance case is commonly used to provide a clear and structured basis for analysing and communicating the assurance arguments and evidence regarding a particular system in a specific environment [11]. An assurance case consists of a related set of auditable elements, such as claims, arguments, and evidence, used to demonstrate that a defined system will satisfy particular properties of interest

N. Selviandro—Supported by Indonesia Endowment Fund for Education (LPDP)

M. Zeller and K. Höfig (Eds.): IMBSA 2020, LNCS 12297, pp. 3–18, 2020.
https://doi.org/10.1007/978-3-030-58920-2_1

(e.g. safety/security requirements). In a complex system, structured arguments will normally be large and complicated, therefore the argument and evidence must be clearly documented to ensure they are communicated in a clear and defensible way between the different system stakeholder (such as developers, reviewers, and regulators).

An assurance case can be represented using a textual (i.e. natural language) and/or graphical approach. The Goal Structuring Notation (GSN) and the Claim-Arguments-Evidence (CAE) are two examples of established assurance case frameworks that can be used to represents an assurance case using graphical representations [7]. These two frameworks have been widely adopted in various domains to represent assurance cases, and examples related to their use can be accessed in the literature, for example, in [3,8,10,13].

The Structured Assurance Case Metamodel (SACM) is a specification that defines a metamodel for representing structured assurance cases. It is issued and published by the Object Management Group (OMG) to improve standardisation and interoperability in assurance case development. SACM is built upon the existing and established assurance case frameworks such as GSN and CAE. However, SACM provides a richer set of features, in terms of expressiveness, than existing assurance case frameworks.

SACM was also developed to better support a model-based approach to assurance case development by supporting high level operations such as model validation, model-to-model transformation and model merging. A number of tools provide some support for model-based assurance case development using SACM. A model-based assurance case tool (the Assurance Case Modelling Environment (ACME)) is currently under development that supports the SACM visual notation. Further discussion of the potential advantages of using SACM for creating assurance cases, including model-based assurance cases, and discussion related to the ACME tool can be found in [15].

To support the adoption of the SACM in assurance case development, we developed a visual notation for representing the SACM using a graphical representation. This was accepted by OMG and incorporated into the latest version of the standard [11]. The visual notation of SACM is developed as an alternative representation to the textual form to represent an assurance case using the SACM specification [14]. There are no publicly available examples of the use of the SACM notation. Other than [15] there is also a lack of literature that discusses the potential benefits of using the SACM in developing assurance cases. In this paper we address these gaps by providing examples based on a concrete case study of the use of the SACM notation for the assurance of machine learning for retinal diagnosis. We also discuss the potential benefits of using the features that SACM provides.

The rest of the paper is organised as follows. In Sect. 2, we briefly discuss different assurance case representation frameworks. In Sect. 3, we present the SACM notation and explain its use in representing assurance cases. The potential benefits of using the SACM specification are presented in Sect. 4. Finally, the conclusion of this paper and discussion of further work are given in Sect. 5.

2 Representation of Assurance Cases

A convincing argument that is supported by evidence is the core of any assurance cases; therefore, they need to be clearly documented and represented. A typical approach used in representing an assurance case is through free text using natural languages. However, some problems can occur when text is used as the only form for representing assurance cases. For example, the language used in the text can be unclear, ambiguous and poorly structured. The limitations regarding the use of free text as the only medium for representing safety cases have been discussed further in [10].

In order to overcome the limitations of using free text in representing assurance cases, graphical representation approaches have been introduced. Graphical notations such as CAE and GSN have been developed and, currently, widely adopted for representing assurance cases in various domains. In this section, we briefly introduce GSN and CAE and provide an overview of the SACM specification.

2.1 Goal Structuring Notation

GSN is a graphical notation for explicitly capturing the different elements of an argument such as claims, evidence, contextual information, and the relationships between these elements. It is a well established graphical argumentation notation that is widely adopted within safety-critical industries for the presentation of safety arguments within safety cases.

An assurance case in GSN can be documented using a claim (represented using *GSN Goal*) that is supported by sub-claims and evidence (represented using *GSN Solution*). The relationship between claims and evidence, can be defined using the *SupportedBy* relationship. A *GSN Context* can be used to scope the asserted claim, wherein this case, the relationship between them can be defined using an *InContextOf* relationship. When documenting how claims are said to be supported by sub-claims, sometimes, it can be useful to document the reasoning step involved, in this case, we can use the *GSN Strategy*. An assumed statement made within the argumentation can be documented using the *GSN Assumption*. Justification is also can be added to the argument structure using the *GSN Justification* in order to represent a statement of rationale. In GSN, the claim structure of the argument progresses downwards (top-down approach), from most abstract claim, recorded in the top-level goal, to an assertion about some item of evidence, recorded in the lowest goal in the structure. A GSN structure should be a directed acyclic graph where loops are not allowed.

Further explanation and complete documentation of the GSN elements can be found in [5]. Literature that discuss the application of the GSN, for example, can be found in [1,6,9].

2.2 Claim-Argument-Evidence

CAE is a graphical notation for representing assurance cases by documenting a set of claims supported by the argument and the related evidence. A *Claim* in CAE can be defined as a statement asserted within the argument that can be assessed to be true or false. An *Argument* is defined as a description of the argument approach presented in support of a claim, and an *Evidence* is described as a reference to the evidence being presented in support of the claim or argument. Other than these elements, CAE also provides elements such as *Side-Warrant*, a statement about the reason behind why we can deduce the top-level claim from the sub-claims and under what circumstances the argument is valid, and different types of relationship such as *Supports* (relation between Argument and Claim), *Is a sub-claim of* (relation between Sub-claim and Argument) and *Is evidence for* (relation between Evidence and Sub-claim). Literature that discuss the application of CAE can be found, for example, in [2,3].

2.3 Structured Assurance Case Metamodel

SACM is a metamodel that defines the specification for representing assurance cases. It was developed to support model-based engineering with existing well-established assurance case frameworks such as GSN and CAE. SACM is composed of the following components:

- the Structured Assurance Case Base that captures the fundamental concepts of SACM;
- the Structured Assurance Case Terminology that defines the mechanism to express; terminology and concept used in the assurance cases
- the Structured Assurance Case Packages that defines the concept of modularity in assurance case development;
- the Argumentation Metamodel that defines a metamodel for representing structured argument; and
- the Artifact Metamodel that specifies the concepts in providing and structuring evidence in assurance cases.

In this paper, we focus on the argumentation part of the SACM since it defines the specification for representing the assurance cases. In the next section, the SACM notation is explained along with examples of its usage.

3   Assurance Case Representation Using SACM Argumentation Notation

To support the adoption of SACM in assurance case development, we developed a visual notation for graphically representing the SACM argumentation specification. The notation was developed using a systematic process we developed for creating visual notations from metamodels [14]. The process is based on the theories of user-centred visual notation design and takes account of existing notations and the hierarchical structure of the elements in the metamodel to create an effective notation. Although SACM models could be represented visually through the transformation of the models to a different argumentation notation such as GSN or CAE, these other notations do not provide the richness of SACM, and the transformations can be complicated and incomplete. It is therefore highly desirable to provide the ability to visually represent SACM models directly. The developed SACM notation was accepted by OMG and is incorporated into the latest version of the standard [11].

3.1 Basic Elements

Structured arguments in SACM are represented explicitly by the Claims, citation of artifacts or ArtifactReferences (e.g. Evidence and Context for Claims), and the relationships between these elements. The Claim and an asserted relationship to connect between Claims and associate a Claim to its supporting context/evidence are defined under the Assertion class in the SACM. It is possible in SACM to associate a Claim to another Claim using a particular relationship type, and it is also possible in SACM to associate a Claim, for example, using a particular relationship type, to a relationship that is used to connect between elements. In this section, there are several examples provided to illustrate this aspect. A Claim in SACM is visually represented using a rectangle where the claim statement can be written within the rectangle, and a unique element identifier is placed at the top-left corner of the rectangle (as shown in Fig. 1). This visual representation is influenced by the GSN. It is being adopted to provide a visual clue to, at least, the assurance case notation user who might be familiar with an existing notation. A Claim can be supported by more than one Claim, and the relationship between them can be defined using an AssertedInference relationship. A line with a solid arrowhead is used to visualise an AssertedInference with a solid dot placed in the middle of the line that can be used as a connection point (as shown in Fig. 1).

In some cases, the relationship that associates more than one Claim may not always be obvious. In such cases, ArgumentReasoning can be used to provide a further description of the reasoning involved. An ArgumentReasoning is visually represented using an annotation symbol (as shown in Fig. 1). It can be attached to the AssertedInference relationship that connect the Claims.

A Claim may require a reference to contextual and/or evidential information. In SACM, both contextual and evidential information is defined as an Artifact, and a reference to this information is defined as ArtifactReference. Therefore, to cite contextual and evidential information to support a particular Claim, we can use an ArtifactReference. An ArtifactReference is visually represented using a note/document symbol to provide a clue to its actual meaning (as an artifact) and with an arrow placed on the top right of the symbol to indicate the meaning of a reference (as shown in Fig. 1).

Since the ArtifactReference as a reference to evidence and contextual information uses the same visual representation, we can differentiate between these in a diagram by identifying the type of relationship that is used to connect the ArtifactReference to its supporting element, and the position of the ArtifactReference relative to its targeted element. For an ArtifactReference that is used as a reference to a Context, the AssertedContext relationship is used to define

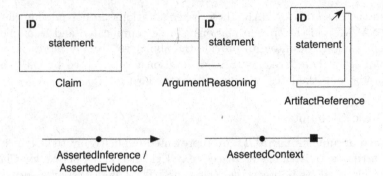

Fig. 1. Visual representation of a Claim, ArgumentReasoning, ArtifactReference, AssertedInference, AssertedContext, and AssertedEvidence relationship

the relationship between the ArtifactReference and its targeted element (e.g. a Claim), and the ArtifactReference is placed horizontally relative to its targeted element. The AssertedContext relationship is visually represented as a line with a solid square placed near to a line-end, and a solid dot placed in the middle of the line that can be used as a connection point (Fig. 1). For the ArtifactReference that is used as a reference to Evidence, we can use the AssertedEvidence relationship. The ArtifactReference, in this case, is located vertically (below) relative to its targeted element (e.g. Claim). The visual representation of the AssertedEvidence in SACM is identical with the visual representation of the AssertedInference, and we can differentiate them when used in a diagram by identifying its source element. For the AssertedEvidence relationship, the source element must be an ArtifactReference, and for the AssertedInference, the source element must be a Claim.

To show the use of the above SACM elements in a graphical diagram, in this paper, we adapted an assurance case [12] for a deep learning system used for retinal disease diagnosis and referral [4]. This system comprises 2 different neural networks. The first network, called Segmentation Network, takes as input three-dimensional Optical Coherence Tomography (OCT) scans and creates a detailed device-independent tissue-segmentation map. The second network examines the segmentation map and outputs one of the four referral suggestions in addition to the presence or absence of multiple concomitant retinal pathologies. The adapted assurance case from [12], originally, was constructed and presented using GSN. In this paper, we modify and reconstruct the assurance case diagram and represent it using the SACM notation. Figure 2 shows the use of the above elements in an assurance case fragment diagram.

In Fig. 2, the top-level claim is the 'ML Assurance Claim'. It is concerning the performance of the system for providing correct diagnosis and referral decisions. This Claim is supported by two references to contextual information (cited via ArtifactReference 'Clinical Setting' and 'Automated Retinal Diagnosis'). The relationship used to associate the ArtifactReference as a reference to a context to

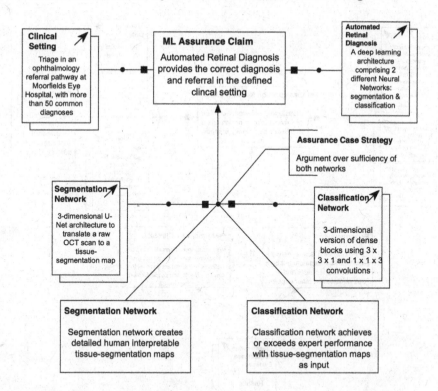

Fig. 2. The used of Claim, ArtifactReference (as a context), ArgumentReasoning, AssertedInference, and AssertedContext in an assurance case fragment

the supported claim is the AssertedContext relationship. The ArtifactReference, in this case, is placed horizontally relative to the claim since it is used as a reference to contextual information. In order to support the top-level claim, there are two sub-claims added to the structure. The relationship between these Claims is defined using the AssertedInference relationship. There are also two ArtifactReference elements (as a reference to contextual information supporting the relationship between Claims), and also an ArgumentReasoning attached to this relationship to provide further explanation regarding the assertion.

In Fig. 3, we show the use of the ArtifactReference as a reference to evidential information. In this case, the 'Classification Performance Evidence' is presented as an ArtifactReference to evidential information. It is located vertically relative to its supporting elements (Claims). The relationship used to associate the Arti-factReference to its supporting Claims is defined using the AssertedEvidence relationship.

In Fig. 3, we also can see the use of ArtifactReference as a reference to a context such as the 'Test Data' Artifact Reference that is placed horizontally relative to its supporting Claim. The relationship used to associate this Artifac-tReference to its supporting element is the AssertedContext relationship.

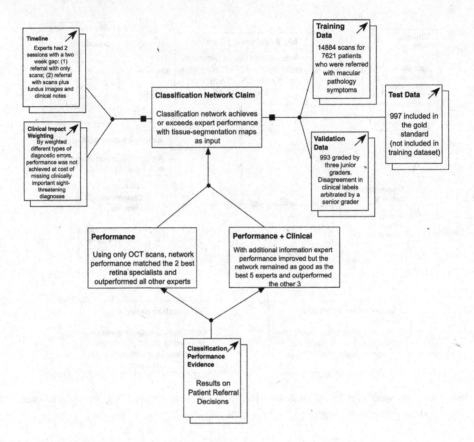

Fig. 3. ArtifactReference as a reference to evidence and ArtifactReference as a reference to context used in a diagram

3.2 Different Types of Claim and Relationship

An Assertion in SACM can be declared into several types:

- **Asserted** that indicates an assertion is asserted
- **Assumed** indicating that the Assertion being made is declared by the author as being assumed to be true rather than being supported by further argumentation
- **Axiomatic** indicates that the Assertion being made by the author is axiomatically true, so that no further argumentation is needed
- **Defeated** indicating that the Assertion is defeated by counter-evidence and/or argumentation;
- **AsCited** indicating that because the Assertion is cited, the AssertionDeclaration should be transitively derived from the value of the AssertionDeclaration of the cited Assertion
- **NeedsSupport** indicating that further argumentation has yet to be provided to support the Assertion.

The concrete example of an assertion in SACM can be either as a Claim or an asserted relationship. AssertedInference, AssertedContext, and AssertedEvidence are examples of asserted relationships in SACM. Therefore, in this case, these elements can be declared into a specific assertion declaration, as mentioned above. In the context of notation design, each specific assertion declaration, as mentioned above, is designed to fit for each assertion declaration type (i.e. the Claim and the asserted relationship).

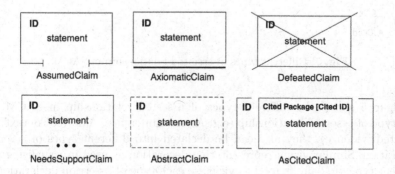

Fig. 4. Different types of Claim in SACM

Figure 4 shows the different types of Claim in SACM. For each different type of Claim, the basic visual representation of a Claim (i.e. a rectangle) is used, a necessary decoration is added to present a particular meaning of the assertion declaration. An AssumedClaim is visualised as a Claim with a line gap on the bottom part of the claim to deliver an assumption meaning which indicates that there is no supporting element that can be attached to this element since it is defined as an assumption. An AxiomaticClaim is visualised as a Claim with a thick line placed below the Claim to indicate that no further argumentation is needed to support this Claim since it is defined as an axiomatic. A DefeatedClaim is visualised as Claim with a cross placed on top of the Claim to indicate this Claim is defeated by a counter argument/evidence. AsCitedClaim is visualised as a Claim placed within square-brackets to indicate that this Claim is a citation claim and further explanation about this claim is presented in another argument structure. The AsCitedClaim notation also can be combined with the others claim, e.g., AsCitedClaim citing an AssumedClaim. A NeedsSupportClaim is visualised as a Claim with three dots placed at the bottom part of the rectangle to indicate further argumentation has yet to be provided to support this claim. A Claim also can be represented as an AbstractClaim. This represents a Claim defined in an abstract form that requires instantiation for a particular argument. Abstract elements, such as claims and relationships, are used to support the construction of assurance case patterns. To provide a visual clue to abstract elements they are rendered using dash-lines, as seen for the AbstractClaim in Fig. 4.

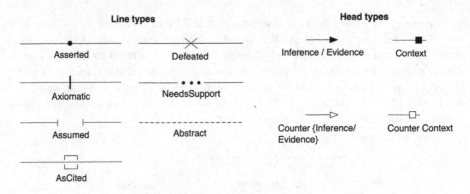

Fig. 5. Different types of asserted relationship in SACM

Figure 5 shows the different types of asserted relationship in SACM. For each type of asserted relationship (e.g. AssertedInference, AssertedContext, and AssertedEvidence), they also can be declared into different types of assertion declaration. Similar visual representation decoration as used in visualising each different type of Claim is used to visualise each type of assertion declaration for the asserted relationship. For example, an Assumed AssertedEvidence is visualised as an arrow headline with a line gap placed in the middle of the line. An Axiomatic AssertedInference is visualised as an arrow headline with a thick line placed in the middle of the line. A Defeated AssertedContext is visualised as a line with a solid square placed near to a line-end and a cross placed in the middle of the line. The use of similar visual representation to represent the same meaning (assertion declaration types) for different elements, such as a Claim and an asserted relationship, was designed to provide a visual clue to the user.

In Fig. 5, we also can see a type of relationship that is defined as Counter. This type of relationship can be used to associate a particular element (e.g. ArtifactReference as a reference to evidence) to counter a particular element such as a Claim. The visual representation of a Counter relationship is visualised as a hollow arrowhead line for an AssertedInference or AssertedEvidence, and a hollow square for an AssertedContext relationship. In order to use this relationship in a diagram, we can declare its specific purpose by combining the type of line and the type of the line-head. For example, we can define an AssertedInference relationship by using the Asserted line-type and the Inference head-line-type with a purpose to make an association between Claims. In case we want to define, for example, an Asserted Counter-Evidence relationship, we can use the Asserted line-type and the CounterEvidence line-head type.

In Fig. 6, we show the use of AssumedClaim to provide an assumption in supporting a particular Claim. The Claim 'Gold Standard' in Fig. 6 is declared without any supporting evidence or argumentation; therefore, this Claim is defined as an AssumedClaim.

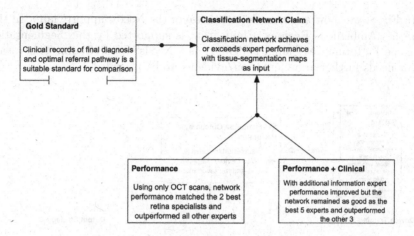

Fig. 6. Example of an AssumedClaim

In Fig. 7, we show an example of the use of an AsCited Claim. In this example, the 'Segmentation Outcome Interpretability' Claim is defined as an AsCited-Claim that means it is citing another Claim ('Segmentation Map Result' Claim) that is defined and developed in a different argument structure (e.g. defined in an ArgumentPackage named Arg.Pkg.1) that deals with human interpretability of segmentation maps.

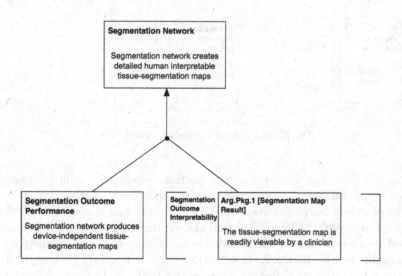

Fig. 7. Example of an AsCitedClaim

In Fig. 8, we show an example of the use of the NeedsSupportClaim. In this case, the 'Ambiguous Regions' Claim, that is supported by the 'Segmentation Outcome Performance' Claim, is defined as a NeedsSupportClaim. This means that it needs further argumentation/evidence to be provided.

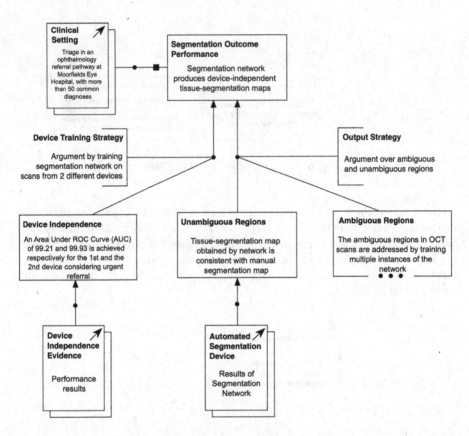

Fig. 8. Example of a NeedsSupportClaim

Figure 9 shows an example of the abstract elements. Claim 'Network' is defined as an AbstractClaim; it concerns the sufficiency of the network in the context of a deep learning system used for retinal disease diagnosis and referral (top-level argument). Claim 'Network' can be instantiated when being implemented in a concrete case such as defining the type of the network (e.g. segmentation network). Similarly, the AbstractArtifactReference that support the Claim can be instantiated further since, in this example, they are defined as an abstract element.

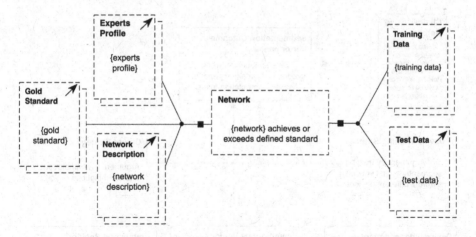

Fig. 9. Example of abstract elements in SACM notation

4   SACM: Potential Benefits

In the previous section, we have discussed the SACM notation based on concrete examples from a clinical diagnosis assurance case. In this section, we discuss the potential benefits of using this notation in assurance case development and review.

SACM is developed to support standardisation and interoperability in assurance case development. SACM provides a richer set of features than existing assurance case frameworks. There are several potential benefits of using SACM in representing assurance cases relative to the existing assurance case notations, for example:

– representing dialectical assurance case argument through the use of Counter-Inference/Evidence.
– presenting an argument concerning a particular Assertion in SACM assurance argument via MetaClaim relationship.
– associating a number of argument elements into a common group with a particular interest, such as different views of stakeholder (via ArgumentGroup).

Figure 10 shows an example dialectical assurance argument in SACM. Here, for purpose of illustration, we modify and reconstruct the assurance argument fragment in Fig. 8. The 'Unambiguous Regions' Claim in Fig. 10 is declared as a DefeatedClaim because it is countered by a counter-evidence cited via Arti-factReference 'Counter-Evidence'. As a result, the tissue segmentation map can not be said to be consistent with the manually-generated one. To associate the counter-evidence (cited visa ArtifactReference) and the targeted claim, in this example, the CounterEvidence relationship is used.

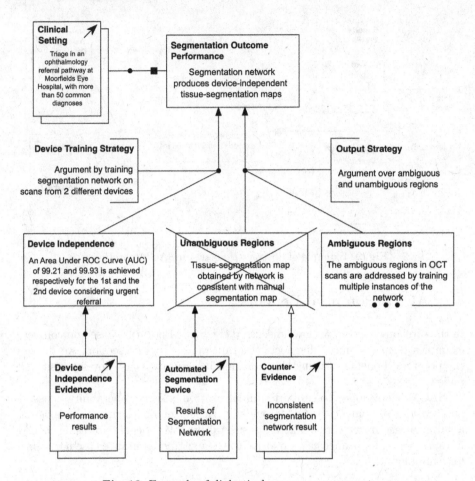

Fig. 10. Example of dialectical assurance argument

5   Conclusion and Future Work

SACM is a metamodel that defines the specification for representing assurance cases. It was developed to support the model-based assurance case development with existing well-established assurance case frameworks such as GSN and CAE. The adoption of the SACM in presenting assurance cases is considered slow. The lack of a visual notation for representing the SACM arguments has been a major factor in this. We developed a visual notation to support the adoption of the SACM. The notation is developed based on visual notation theories and considered the hierarchical structure of the elements in the metamodel. The developed notation was accepted by OMG and was incorporated into the latest version of the standard.

This paper provides, for the first time, an explanation of how to use the SACM notation in presenting assurance cases. The use of SACM elements such as

Claim, ArtifactReference, and different types of relationship that can be used to associate these elements have been demonstrated and described through several concrete examples from a clinical diagnosis assurance case.

As for the future work, we are currently empirically evaluating the effectiveness of the new graphical notation in different domains. We are also developing model-based tools that integrate the notation into established model-based assurance case frameworks that traceably link the assurance case model with external artefacts, e.g. design models and service data.

References

1. Bate, I., Hawkins, R., McDermid, J.: A contract-based approach to designing safe systems. In: Proceedings of the 8th Australian Workshop on Safety Critical Systems and Software-Volume 33, pp. 25–36. Citeseer (2003)
2. Bishop, P., Bloomfield, R., Penny, J., Eaton, A.: A methodology for safety case development. In: Safety-Critical Systems Symposium (1998)
3. Bloomfield, R., Bishop, P.: Safety and assurance cases: past, present and possible future–an adelard perspective. In: Dale, C., Anderson, T. (eds.) Making Systems Safer, pp. 51–67. Springer, London (2010). https://doi.org/10.1007/978-1-84996-086-1_4
4. De Fauw, J., Ledsam, J.R., Romera-Paredes, B., et al.: Clinically applicable deep learning for diagnosis and referral in retinal disease. Nat. Med. **24**(9), 1342–1350 (2018)
5. GSN: Goal structuring notation (GSN) community standard. Version 2 (2018). https://scsc.uk/r141B:1?t=1
6. Hawkins, R., Clegg, K., Alexander, R., Kelly, T.: Using a software safety argument pattern catalogue: two case studies. In: Flammini, F., Bologna, S., Vittorini, V. (eds.) SAFECOMP 2011. LNCS, vol. 6894, pp. 185–198. Springer, Heidelberg (2011). https://doi.org/10.1007/978-3-642-24270-0_14
7. Hawkins, R., Habli, I., Kolovos, D., Paige, R., Kelly, T.: Weaving an assurance case from design: a model-based approach. In: 2015 IEEE 16th International Symposium on High Assurance Systems Engineering (HASE), pp. 110–117. IEEE (2015)
8. Hawkins, R., Kelly, T., Knight, J., Graydon, P.: A new approach to creating clear safety arguments. In: Dale, C., Anderson, T. (eds.) Advances in Systems Safety, pp. 3–23. Springer, London (2011). https://doi.org/10.1007/978-0-85729-133-2_1
9. Kelly, T., McDermid, J.: Safety case patterns-reusing successful arguments (1998)
10. Kelly, T., Weaver, R.: The goal structuring notation-a safety argument notation. In: Proceedings of the Dependable Systems and Networks 2004 Workshop on Assurance Cases, p. 6. Citeseer (2004)
11. (OMG), O.M.G.: Structured assurance case metamodel (SACM) Version 2.1 (2020). https://www.omg.org/spec/SACM/About-SACM/
12. Picardi, C., Habli, I.: Perspectives on assurance case development for retinal disease diagnosis using deep learning. In: Riaño, D., Wilk, S., ten Teije, A. (eds.) AIME 2019. LNCS (LNAI), vol. 11526, pp. 365–370. Springer, Cham (2019). https://doi.org/10.1007/978-3-030-21642-9_46
13. Picardi, C., Hawkins, R., Paterson, C., Habli, I.: A pattern for arguing the assurance of machine learning in medical diagnosis systems. In: Romanovsky, A., Troubitsyna, E., Bitsch, F. (eds.) SAFECOMP 2019. LNCS, vol. 11698, pp. 165–179. Springer, Cham (2019). https://doi.org/10.1007/978-3-030-26601-1_12

14. Selviandro, N., Kelly, T., Hawkins, R.D.: The visual inheritance structure to support the design of visual notations. In: 3rd International Workshop on Human Factors in Modeling (HuFaMo 2018), York (2018)
15. Wei, R., Kelly, T.P., Dai, X., Zhao, S., Hawkins, R.: Model based system assurance using the structured assurance case metamodel. J. Syst. Softw. **154**, 211–233 (2019)

Argument-Driven Safety Engineering of a Generic Infusion Pump with Digital Dependability Identities

Jan Reich[1]([⊠]), Joshua Frey[1], Emilia Cioroaica[1], Marc Zeller[2], and Martin Rothfelder[2]

[1] Fraunhofer IESE, Kaiserslautern, Germany
{jan.reich,joshua.frey,emilia.cioroaica}@iese.fraunhofer.de
[2] Siemens AG, Munich, Germany
{marc.zeller,martin.rothfelder}@siemens.com

Abstract. Creating a sound argumentation of why a system is sufficiently safe is a major part of the assurance process. Today, compiling a safety case and maintaining its validity after changes are time-consuming manual work. By using the concept provided by *Digital Dependability Identities (DDI)*, we present a systematic approach for creating a model-connected safety argument that is formally related to safety models such as hazard and risk assessment, safety analysis, architecture, safety requirements or validation. The comprehensively traced DDI model provides the traceability basis to guide argument-driven safety engineering processes. Flaws in arguments or evidence emerging through changes in the product development process are addressed by DDI-based automation. The case study described in this paper evaluates the DDI approach based on the publicly available safety assurance documentation of a Generic Infusion Pump (GIP) system. The evaluation demonstrates that DDIs can capture the relevant safety aspects of the GIP system.

1 Introduction

The growing complexity of safety-critical systems in many application domains such as medical, automotive or avionics poses new challenges for system development. Along with the growing system complexity, the effort for safety assurance is drastically increasing, too. Safety assurance is mandatory to pass certification and to satisfy the high-quality demands imposed by the market. Consequently, without safety assurance, market introduction and success of a product is in jeopardy. Functional safety standards such as IEC 62304 [1] for medical software specifically define normative goals to be met by safety assurance processes. Their objectives are to identify all system-internal failures that can cause hazardous situations and to demonstrate the system's residual risk is acceptable at product release. Typical activities are the identification and assessment of hazards, safety analyses (e.g. using fault tree analysis (FTA) or failure mode and effect analysis (FMEA)) and the creation of a sound safety argument as to why trust in the safety property is ensured. The safety argument clearly has a central role as it communicates the relationship between safety objectives and their supporting evidence [2]. The argument

© Springer Nature Switzerland AG 2020
M. Zeller and K. Höfig (Eds.): IMBSA 2020, LNCS 12297, pp. 19–33, 2020.
https://doi.org/10.1007/978-3-030-58920-2_2

is often part of a safety case and its creation can generally be considered a major task of the assurance process.

Compiling a safety case is typically very laborious and, as of today, is often manual work performed by safety experts based on their experience about the applied safety standard and the developed system. There is a lack of methodological guidance for producing a sound safety argument and matching evidence, in particular, when changes to the safety artifacts are performed and consistency needs to be ensured.

By using the concept of *Digital Dependability Identities* (DDIs) [3] developed in the H2020 DEIS Project[1], in this paper we present an argument-driven safety engineering approach that starts at the safety objectives and systematically employs safety models to build and support the argument. These safety models are formally integrated with each other and are traceable to the claims of the argument. Particularly, by using DDIs, the safety case's quality is improved by having a clear picture at every point in time, which models need to be created to support a claim of interest and whether the defined confidence is achieved. In addition, the model-based integration of the aspects enables automation to reduce effort for the reassessment after performing system changes. We illustrate our approach using a case study from the medical domain, which focuses on the safety assurance of a generic infusion pump (GIP) as a running example.

The rest of the paper is organized as follows: In Sect. 2, we set the stage by introducing the concept of DDIs, the case study and related work. Afterward in Sect. 3, we describe the GIP system DDI and illustrate the DDI safety engineering procedure by example. Section 4 concludes the paper.

2 Problem Description and Related Work

2.1 DDIs and Open Dependability Exchange (ODE) Meta-model v2.0

A fundamental problem of current safety engineering processes hampering effective and confident safety assurance lies in the fact that safety argument models are not formally related to the evidence models supporting the argument. Concrete examples for such evidence are hazard and safety analysis models, architecture models or verification and validation (V&V) models. As all those artifacts refer to the same system and therefore are naturally interrelated with each other, we claim this should also be the case for the system's model-based safety reflection: The *Digital Dependability Identity (DDI)*. By establishing this kind of traceability, DDIs represent an integrated set of safety data models that are generated by multiple engineering roles. A DDI (Fig. 1, left) is therefore an evolution of classical modular safety assurance models in that several separately defined aspect models are now formally integrated allowing for comprehensive and semi-automatic construction and reasoning, in particular when changes occur during product development. DDIs are used for safe integration of components into systems at design time, certified when the system is released, and then continuously maintained over the lifetime of a system.

A DDI contains information that describes the safety characteristics of a system in a comprehensible and transparent manner organized in a modular assurance case. The

---

[1] Dependability Engineering Innovation for Cyber-Physical Systems: www.deis-project.eu/.

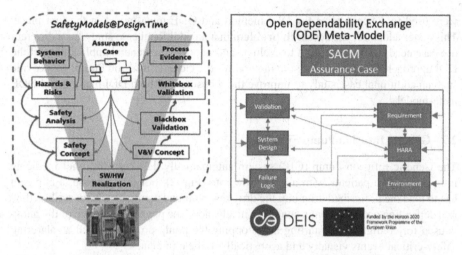

Fig. 1. DDI concept overview (left: Conceptual GIP DDI, right: technical DDI meta-model)

assurance case contains assurance claims about the safety guarantees given by a system or component and supporting evidence for those claims in the form of various integrated models and analyses. Each assurance activity and their artifacts contained in a DDI is motivated by at least one claim that demands the satisfaction of a safety property with a given integrity. Depending on the criticality of a specific risk, functional safety standards define safety processes and claims to achieve the desired integrity in risk assessment and reduction.

Thus, a DDI is powered by a set of safety claims, for which the models produced during safety activities shall provide convincing evidence of satisfaction for the developed system. For both risk management planning and safety assessment purposes, an explicit argument is indispensable inductively relating the created evidence to the top-level claim through several step-wise layers of argumentation. As of now, DDIs can deal with safety and security risks, thus the set of currently supported assurance activities focus on well-established methods such as hazard and risk analysis, safety analyses, safety design concepts, validation, and verification. These activities proved sufficient over the last decades in demonstrating the functional safety of embedded systems.

The advantage of continuous traceability in DDIs between a safety argument expressed in the Goal Structuring Notation (GSN/SACM) [4] and safety-related evidence models is enabled by an integrated meta-model, the *Open Dependability Exchange* (ODE) meta-model v2.0 (Fig. 1, right). Around this technical DDI backbone, an automation framework was built to support automated change impact or argument validity analyses on the DDI data contents [5]. Details on the DDI framework as well as an open-source version of the technical ODE meta-model can be found at GitHub[2].

The DDI method was already successfully applied in DEIS to four use cases from automotive (Platooning, Driver Health Monitoring), railway (European Train Control System) and medical (GDPR for Oncology app) domains. However, these use cases

---

[2] https://github.com/DEIS-Project-EU.

were used to conceptualize the DDI method and ODE meta-model in the first place. This paper addresses the **research problem** that an additional case study for a different use case needs to be carried out to evaluate and improve the general applicability of the DDI approach. By instantiating the method for the Generic Infusion Pump, we provide such an additional case study to improve the robustness of both DDI method and ODE meta-model.

2.2 Generic Infusion Pump System

The Generic Infusion Pump (GIP) system automatically delivers pain relief medicine intravenously to patients with a basal flow rate (Fig. 2). For this purpose, a clinician has to load the prescribed drug into the drug reservoir and configure the prescribed flow rate depending on the patient's condition in advance. The physical interface of the pump is used for configuration, starting and stopping the pump process as well as alarming safety-critical events visually and acoustically to the clinician.

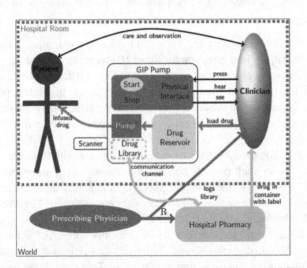

Fig. 2. Generic Infusion Pump system (adapted based on [6])

The creation of the GIP DDI described in this paper was based on publicly available safety engineering artifacts provided by the *Generic Infusion Pump Research Project*[3] carried out by thirteen U.S. academic, industrial and regulatory partners. This enabled a realistic evaluation of the DDI technology robustness for its application in new use cases. Since for some aspects such as the safety case, multiple documents from different sources existed, the study inputs are selected to contain DDI-relevant safety aspects and that those aspects are consistent with each other. Concretely, the considered aspects were functional requirements and use cases, functional architecture, hazard- and safety analysis, safety requirements and safety concept, assurance case, software design and the

---

[3] https://rtg.cis.upenn.edu/gip/.

implementation. For the purpose of the study, the documents from the Kansas State University (KSU) were applicable well as they covered the majority of the above-mentioned aspects and most importantly, the conceptual traceability from safety case to safety models was established. For illustrating the DDI safety assurance method in this paper, we focus on the *Too High Drug Flow* hazard of the *Basal Rate Infusion* function.

2.3 Related Work

Argument-driven safety engineering is not a new paradigm, as basically any safety assurance follows an implicit safety argument and produces evidence to support it. There exist numerous model-based approaches to develop an explicit safety case, mostly based on the Goal Structuring Notation (GSN) and its successor, the OMG Structured Assurance Case Metamodel (SACM) [4]. Based on those models, patterns are created for providing argued support for specific assurance problems [7]. For modeling the evidence, integrated meta-models for various safety-related aspects [8] and approaches for modeling the process-wise management of the evidence evolution and the safety case artifacts over time [9] were developed.

All of these works have in common that they focus on formalizing specific important parts of the safety assurance process. The DDI concept, its meta-model and the accompanying engineering method aim at building a superordinate model-based framework, which provides mechanisms to integrate all of the mentioned aspects into one integrated meta-model and enable comprehensive dependability reasoning for safety-critical embedded systems. In particular, DDIs enable the formal integration of the SACM-based argument with the concrete product safety evidence models.

3 Digital Dependability Identity for GIP System

In this section, the existing GIP development artifacts are transferred into a GIP representative DDI. Note that the contribution of this paper only addresses the systematic argument-driven creation of the DDI with the given content, but it does not cover an evaluation of the provided GIP artifacts regarding their correctness or completeness.

3.1 GIP System DDI Overview

Following the notion of argument-driven safety engineering, Fig. 3 depicts at the top a generic model of how a systematic safety argument fragment for each safety-related activity can be constructed in principle and at the bottom the concrete GIP system functional safety argument mapped to those DDI evidence models supporting it. When a safety argument should be systematically built up demonstrating the absence of critical risks, safety engineers produce various kinds of safety artifacts for the system under development (SUD) each reflecting a different safety aspect with the intention to provide confidence in the satisfaction of a claim. A flaw in the artifact quality impedes this confidence and thus has to be avoided. Therefore, the argument is structured to make sure that all causal influences leading to a degraded artifact quality are mitigated appropriately. The first major cause is a limited understanding of the SUD or its environment leading to incomplete or incorrect modeling of its safety aspects. The second cause is an incorrect execution of the safety process leading to a mismatch between the produced contents of the artifact and the needed evidence for satisfying a claim. These issues can be addressed separately and thus the argument is decomposed into *product* and *process* parts. While the process argument describes, why there is confidence that involved engineers produce complete and qualitatively sufficient artifacts, the product argument argues, why evidence models properly reflect the SUD and its environment.

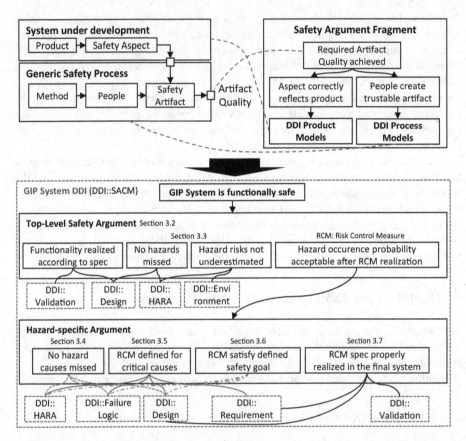

Fig. 3. High-Level Overview GIP DDI with mapping between argument and evidence models

The bottom of Fig. 3 instantiates this notion multiple times for the GIP functional safety claims that have to be satisfied. On the first level, the argument modeled in the DDI package *DDI::SACM* consists of a top-level safety argument that is concerned with setting a functional basis to analyze critical behavioral deviations and their potential to cause harm in the SUD environment. The relevant DDI packages (dashed red boxes) to support the top-level claims are *DDI::Validation* (test evidence for functionality), *DDI::Design* (system and safety functions), *DDI::Environment* (safety-relevant system context), *DDI::HARA* (hazard and risk assessment model). For critical hazards, a dedicated hazard-specific argument is specified analyzing critical hazard causes, defining risk control measures (RCM) and providing verification and validation evidence that RCMs lead to acceptable risk reduction. The DDI packages supporting those claims are *DDI::HARA* (Starting point for safety analysis), *DDI::Design* (System-internal structure, data-flow and RCM design), *DDI::FailureLogic* (System-internal fault definition and fault propagation logic), *DDI::Requirement* (Safety requirements addressing critical faults) and *DDI::Validation* (test evidence for safety requirement validation).

The upcoming subsections sequentially describe the argument parts in order as they occur in the safety engineering lifecycle. The explanation in each subsection is split into process and product part.

3.2 Top-Level Safety Argument

The purpose of the top-level safety argument is the decomposition of the overall system safety claim in its different aspects. While in this paper, the functional safety aspect (hazards due to malfunctioning behavior) is addressed, there are other relevant safety aspects such as arguing that the nominal behavior specification is safe or that functional insufficiencies (e.g. incapability of sensors to correctly measure patient health state) and unsafe operator misuse (e.g. wrong usage of system) are prevented. For each of those aspects, safety engineering lifecycle activities in combination provide evidence that the GIP system is acceptably safe for public release.

The functional safety claim in Fig. 3 is decomposed according to the safety lifecycle activities and therefore decomposition completeness can be argued: If the intended functionality specified through use cases and functional requirements is validated, a sound basis for analyzing FuSa deviations is created. Building on this basis, hazards for the system's outputs potentially leading to harm need to be completely identified for the intended operating environment. Subsequently, the risks of hazardous situations need to be correctly assessed, where a too low risk assessment has to be avoided by all means. These two claims are of outmost importance, as missed hazards and underestimated risks will in many cases stay undiscovered in the remaining lifecycle, as the following activities focus on realizing and validating safety goals derived from hazardous situations. Assuming safety goals have been defined with a correct integrity level, the following hazard-specific activities have to ensure that the hazard occurrence probability *is reduced* by the use of mitigation measures to an *acceptable* level (i.e. appropriate for the hazardous situation criticality). Demonstrating proper risk reduction is carried out through evidence provided through analytic safety analysis and through testing of the actual system against its safety specification (validation).

3.3 Hazard Identification and Risk Assessment Argument

Process-wise, the identification of a complete hazard list can be achieved by applying systematic methods, where the experience of involved people is carefully balanced with the strictness dictated by specific hazard identification methods, e.g. Functional Hazard Analysis (FHA), which is a guideword-based approach for systematic identification of malfunctions and hazards. Note that also the innovation degree of a system is a factor influencing the required level of process rigor. While for well-understood system types and operating environments, existing hazard analyses can be reused, this situation changes for innovative systems, where more thorough analyses are required. For the correct assessment of hazard risks for the GIP system, the well-established medical risk management standard ISO 14971 [10] has been used as reference process. Note that a common cause for incorrect risk assessment is that the most critical environmental situations are not identified for a particular hazard. This issue can be tackled with a systematic situation space partitioning method aided by operating environment ontologies.

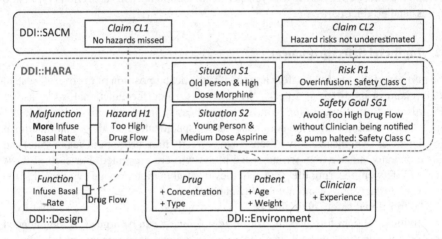

Fig. 4. Hazard identification and risk assessment argument support

The DDI supports the hazard identification and risk assessment claims with three modeling aspects: *DDI::HARA, DDI::Design* and *DDI::Environment*. As hazards are critical states at the system boundary potentially causing harm, they can be systematically analyzed by looking at the functional outputs modeled at the system boundary. Both system functions and their interface are expressed in *DDI::Design*. To support the identification of environmental situations, in which the potential hazards may be critical, a model of the safety-relevant environment is required. *DDI::Environment* supports this by providing capabilities to model environmental entities along with their attributes. *DDI::Environment* is a highly-reusable model, as many systems in a domain share similar environment (e.g. clinician, patient, drug are typical entities of the medical domain). By permutating the entities and attributes of the environment, a complete set of situations can be systematically generated for risk assessment. *DDI::HARA* finally puts together design and environment elements into a model-based version of the HARA process and thus establishes continuous traceability from functions and their outputs over hazards and situations to safety goals addressing hazardous situations.

For the GIP system, Fig. 4 demonstrates the instantiation of the hazard identification and risk assessment argument with the help of DDI contents. We need to achieve confidence that we do not miss important hazards (CL1) and that their risks are not underestimated (CL2). To support CL1, we systematically analyze all *Outports* of the system

Functions for *Malfunctions*. This activity makes use of a set of HAZOP guidewords assumed to be covering all potential deviations. This leads to the *Malfunction* "More Infuse Basal Rate" and the related *Hazard* "Too High Drug Flow". In order to avoid risk underestimation, the situation space is constructed by permutating the GIP context elements in *DDI::Environment*. In the example, the *Patient* with its attributes age and weight as well as the characteristics of the specific *Drug* are considered risk-influencing factors. Elder persons are assumed to be more vulnerable to severe consequences due to their weaker immune system than younger persons. Similarly, an over-infusion of morphine leads to more severe consequences than ibuprofen. The completeness of the assessed situations is argued by making sure that the *DDI::Environment* package has been modeled with specific care and that all relevant combinations of context elements have been analyzed regarding likelihood and severity of the accident "Over-Infusion".

3.4   Critical Cause Identification Argument

After identifying hazards and assessing their risk, the analysis focus is switched from the system environment to the system itself, where critical causes (i.e. faults) for the hazards are analyzed. For arguing completeness of the cause analysis, two strategies are employed: Process-wise, the combination of inductive (e.g. FMEA) and deductive (e.g. FTA) analysis techniques create a methodical redundancy. Product-wise, we can use the fact that system failures always originate in system components and that they propagate to the system boundary through component interfaces. Thus, if the cause analysis method systematically covers all existing system components, their functional interfaces and the potential inter-component propagation paths (i.e. data flow paths), confidence in hazard cause completeness can be argued.

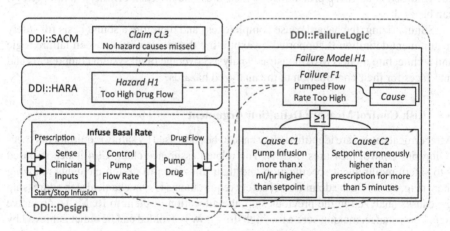

Fig. 5. Critical cause identification argument support

The DDI supports the hazard cause completeness claim CL3 with three aspect packages: *DDI::HARA*, *DDI::Design* and *DDI::FailureLogic*. While *DDI::HARA* establishes the traceability to the hazard and its criticality source, *DDI::Design* and

DDI::FailureLogic serve as the basis for the cause completeness argument. They model the system's functional architecture, i.e. the decomposition of functionality into sub functions and their interfaces, as well as the failure propagation logic. The essential property being exploited for the completeness argument is the traceability between hazard, system-level failure and its causes on the one hand and between the failure logic and functional components on the other hand (Fig. 5). *DDI::FailureLogic* generally contains capabilities for commonly used analysis techniques FMEA, FTA and Markov. Based on those models, critical cause combinations leading to hazard occurrence with high likelihood can be systematically analyzed qualitatively and quantitatively. This establishes a suitable basis for deriving risk control measures (Sect. 3.5).

For the GIP system, the system function *Infuse Basal Rate* is decomposed into sensing, control and actuator components. The flow rate prescription and start command are sensed by *Sense Clinician Inputs*. From that point on, the flowrate set point is determined by *Control Pump Flow Rate* and a periodic infusion process from drug reservoir to patient is carried out by *Pump Drug*, until the infusion is stopped. Note that the actual GIP architecture is more complex, but has been simplified for the sake of clarity. The failure logic has been modeled as a component fault tree analyzing the causes of the system failure "Pumped Flow Rate Too High". This failure may be caused for instance if the controller is computing a wrong setpoint OR if a correct setpoint is incorrectly actuated by the pump. The whole set of potential causes and their combinations are traced to the concrete functions, where they occur and the data flow interfaces over which failures propagate towards the system output. Component Fault Trees have the advantage that they mirror the structure of the functional architecture and therefore simplify the systematic coverage of functions and their interfaces regarding failure propagation analysis. Note that for the prioritization of cause combinations, various metrics such as minimal cut set order, occurrence probability or measures like the Risk Priority Number (RPN) can be used.

Summarizing, the hazard cause completeness and therefore a sound basis for safety requirement definition is supported by exploiting the traceability between failure logic and architecture models to demonstrate analysis coverage of all system components and interfaces for their contribution to the analyzed hazards.

3.5   Risk Control Measure Definition Argument

After critical causes are identified, they have to be addressed by safety requirements specifying risk control measures (RCM). The related assurance claim CL4 is decomposed into safety requirement specification and their allocation to design elements realizing them (Fig. 6). While the definition of safety requirements is a mechanical step addressing the causes analyzed in the previous step, the allocation of them to RCMs is a creative step. For instance, making sure a too high drug flow is avoided can be either achieved by ensuring the nominal function acts according to its specification or by adding a safety function performing shut-off after a detected but non-dangerous deviation.

For both cases, the DDI supports the argument by providing on the one hand traceability between the identified causes (*DDI::FailureLogic*) and the resulting derived safety requirements (*DDI::Requirement*). On the other hand, safety requirements are explicitly allocated to (new) design elements (*DDI::Design*).

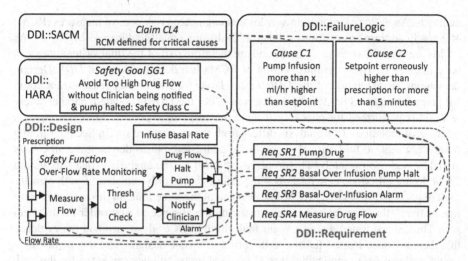

Fig. 6. Risk Control measure definition argument support

For the GIP system, four exemplary safety requirements are defined to realize the safety goal by means of a dedicated over-flow rate monitoring *safety function*:

SR1 The mechanical pump shall halt the infusion (rate = 0) when commanded.

SR2 If delivered flow rate exceeds the prescribed rate by more than its allowed tolerance over a period of more than 5 min, or immediately if the pump goes into free flow, the infusion shall be halted latest after 50 ms.

SR3 If delivered flow rate exceeds the prescribed basal rate by more than its allowed tolerance over a period of more than 5 min, a basal over-infusion alarm shall be issued to the clinician visually and acoustically latest after 500 ms.

SR4 The down-stream drug flow between GIP and patient shall be measured with max. deviation of $-0,1$ ml/hr relative to the actual flow rate

These address the single-point failures *C1* (*SR1*) and *C2* (*SR2, 3, 4*) and are allocated to sub safety functions for measuring the drug flow (*Measure Flow*), checking against a critical threshold (*Threshold Check*) and transforming the system into a safe state (*Halt Pump, Notify Clinician*).

Up to this point, the constructive safety assurance tasks of creating a safe design to address system hazards is carried out and argued. The seamless traceability between the argument and the modeling aspects builds trust that the safety claims are sufficiently supported by a safe design. What is missing at this point is the confidence that the safety design is reducing system risk appropriately and that the final system realizes that design. Those claims are addressed in the upcoming two sections, respectively.

3.6 Analytic Risk Reduction Argument

After having systematically derived a safe design, the next step is to provide validation and verification (V&V) evidence that the design satisfies the safety goal's integrity demands. Analytic risk reduction verifies that engineered risk control measures (RCM) effectively address hazards and all critical faults are actually addressed by RCMs. As RCMs are often realized in software and are therefore part of the final system, they can have faults, too. Thus, the introduction of RCMs is a design change in *DDI::Design*, demanding an adaptation of the *DDI::FailureLogic* for consistency reasons to account for potential faults in the RCMs themselves. After the DDI is updated, another safety analysis is performed for checking if there are still single-point failures leading to a safety goal violation. This analysis differs from the one carried out in Sect. 3.4 in that it does not seek to find critical causes to be addressed, but to demonstrate all causes are addressed appropriately. The property exploited for the analysis is that – assuming RCM do not introduce new hazards – the safety goal is only violated, if both primary fault (e.g. C1 in Fig. 7) *AND* RCM failure occur at the same time. In the context of fault tree analysis, this translates into demonstrating the absence of first-order minimal cut sets. Thus, if we found a single-point fault during this analysis, we had the evidence that there are unaddressed faults and therefore an unsafe design. Note that quantitative safety analyses or, if applicable, formal verification techniques can serve for this task similarly. The important point is to reanalyze the system *after* RCMs have been added.

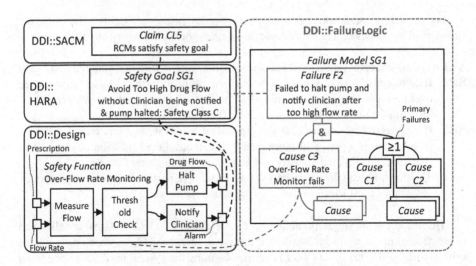

Fig. 7. Analytic risk reduction argument support

3.7 Safety Validation Argument

The validation activities produce evidence that a system component, the interplay of multiple components or the final product actually realizes the engineered safety design. Note that, although often not explicitly mentioned, one assumption behind inferring functional safety from successfully run safety tests is that the intended functionality is correctly realized in the system. Since functional safety aims at safely controlling *deviations* from intended functionality, its correct realization is a necessary precondition that the right conclusions can be drawn from safety tests. The overall safety validation claim (CL6 in Fig. 8) can be decomposed into two sub claims to be supported:

CL7 The derived safety test set provides sufficient coverage to demonstrate the satisfaction of the safety goal.

CL8 The concrete test case execution covers all safety design elements and test results are successful

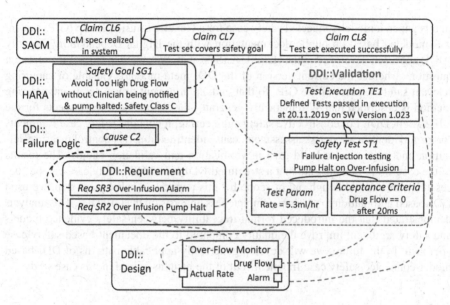

Fig. 8. Safety validation argument support

Safety Tests are part of the *DDI::Validation* package and validate safety requirements from *DDI::Requirement* by inducing *Test Parameters* at system or software inputs and checking *Acceptance Criteria* at system outputs. To support the argument of CL7, the DDI contains the traceability between safety tests and requirements, as each safety requirement needs to be covered by at least one test case. The argument for completeness of safety requirements regarding the safety goal and their proper allocation to design elements is built up in Sects. 3.4, 3.5 and 3.6. Thus, the established traceability down the left side of enables a seamless argument basis for test set completeness. The *Safety Test* "Failure Injection testing Pump Halt on Over-Infusion" refers to SR2 (see Sect. 3.5), defines test triggers ("Actual Rate = 5.3 ml/hr with Prescription of 5 ml/hr") and measurable criteria ("Drug Flow == 0 after 20 ms"). These are formally traced to system input ("Actual Rate, Prescribed Rate") and output ports ("Drug Flow"). To create and relate supporting evidence for CL8 about successful text execution into the safety argument, *DDI::Validation* offers the possibility to document *Test Execution* results for the executed *Safety Tests*. Note that assuring a proper test execution (e.g. correct product version tested, documented tests have been actually carried out, etc.) is a very important topic to be addressed with process measures, but was out-of-scope in this study.

In summary, DDIs support safety validation arguments through the elements of the *DDI::Validation* package and their seamless traceability to modeling elements in the constructive safety packages *DDI::Requirement* containing the safety requirements to be tested and *DDI::Design* containing the design model of the system under test.

4 Conclusion

In this paper, a model-connected safety case for a Generic Infusion Pump (GIP) system was modeled based on public documentation with the Digital Dependability Identity (DDI) approach developed in the H2020 DEIS project. We aimed to answer the research questions whether the current version of the DDI meta-model is capable of capturing relevant safety aspects of the GIP. To that end, an argument-driven safety engineering method is described that systematically generates the functional safety aspects for the GIP system DDI. For constructive safety engineering, it contains safety case fragments for hazard identification, risk assessment, cause identification, risk control measure definition and fragments to build trust in verification and validation claims. The results of the case study demonstrate that a structured DDI-based GIP safety case can be successfully created. Although out of scope for this paper, in a subsequent step, we used DDI-based automation to perform completeness analysis on the GIP DDI. This analysis demonstrated that the introduced formal traceability between safety evidence models and safety argument improve the quality compared to the document-based safety case approach. In the future, we will develop generically applicable patterns of DDI-based model-connected safety case fragments out of the insights gained in this case study.

References

1. International Electrotechnical Commission: IEC 62304:2006 – Medical device software – Software life cycle processes (2006)
2. Kelly, T.P.: Systematic approach to safety case management. In: Proceedings of SAE World Congress (2004)
3. Schneider, D., et al.: WAP: digital dependability identities. In: Proceedings of IEEE International Symposium on Software Reliability Engineering (ISSRE), pp. 324–329 (2015)
4. Wei, R., Kelly, T.P., et al.: Model Based System Assurance Using the Structured Assurance Case Metamodel (2019). https://arxiv.org/pdf/1905.02427
5. Reich, J., Zeller, M., Schneider, D.: Automated evidence analysis of safety arguments using digital dependability identities. In: Romanovsky, A., Troubitsyna, E., Bitsch, F. (eds.) SAFE-COMP 2019. LNCS, vol. 11698, pp. 254–268. Springer, Cham (2019). https://doi.org/10.1007/978-3-030-26601-1_18
6. Kansas State University: Open Patient-Controlled Analgesia Infusion Pump System Requirements 1.0.0. (Report: SanToS TR 2018-4-1) (2018)
7. Gleirscher, M., Carlan, C.: Arguing from hazard analysis in safety cases: a modular argument pattern. In: IEEE 18th International Symposium on High Assurance Systems Engineering (HASE), Singapore, pp. 53–60 (2017)

8. Pohl, K., Hönninger, H., Achatz, R., Broy, M. (eds.): Model-Based Engineering of Embedded Systems – The SPES 2020 Methodology. Springer, Heidelberg (2012). https://doi.org/10.1007/978-3-642-34614-9

9. de la Vara, J.L., et al.: Model-based specification of safety compliance needs for critical systems: a holistic generic metamodel. Inf. Softw. Technol. **72**, 16–30 (2016)

10. International Standardization Organization: ISO 14971:2019 – Medical devices – Application of risk management to medical devices (2019)

Model-Based Risk Analysis
for an Open-Source PCA Pump Using
AADL Error Modeling

Hariharan Thiagarajan[1]([✉]), Brian Larson[2]([✉]), John Hatcliff[1]([✉]),
and Yi Zhang[3]([✉])

[1] Department of Computer Science,
Kansas State University, Manhattan, KS, USA
{thari,hatcliff}@ksu.edu
[2] Multitude Corporation, St. Paul, MN, USA
brl@multitude.net
[3] The MD PnP Interoperability & Cybersecurity Program,
Massachusetts General Hospital, Boston, MA, USA
yzhang134@mgh.harvard.edu

Abstract. Risk management is a key part of the development of medical devices to achieve acceptable product safety and pass regulatory scrutiny. As model-based development (MBD) techniques gain ground in the medical device industry, the medical device industry needs guidelines on the best practices of integrating risk management principles and activities in MBD-driven product development.

In this paper, we demonstrate how the SAE standard Architecture, Analysis, and Definition Language (AADL) and its Error Modeling (EM) annex can be applied in the development of an open-source patient-controlled analgesic (PCA) pump to support the risk management tasks of ISO 14971 - the primary risk management standard in the medical device domain. While AADL EM has been applied in other domains, our work provides the first mapping of AADL EM to ISO 14971 concepts. It not only represents one of the largest applications to-date of AADL's EM framework, but also provides the industry and academia an example with considerable complexity to investigate methodologies and methods of integrating MBD and risk management. This work is part of the Open PCA Pump project, which presents a variety of open source integrated development artifacts for a realistic medical device.

Keywords: Error modeling · Medical device · Risk analysis ·
Architecture Analysis and Design Language (AADL)

1 Introduction

The medical device domain, like other safety-critical domains, includes risk management as a key activity in development and certification. The international

This work was supported in part under the U.S. Army Medical Research Acquisition Activity Contract W81XWH-17-C-0251.

standard ISO 14971 [14] describes a risk management process for medical devices. The 14971 process includes identifying hazards (things associated with the device and its use that might cause harm), performing risk analysis (including hazard analysis) to identify hazardous situations (causal chains leading from root causes to device-user/device-patient interactions that might cause harm), developing risk controls (mitigations of hazard situations), verifying risk controls, and determining if residual risks are acceptable.

The Open PCA Pump project [12,19] was created to illustrate rigorous model-driven engineering (MBE) and formal methods on realistic medical device artifacts. With team members from industry, healthcare delivery organizations, regulatory agencies, and academia, the project aims to overcome barriers between these groups that have hindered the explanation of development and verification challenges, certification and regulatory concerns, and benefits of formal development techniques. The project addresses patient controlled analgesic (PCA) pumps – patient bedside pain relief devices that are widely used in clinical care, despite having a history of safety problems. The project produces a broad collection of linked and deeply integrated artifacts including use cases, concepts of operation, requirements, formal architectural models, formal behavioral specifications, testing and verification artifacts, and assurance cases.

As part of this effort, the Open PCA project is investigating the use of model-based safety analysis (MBSA) techniques in the context of the SAE standard Architecture, Analysis, and Definition Language (AADL) [1] – the modeling framework used in the project. AADL includes a standardized Error Modeling (EM) annex [2] that provides modeling annotations for MBSA, and the Eclipse-based OSATE integrated development environment for AADL provides basic analysis and reporting capabilities for the EM annex.

Unfortunately, there are few publicly available completely worked examples of AADL EM for large systems. The examples that exist are related to the avionics domain, and the EM annotation libraries supplied with OSATE are oriented to the avionics domain (e.g., ARP 4761). Thus, in its current state, AADL EM and associated tooling does not include infrastructure to directly support the concepts, terminology, and reporting for medical device risk management (ISO 14971), and there are no realistic medical device examples that could help players in the medical device domain understand AADL-based MBSA, its integration into the medical device development lifecycle, and its potential benefits.

The contributions of this paper are as follows:

- We report on an MBSA analysis for one of the largest, most complex medical device examples considered in the academic/industry literature to date. This work also represents one of the most complete to-scale application of the SAE's AADL EM standard in any domain.
- We illustrate an approach to developing model annotation libraries that instantiate the AADL EM framework to support ISO 14971 risk management,

– We demonstrate how a scalable dependence and error flow analysis framework called Awas [5] that we have developed for AADL can support the key steps of ISO 14971 risk analysis that uses AADL EM.

All of the artifacts described in this paper including AADL models, EM specifications, and analysis reports are freely available under an open source license, along with other Open PCA Pump artifacts (requirements, formal specifications, assurance cases, etc.) on our project website [19].[1]

2   Background - PCA Infusion Pump

A PCA infusion pump is a medical device intended to administer intravenous (IV) infusion of pain medication to the patient in a variety of clinical settings. During clinical use, a caregiver (typically nurse) first prepares the PCA pump by loading a vial of medication, priming the pump's infusion set (tubing and needle), and connecting the pump to the patient via the infusion set. The caregiver then configures infusion parameters (e.g., infusion volume, rate, and duration) on the pump's operator interface and initiates the infusion.

A PCA pump is able to deliver medication in either a basal or bolus mode, where the former continuously delivers medication at a low rate and the latter delivers a bulk of medication in a short period of time. The patient can request for additional boluses for further pain relief by pressing a hand-held button provided by the pump, although too many patient-requested boluses can pose severe overdosing risks to the patient.

While PCA pumps (and infusion pumps in general) have allowed for a greater level of control and accuracy in drug delivery, they have been associated with persistent safety problems [26]. This led FDA to take a broad set of steps to enhance infusion pump safety [27], including imposing special design control over infusion pumps coming to the market [9]. This special control requires, among many other things, manufacturers to use risk management best practices in identifying and controlling risks associated with their products.

3   Open PCA Pump Architecture

Many of the Open PCA Pump artifacts integrate with or have traceability to AADL EM MBSA. The most closely related artifact is the architecture model, into which the annotations for the AADL EM MBSA are integrated. This section provides a brief summary of the architectural model, with a focus on attributes related to the MBSA. Readers can download the full models from the project website [19] and find a high-level description in [13].

The Open PCA Pump extends and specializes the ISOSCELES medical device reference architecture [8]. The ISOSCELES reference architecture is essentially an AADL model that separates functional architecture (including software) from the physical architecture (components, wires and assemblies), and

---

[1] The following is a direct link to the artifacts for this paper https://awas.sireum.org/doc/03-risk-analysis/index.html.

includes generic subsystems for operation, safety, user interface, network interface, power, and sensors/actuators. The Open PCA Pump AADL model extends
the ISOSCELES architecture with sensors and actuators for drug infusion, and
detailed software behavior.

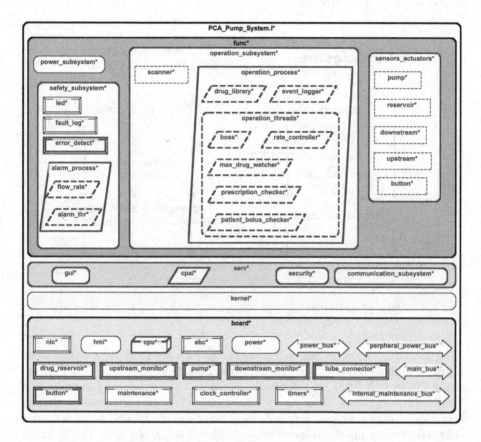

Fig. 1. Open PCA Pump containment hierarchy

Figure 1 shows the Open PCA Pump containment hierarchy which retains the
ISOSCELES architectural layering of a functional architecture using ISOSCE-
LES runtime services, isolated by a separation kernel, executed by physical hardware. The full architecture includes separate AADL projects for the ISOSCELES
medical device platform and its Open PCA Pump refinement, having thirty-nine
packages together. AADL distinguishes component *types* which define externally-
visible interfaces, from component *implementations* which define internal behavior and decomposition into subcomponents. The Open PCA Pump AADL model
defines in total 121 component types and implementations.

It is noteworthy that the Safety subsystem exemplifies a medical device
safety architecture that separate software and hardware used for detecting unsafe

conditions and mitigating hazards from those used for normal device operation. Following the principles in [17], the Safety subsystem is designed to have three physical devices that can detect, react to, annunciate, and log faults. More complex faults are detected by software (AADL threads), executing in a protected address space (AADL process).

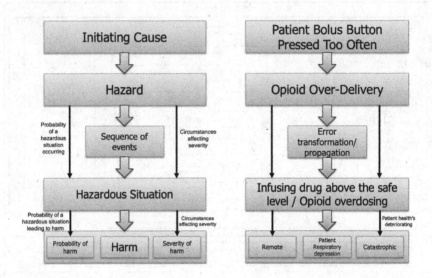

Fig. 2. ISO 14971 key risk analysis terms and relationships

In these models, important behavioral properties are formally specified using contracts and assertions from the Behavior Language for Embedded Systems with Software (BLESS) [16]. Similarly, behavior can be formally expressed as BLESS state machines. One can formally verify that the state machine implementations conform to contracts and assertions using the BLESS proof assistant, which transforms proof outlines into deductive, human-readable, proofs under human guidance.

4   Medical Device Risk Management Concepts

ISO 14971 defines a number of concepts that need to be reflected in medical device MBSA. *Harm* is defined as "injury or damage to the health of people, or damage to property or the environment". *Hazard* is a "potential source of harm", and a *hazardous situation* is a "circumstance in which people, property or the environment is/are exposed to one or more hazards." *Initiating cause* is not a ISO 14971 defined term, but it is used in the standard to refer to faults or other issues that lead to a hazard.

The left side of Fig. 2 (slightly adapted from ISO 14971 Annex C) illustrates the relationships between these terms. The scope of our work is *functional safety*

– potential harms associated with incorrect function of software and hardware elements of the device, rather than physical, chemical, mechanical, electrical, and biological safety discussed in ISO 14971. Table 1 provides instances of the terms of Fig. 2 related to the functional safety of the PCA Pump. The two primary hazards are opioid over-infusion and infusion of air bubbles into the patient blood stream – in both situations, severe consequences including death can be caused to the patient. Both of these hazards can have multiple initiating causes (excerpts are shown in Table 1), and our full models capture these along with associated mitigations. Due to space constraints, we limit detailed discussion to selected cases.

Table 1. ISO 14971 risk analysis concepts applied to the PCA Pump (excerpts)

Harm	Hazardous situation	Hazard	Initiating cause
Cardiac arrest	Infusing Opioid when patient's respiration is deteriorating	Opioid over-infusion	a. Bolus button pressed too frequent b. Incorrect pump calibration
Tissue or organ damage	Infusing air bubbles into the patient's blood stream	Air embolism	Continue infusion i) after inappropriate priming, ii) with empty reservoir, or iii) under tubing leakage

The right side of Fig. 2 provides one such case in which opioid over-infusion has an initiating cause associated with the patient bolus button being pressed too frequently. One of the purposes of risk analysis is to identify causal relationships between the ultimate harm and potential causes – either working top-down (starting from the harm to the patient and hazardous situation at the boundary of the system and environment and working "down" through various notions of dependence in the system (control actions, information flows from sensors through system state and control laws, and other less direct notions such as interference between functions due to resource constraints)) or bottom up (starting from failures of components or communication, or events in the environment that may cause the system to move to an unsafe state). Looking at Fig. 2 from a bottom-up view, causality flows from events in the environment (i.e., the patient pushing the bolus button repeatedly over a period of time) through button press detection, through the system's logic that calculates pump flow rate, through commands to the pump motor, triggering increased opioid flow rates from the pump into the patient's blood vessels. In this scenario, the initiating cause is the repeated bolus button pushes over time. The system control logic commands the pump motor to increase flow rates, resulting in hazard (potential source of harm) of a high drug flow rate. The hazardous situation is the patient being exposed to a high drug flow over time, leading to a harm of cardiac arrest.

If risk reduction is needed to bring risk to an acceptable level, risk controls are designed, implemented, and verified. Risk controls can involve (a) removing the source of harm, (b) reducing the probability of occurrence of harm (either by the device controlling aspects of the system or environment) and/or severity of the harm, or (c) detecting the occurrence of a harm and calling for user intervention. In the hazardous situation of Fig. 2, the hazard (related to the presence of opioid) cannot be eliminated since that is the source of therapy (pain relief). However, probability of occurrence and severity can be reduced via pump controls to limit the maximum dosage of opioid that the patient can receive over a period of time. In addition, detection of harm occurrence can include the simultaneous use of additional medical devices (e.g. pulse oximetry and capnography) that monitor patient vital signs.

In addition to capturing causality information with mappings to initiating cause, hazards, and hazardous situations, the broader risk management process benefits from model-based capture of device-based risk controls and indication of the scope of verification of risk-based controls. Note that risk controls of type (a) or (b) above are properties of the design design/function can be captured via "before" and "after controls" device models, whereas type (c) is a property of the broader environment (outside of the boundary of the device). Our focus in this paper is on types (a) and (b).

5   AADL Error Modeling for the OpenPCA System

As described in [2], the AADL Error Modeling annex document enables modeling of different types of faults, fault behavior of individual components, fault propagation across components in terms of peer-to-peer interactions and deployment relationships between software components and their execution platform, and aggregation and propagation of fault behavior across the component hierarchy.

AADL EM provides an *error type* facility to specify categories of errors and faults for a particular application or organization, each of which are represented as *error tokens* – values of error types. One main activity in AADL EM modeling is to specify error propagation rules within the model that describe how error tokens propagate from component inputs to outputs and along other model relationships (e.g., deployment bindings). The basic causality and dependence information captured in the AADL EM error propagation annotations can be used to support both forwards and backwards analyses of causality chains.

Using AADL EM involves a *layering* of concepts and annotations. On top of the architecture definitions (e.g., as presented Sect. 3), error flow/propagation annotations describe how errors propagate between component inputs and outputs (intra-component). In underlying tools, these are combined with model associations such as component connections and bindings to create a error flow graph. The elements that flow along the arcs in the graph are error tokens defined using the EM error token/type facility.

To design the framework, we used AADL's *property set* extensibility mechanism to add schemas for new properties capturing the ISO 14971 notions of harm, hazard, hazardous situation, and initiating cause. We configured AADL's property association mechanism to allow the analyst to associate declarations of hazard, hazardous situation, and initiating cause to various points in the architecture and to specific error tokens. The analyst uses the existing AADL EM error type mechanism to declare fault/error classifications appropriate to the product. Further, the analyst uses the EM error propagation rules to indicate how error, faults, and their effects propagate through the system, according to their knowledge of the system's behavior and structure. Section 6 describes new analysis automation and reporting mechanisms that we have developed that aggregate all of these annotations into structure information that can be actively browsed, queried, and used to generate ISO 14971 aligned risk analysis reports with active elements that link directly to models and causality visualizations.

Preparing the ISO 14971 Framework – Tool Designer: Part of our effort to configure AADL EM for ISO 14971 involved defining schemas for related properties. The listing below shows the schema for the notion of harm. Schemas for Hazard, Hazardous Situation, and Cause are similar.

```
Harm: type record ( ID: aadlstring; -- unique ID used as reference to the harm
  Description: aadlstring; -- description used in report generation
  Severity: ISO14971_80001::SeverityScales;); -- associate severity
```

AADL EM includes a standard error type library that captures many of the notions in the fault taxonomy of [4]. For this paper, we configured a simplified type library that is sufficiently general for supporting medical device risk analysis. Device manufacturers can further specialize the library to introduce notions of fault and error specific to their products. As an example of such customization, previous work from our research group created specializations for supporting risk analysis for interoperability and security related issues [22].

Identifying Harms, Hazards, and Hazardous Situations for a Device – Analyst: Drawing on information gathered from the ISO 14971 process steps of "gathering characteristic related to safety" and "identifying hazards" (clauses 5.3 and 5.4) the analyst introduces model annotations to capture harms and hazards. The discovery of harms/hazards cannot be supported to any significant degree by automated tooling, but instead relies on domain knowledge, experience, clinical trials, and medical domain literature to identify relevant harms and hazards. The listing below illustrates the definition of an over-infusion hazard and an associated harm of respiratory depression.

a. Harm and Hazard instance   b. Cause Instance

```
--Harm
H1: constant ISO14971_80001::Harm => [
   ID => "H1";
   Description => "Respiratory Depression";
   Severity => Catastrophic; ];
--Hazards
Haz1: constant ISO14971_80001::Hazard => [
   ID => "Haz1";
   Description => "Drug over-infusion"; ];
```

```
FrequentButtonPress : constant
   ISO14971_80001::Cause => [
   ID => "FrequentButtonPress";
   Description => "";
   Probability =>  Frequent; ];
```

Similarly, the analyst introduces property that will label events/state in the device or environment that represent an initial step in a causality chain. The example below illustrates the introduction of a reporting label for a frequent bolus button press (one of the root causes of a potential over-infusion hazard). Additional causes may also be discovered and added in the process of the analysis (e.g., applying the tools of Sect. 6).

To configure the error propagation layer, based on their domain knowledge, analysts introduce EM error types representing different types of root causes and observable problematic device behaviors that may contribute to harms. The listing below shows excerpts that define error types for problematic environment actions that (without mitigation) may cause harms as well as observable device behaviors that may lead to harms.

```
annex EMV2 {**
   error types --errors caused in the environment
   DrugKindError : type;   --wrong drug is loaded into reservoir
   TooSoonPress : type;    -- patient button pressed too soon/often
   ThirdPartyPress : type; --someone other than the patient presses the button
      ...
   -- errors indicating patient harm
   AirEmbolism : type;   -- air bubble in fluid emitted from device
   DrugOverInfusion : type; -- too much drug, possibly harmful
   DrugUnderInfusion : type; -- too little drug, insufficient to reduce pain
**}
```

Now the analyst uses AADL EM annotations to connect the layers in the framework – linking the elements above to the architecture description. Such annotations are added throughout the architecture, but an especially important step is the treatment of the system boundary to reflect both environmental causes of hazards (typically associated with device inputs) and observable device behaviors that may lead to harm (typically associated with device outputs). The listing below shows excerpts of the system boundary model – focusing on annotations that address frequent bolus request/over-infusion.

```
system PCA_Pump_System extends Platform::Generic_System
 features
  sense: refined to feature group iPCA_Feature_Groups::Sensing_iPCA;
  act: refined to feature group iPCA_Feature_Groups::Actuation_iPCA;
  fill_drug: in data port Physical_Types::Fluid_Volume;
 properties
  ISO14971_80001::SystemInfo => [
   Name => "Open PCA Pump";
   Description => "Patient-Controlled Analgesic infusion pump";
   IntendedUse => "patient for pain management"; ];
  ISO14971_80001::Hazardous_Situations => (HazardousSituations::OverInfusion,
       HazardousSituations::UnderInfusion, HazardousSituations::IncorrectDrug);
  annex EMV2 {**
   use types iPCA_Error_Model, ErrorLibrary;      -- import error types
   error propagations
    -- drug output may be wrong flow rate, kind of drug, or air bubble
    act.drug_outlet: out propagation {DrugStopped, DrugOverInfusion,
       DrugUnderInfusion, DrugKindError, AirEmbolism};
    fill_drug: in propagation {DrugKindError};   -- wrong drug filled
    -- button pressed before next bolus permitted
    sense.patient_button_press: in propagation {TooSoonPress, ThirdPartyPress};
    sense.barcode_signal: in propagation {ValueError};   --barcode corruption
    sense.ui_touch: in propagation {OperatorError};   -- clinician error
   end propagations;
   properties   -- AADL properties specify error sources and resulting harms
    ISO14971_80001::causes => (Causes::FrequentButtonPress)
         applies to sense.patient_button_press.TooSoonPress;
    ISO14971_80001::causes => (Causes::IncorrectDrug)
         applies to fill_drug.DrugKindError;
    ISO14971_80001::Hazards => (Hazards::Haz1)
         applies to act.drug_outlet.DrugOverInfusion;
    ISO14971_80001::Hazards => (Hazards::Haz2)
         applies to act.drug_outlet.DrugUnderInfusion;
    ISO14971_80001::Hazards => (Hazards::Haz3)
         applies to act.drug_outlet.DrugKindError;
  **};
 end PCA_Pump_System;
```

In particular, on the `patient_button_press` sensor input, an EM flow annotation of `ButtonError` models button presses that occur too often. The AADL EM `applies` construct associates the `Cause::FrequentButtonPress` cause with the `ButtonError` flow token, which has the effect of linking the error token (and flows proceeding) from the token to the reporting framework as a possible cause of (and causality chain leading to) a hazard. Similarly, the `DrugOverInfusionToken` is associated with `drug_outlet` output, and then associates flow leading into that token as well as the token itself with the `Haz1` annotation which is understood by the reporting framework.

Using the Analysis Framework to Identify Sequences of Events – Analyst: The analyst adds flow annotations to components throughout the architecture to model causality paths and then uses the analysis capabilities in Sect. 6 to compute various forms of reachability and report generation.

The fragments in the listing below illustrates how flow annotations are added to capture error propagations indicating that a component (a) may be a *source* of an error, (b) may propagate errors (and possibly transform the type of error), and (c) may *sink* an error (i.e., serve as a mitigation for an error).

```
calibration_over : error source drug_outlet{DrugOverInfusion};
mp_err: error path drug_intake{DrugKindError} -> drug_outlet{DrugKindError};
over: error path bindings {HighValue} -> drug_outlet{DrugOverInfusion};
pbc: error sink patient_button_request {TooSoonPress, ThirdPartyPress};
```

In the component for the mechanical pump which takes actuation commands from the control logic (including setting the flow rate), the first line in the listing models the fact that a lack of calibration of the pump itself could cause fluid to be moved out of the `drug_outlet` port at a rate that exceeds the pump's specification, resulting in an drug over-infusion error (a corresponding under-infusion error is omitted). The second line models a situation where the wrong drug enters the `drug_intake` port (intuitively, because the nurse has entered a vial in the drug reservoir with the wrong drug) – in this case, the error propagates from the input to the output (i.e., the wrong drug flows through mechanical pump). The third line models a situation where the control logic has commanded a flow rate that is too high: the `HighValue` error is transformed to a `DrugOverInfusion` error indicating that the bad command causes a problematic high flow out of the mechanical pump. The final line models the patient bolus checker component that (partially) mitigates errors related to the bolus button being pushed too soon or by a third party by limiting the number of active button pushes over a time period. In this case, the component acts as a sink for the errors.

As flows are explored using the tools in Sect. 6, the analyst is interested in understanding the relationships between causes, hazards, and harms. A hazardous situation describes relationships between a hazard and a harm. The analyst records a hazardous situation by introducing a model property such as in the listing below. The hazardous situation instance below describes a scenario in which the Haz1 leads to the harm H1. During the analysis, the causality relationship between hazards and initiating causes are computed. Hence, providing a complete scenario of error flow from initiating cause to hazards to hazardous situation and finally leading to harms (this is reflected in the 14971 reports described in the following section).

```
OverInfusion : constant ISO14971_80001::Hazardous_Situation => [
 ID => "OverInfusion";
 Description => "Infusing drug when the patient's health is deteriorating";
 Hazard => Hazards::Haz1;
 Paths_to_Harm => ([
  Harm => Harms::H1;
  Contributing_Factors => (ContributingFactors::HealthDeteriorating);
  Probability_of_Transition => Remote;]);
 Risk => High;
 Probability => Remote; ];
```

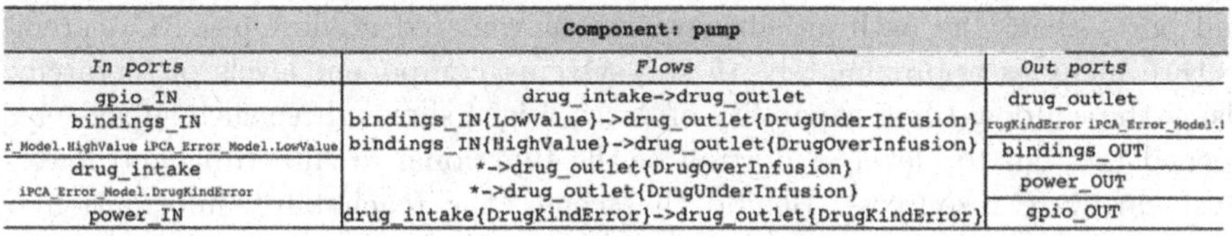

Component: pump		
In ports	*Flows*	*Out ports*
gpio_IN	drug_intake->drug_outlet	drug_outlet
bindings_IN	bindings_IN{LowValue}->drug_outlet{DrugUnderInfusion}	rugKindError iPCA_Error_Model.i
r_Model.HighValue iPCA_Error_Model.LowValue	bindings_IN{HighValue}->drug_outlet{DrugOverInfusion}	bindings_OUT
drug_intake	*->drug_outlet{DrugOverInfusion}	power_OUT
iPCA_Error_Model.DrugKindError	*->drug_outlet{DrugUnderInfusion}	power_OUT
power_IN	drug_intake{DrugKindError}->drug_outlet{DrugKindError}	gpio_OUT

Fig. 3. Awas AADL intra-component error flows visualization

6   AADL Error Modeling Analysis Support

The OSATE AADL EM plug-in provides several different forms of safety analysis including fault tree analysis and a simple functional hazard analysis. In this section, we illustrate Awas [5] which complements these existing analysis with a scalable interactive visualizations and queries of error flows. In the ISO 14971 context, these capabilities are applied to automated discover and visualize potential "sequence of events" leading from causes to hazards, to hazardous situations, to harms.

Awas builds *component* and *system* visualizations that are tailored to illustrating *flow-related* aspects. Figure 3 illustrates how Awas builds a component-level summary of flow properties that show component inputs (left side), outputs (right side), and the error flow rules (middle) that the analyst has specified to capture how error tokens propagate from inputs to outputs.

Awas builds a dependence graph composed from intra-component flows (as in Fig. 3) together with several forms of inter-component dependences including port connections, component bindings, etc. The flow graph representation and analysis algorithms are written in Scala and compiled to Javascript using the Scala.js framework[2]. This generates a highly navigable, dynamic visualization of flows integrated across all levels of the system hierarchy. The most basic capability is forward/backward reachability analysis. Analysts simply click on a component or port and press a button to carry out basic queries such as "where in the system do the modeled errors (and their subsequent impacts) from this port/component flow?" or "what system elements are contributing errors that flow into this port/component?".

In the example of Fig. 4[3], the analyst clicks on the system boundary sense.patient_button_press input port with an error token indicating a possible "too frequent" bolus button push and presses the Forward analysis button to have the tool discover and mark up to the where in the architecture the effects of this error may propagate (paths are shown in red, and components

---

[2] www.scalajs.org.

[3] Note that the purpose of these screenshots is to illustrate application of the Awas tools at scale (capturing system-wide browsing across a large system with many complex components). The screen captures of the tool cannot capture both the scalability aspect while preserving the readability of the component/port/details, etc. In the Awas tool, mouse scrolling easily zooms in and out to reveal details.

and ports along the path are shown in green and red). The Open PCA architecture includes approximately 19 sub-systems/component levels of hierarchy. Using the window-tiling capability of Awas, Fig. 4 shows three such subsystems opened (system top-level, a portion of the functional architecture, and lower-level hardware resources). Behind the scenes, the reachability information is computed almost instantaneously across the entire system, A simple scroll of a mouse wheel zooms into a particular system section or component of interest. Double-clicking on components drills down to their subcomponent models. Projections of the system can be performed on components/flows of user-specified categories, or components along user-specified paths.

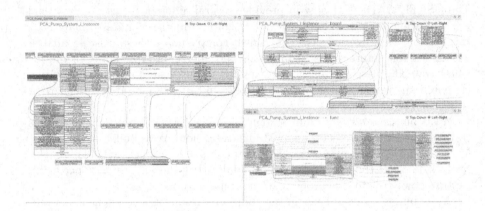

Fig. 4. Awas AADL system-wide error flow visualization (selected sub-systems)

This supports expected ISO 14971 workflows as follows. Working in either a bottom up manner (from causes to hazardous situations) or top-down manner (from hazardous situations to causes), the analyst uses both forward and backward Awas reachability to discover causality chains in the error-flow annotated architecture. Annotations marking causes and hazardous situations are incrementally added to the model as important aspects of error propagations are revealed in Awas. The web-site supporting this submission illustrates further capabilities in the browser-based deployment of Awas (no tool installation needed) including the ability to define and save more sophisticated queries written in a form of path logic. As the analyst discovers error propagations and begins to annotate the architecture for mitigation strategies, this enables common queries corresponding to hazardous situations to be replayed as mitigations are added to confirm that impacts of causes are eliminated or reduced.

On top of the general Awas capabilities, we have developed a reporting tool that produces information in the formats suggested by ISO 14971 and associated medical domain risk management guidance. Figure 5 illustrates an excerpt of this report that captures the association between hazardous situations and related concepts. This information is automatically extracted from the model

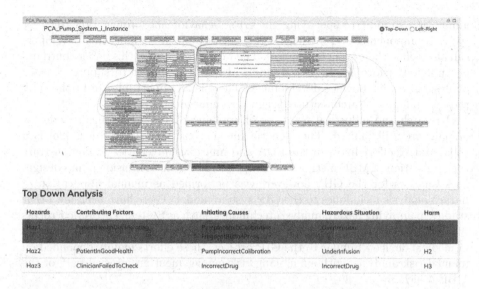

Fig. 5. Awas ISO 14971 report (excerpts) illustrating sequence of events leading to hazardous situation (Color figure online)

based on the model annotations of Sect. 5 and the Awas reachability analysis. Both PDF and HTML versions of the report are produced. The HTML report (Fig. 5) is "animated" in the sense that one can highlight a certain hazardous situation (the selection is shown in blue), the Awas visualization for the causality chain from cause through hazardous situation to harm is automatically computed and displayed in the report, corresponding to the ISO 14971 requirement that the analyst uncover "series of events" (see Fig. 2) along the causality pathway). Figure 5 shows excerpts capturing only a portion of information related to the over-infusion hazard. The website artifacts show a much expanded report capturing a number of other hazardous situations.

7   Related Work

The development and application of MBSA techniques have been widely studied in other safety-critical domains such as avionics and automotive, with the goals to support system-level safety assurance and to help manufacturers better comply with the mandatory safety standards (such as ISO 26262). These techniques combine safety analysis techniques (such as HiP-HOPS [20]) with system design models specified in languages like AADL, SysML, and Mathworks' Simulink, to provide the developers better visibility into how design changes or errors within the system model propagate across the system and give rise to risks. Extensive review of MBTA techniques in these domains can be found in [3,23].

MBSA techniques based on AADL EM, like [7,10] and the one presented in this paper, follow the same safety analysis paradigm. AADL EM provides strong annotation support to specifying the error behavior and propagation rules for system components, and includes a rich set of built-in errors (while developers can also define their own error types). The work presented in this paper continues our previous effort [15,21] in extending the AADL toolset to support hazard analysis in medical device development. There is an opportunity to further link these techniques to architecture design techniques for safety (e.g., [17,24]).

Research and industrial practices of applying MBSA to the medical device domain are still limited. The Generic Infusion Pump (GIP) project [25] is a collaborative effort between the FDA and multiple universities to demonstrate the application of MBE methods to an open-source generic infusion pump design. Risk analysis for the GIP, however, was performed as manual application of hazard analysis techniques to the GIP system model. There have been few other studies in applying hazard analysis techniques, such as System Theoretic Process Analysis (STPA) [6,18] and HAZOP (Hazard Operability) [11], to different types of medical devices. Similar to the GIP project, these efforts mainly depended on manual risk analysis, without making risk management an integral part of the MBE toolchain.

8   Conclusion

We have provided an overview of how AADL EM can be used to support MBSA for medical devices in alignment with the ISO 14971 standard. For medical device manufacturers and regulators that may be unfamiliar with any form of MBSA, this work illustrates how an architecture-integrated MBSA may be carried out with a broader collection of artifacts that are part of the Open PCA project.

We have also demonstrated how the Awas AADL dependence analysis and visualization tool can be applied to support specific steps in AADL safety analysis and how reporting capabilities can be developed to support the ISO 14971 risk management process. We believe that the visualizations and error flow browsing capabilities can provide multiple practical benefits to practitioners working on full-scale systems.

References

1. Architecture Analysis & Design Language (AADL) (Rev. C). Aerospace Standard AS5506C (2017)
2. Architecture analysis and design language (AADL) annex volume 1: Annex E: Error model annex (2015)
3. Aizpurua, J.I., Muxika, E.: Model-based design of dependable systems: limitations and evolution of analysis and verification approaches. Int. J. Adv. Secur. 6(1&2), 12–31 (2013)
4. Avizienis, A., Laprie, J.C., Randell, B., Landwehr, C.: Basic concepts and taxonomy of dependable and secure computing. IEEE Trans. Depend. Secure Comput. 1(1), 11–33 (2004)
5. Sireum Awas (2018). https://awas.sireum.org

6. Blandine, A.: Systems Theoretic Hazard Analysis (STPA) applied to the risk review of complex systems: an example from the medical device industry. Ph.D. dissertation, Massachusetts Institute of Technology (2013)

7. Brunel, J., et al.: Performing safety analyses with AADL and AltaRica. In: Proceedings of 4th International Symposium on Model-Based Safety and Assessment, pp. 67–81 (2017)

8. Carpenter, T., Hatcliff, J., Vasserman, E.Y.: A reference separation architecture for mixed-criticality medical and IoT devices. In: Proceedings of the ACM Workshop on the Internet of Safe Things (SafeThings). ACM, November 2017

9. Center for Devices and Radiological Health: Infusion Pumps Total Product Life Cycle-Guidance for Industry and FDA Staff. Technical report FDA-2010-D-0194, US Food and Drug Administration (2014)

10. Delange, J., Feiler, P.: Architecture fault modeling with the AADL error-model annex. In: 2014 40th EUROMICRO Conference on Software Engineering and Advanced Applications, pp. 361–368 (2014)

11. Guiochet, J., Hoang, Q.A.D., Kaaniche, M., Powell, D.: Model-based safety analysis of human-robot interactions: the MIRAS walking assistance robot. In: Proceedings of IEEE 13th International Conference on Rehabilitation Robotics, pp. 1–7 (2013)

12. Hatcliff, J., Larson, B., Carpenter, T., Jones, P., Zhang, Y., Jorgens, J.: The Open PCA pump project: an exemplar open source medical device as a community resource. SIGBED Rev. **16**, 8–13 (2019)

13. Hatcliff, J., Larson, B.R., Belt, J., Robby, Zhang, Y.: A unified approach for modeling, developing, and assuring critical systems. In: Margaria T., Steffen B. (eds.) Leveraging Applications of Formal Methods, Verification and Validation. Modeling, ISoLA 2018. LNCS, vol. 11244, pp. 225–245. Springer, Cham (2018). https://doi.org/10.1007/978-3-030-03418-4_14

14. ISO: ISO 14971:2019(E) Medical devices - Application of risk management to medical devices (2019)

15. Larson, B., Hatcliff, J., Fowler, K., Delange, J.: Illustrating the AADL error modeling annex (v.2) using a simple safety-critical medical device. In: Proceedings of the 2013 ACM SIGAda Annual Conference on High Integrity Language Technology, HILT 2013, pp. 65–84. ACM, New York (2013)

16. Larson, B.R., Chalin, P., Hatcliff, J.: BLESS: formal specification and verification of behaviors for embedded systems with software. In: Brat, G., Rungta, N., Venet, A. (eds.) NFM 2013. LNCS, vol. 7871, pp. 276–290. Springer, Heidelberg (2013). https://doi.org/10.1007/978-3-642-38088-4_19

17. Larson, B.R., Jones, P., Zhang, Y., Hatcliff, J.: Principles and benefits of explicitly designed medical device safety architecture. Biomed. Instrum. Technol. **51**(5), 380–389 (2017)

18. Masci, P., Zhang, Y., Jones, P., Campos, J.C.: A hazard analysis method for systematic identification of safety requirements for user interface software in medical devices. In: Cimatti, A., Sirjani, M. (eds.) SEFM 2017. LNCS, vol. 10469, pp. 284–299. Springer, Cham (2017). https://doi.org/10.1007/978-3-319-66197-1_18

19. Open PCA Pump Project (2018). http://openpcapump.santoslab.org

20. Papadopoulos, Y., McDermid, J.A.: Hierarchically performed hazard origin and propagation studies. In: Felici, M., Kanoun, K. (eds.) SAFECOMP 1999. LNCS, vol. 1698, pp. 139–152. Springer, Heidelberg (1999). https://doi.org/10.1007/3-540-48249-0_13

21. Procter, S., Hatcliff, J.: An architecturally-integrated, systems-based hazard analysis for medical applications. In: 2014 Twelfth ACM/IEEE Conference on Formal Methods and Models for Codesign (MEMOCODE), pp. 124–133, October 2014

22. Procter, S., Vasserman, E.Y., Hatcliff, J.: Safe and secure: deeply integrating security in a new hazard analysis. In: Proceedings of ASSURE 2018 International Workshop on Assurance Cases for Software-Intensive Systems, pp. 1–10, September 2018

23. Sharvia, S., Kabir, S., Walker, M., Papadopulos, Y.: Model-based dependability analysis: state-of-the-art, challenges, and future outlook. In: Software Quality Assurance, pp. 251–278. Morgan Kaufmann (2016)

24. Sun, M., Meseguer, J., Sha, L.: A formal pattern architecture for safe medical systems. In: Ölveczky, P.C. (ed.) WRLA 2010. LNCS, vol. 6381, pp. 157–173. Springer, Heidelberg (2010). https://doi.org/10.1007/978-3-642-16310-4_11

25. University of Pennsylvania Real Time Systems Group: The Generic Infusion Pump (GIP). http://rtg.cis.upenn.edu/gip.php3

26. US Food and Drug Administration: Examples of Reported Infusion Pump Problems. https://www.fda.gov/medical-devices/infusion-pumps/examples-reported-infusion-pump-problems

27. US Food and Drug Administration: Infusion Pump Improvement Initiative. https://www.fda.gov/medical-devices/infusion-pumps/infusion-pump-improvement-initiative

State-Space Modeling

Reliability Evaluation of Reconfigurable NMR Architecture Supported with Hot Standby Spare: Markov Modeling and Formulation

Koorosh Aslansefat[1](✉), Gholamreza Latif-Shabgahi[2], and Mehrdad Mohammadi[2]

[1] Department of Computer Science and Technology, University of Hull, Hull, UK
k.aslansefat-2018@hull.ac.uk

[2] Department of Electrical Engineering, Shahid Beheshti University, Tehran, Iran

Abstract. Reliability is a major issue for fault-tolerant systems used in critical applications. N-modular redundancy (NMR) is one of the traditional approaches used for fault masking in fault-tolerant systems. Reconfigurable NMR architecture supported with hot or cold standby spares is a common industrial method. So far, no systematic method for creating the Markov model of reconfigurable NMR systems supported with hot standby spares has been presented. Likewise, there is no explicit parametric formula for the reliability of these systems in the literature. This paper focuses on two issues: the systematic construction of the Markov model of reconfigurable NMR system, and its evaluation through a precise and explicit formula introduces in this paper. The introduced formula gives for system designer a good view of reliability behaviour of the reconfigurable NMR systems.

Keywords: Hot standby spare · Hybrid redundancy · Markov modelling · Reconfigurable TMR architecture · Reliability

1 Introduction

A group of systems like aeroplane control and protection equipment, medical devices, and nuclear reactors must be designed fault-tolerant. In these systems, the occurrence of hardware faults or software errors does not cause irrecoverable catastrophic consequences or financial losses [1, 2]. The use of redundancy is one of the effective ways to design high reliable systems at the cost of increased weight, size, energy consumption and system complexity. N-modular redundancy (NMR) is one of the most used approaches for fault masking in fault-tolerant systems. It uses N similar modules, works in parallel with the same input, and subject their outputs to an adjudicator to generate a single value as system output. This architecture creates a correct output as long as $(N + 1)/2$ of its modules works fault free. In other words, this architecture masks $(N-1)/2$ faults of its inputs. The adjudicator is usually called "voter", and it can be implemented in software or hardware [3]. This architecture is as "static redundancy" or "masking redundancy" has referred in fault-tolerant textbooks. Another form of redundancy which is called "dynamic redundancy", is based on standby spare modules. This form has the potential to

© Springer Nature Switzerland AG 2020
M. Zeller and K. Höfig (Eds.): IMBSA 2020, LNCS 12297, pp. 53–67, 2020.
https://doi.org/10.1007/978-3-030-58920-2_4

detect, locate and isolate faulty modules to recover the system into operation. The combination of static and dynamic redundancy which is called "hybrid redundancy" offers a higher level of reliability than that of the static and dynamic systems alone [4, 5]. This paper investigates the reliability of "NMR architecture with reconfiguration capability" which has been used in many highly reliable applications such as flight control systems [6] and subsea blowout preventer control systems [7, 8].

There are various methods for evaluating the reliability of fault-tolerant systems from which Fault Tree (FT), Reliability Block Diagram (RBD), Continuous Time Markov Chain (CTMC) and Petri Net (PN) can be referred [9, 10]. The "reconfigurable NMR architecture" has temporal behaviour and this is why for its reliability evaluation either "CTMC" or "PN modelling" approach must be used [11]. In the literature, there is not a systematic way neither for creation the Markov model of "reconfigurable NMR architecture supported with n hot standby spares" nor for formulation its reliability. This paper presents a systematic way for creating the Markov model of "reconfigurable NMR architecture supported with n hot standby spares", and gives a general formula for its reliability. The organization of this paper is as follows

In Sect. 2, some previous research works on hybrid redundancy and their modelling are studied. In Sect. 3, systematic Markov modelling of NMR architecture supported with n hot standby spares is presented and in the next section, reliability solution and formulation for NMR architecture supported with a hot standby spare is achieved. Section 5 discusses the numerical results.

2   Hybrid Redundancy and Its Modelling

In the literature, several structures have been introduced as "Hybrid Redundant Systems". Examples are: a TMR architecture with modules each supported with one/two spares, a TMR architecture with self-diagnosis modules, a reserve system with modules each has TMR structure, a TMR architecture with duplicated modules, and a TMR architecture in which faulty modules can be automatically replaced by some extra spares. Moreover, in all mentioned structures, spare modules can appear in Cold, Warm or Hot type. This paper considers the last structure to study. The reason is that this structure is one of the widely used approaches in the industry. There have been some research works on the reliability evaluation of reconfigurable redundant systems.

In [4, 12, 13] the Markov model of different types of reconfigurable NMR has been addressed in which the representation of architectural features of the system in mathematical forms is emphasized. Reference [14] provided some reliability formulas for self-repairable TMR architecture supported with spares. This paper studied hybrid redundant system's reliability versus the failure rate of its constituent modules. References [15, 16], developed a mathematical model for Triple Modular Redundancy with Standby (TMRSB) systems for FPGA devices in which reconfiguration time overheads and imperfect switching effect are taken into account. The paper has shown that a TMRSB system is superior to the conventional TMR system with components for which failure rates obey from exponential distribution function. Reference [17] presented an approach to model fault-tolerant systems able to express dynamic attributes of fault-tolerant systems, such as reconfigurable redundancy, imperfect coverage, common cause errors, and failure propagation. Reference [18], evaluated the reliability and availability of a hybrid redundancy system in which each module of the NMR core can be replaced by one of k cold spares (k, N) and a repair facility. It uses the semi-Markov modelling approach. In reference [19], failure and repair rates have been assumed as fuzzy numbers and the results of two Markov models: one with fuzzy transition rates and the other with constant transition rates, have been compared. The Markov model of reconfigurable TMR architecture supported with standby spares along with reliability and sensitivity assessment was presented in [20]. This paper evaluated the reliability of systems with one and two cold spares without giving a systematic way for construction of the related Markov model and its solution. In two references of [21, 22], the authors of current paper provided a systematic method for Markov modelling of NMR architecture supported with n cold spares and suggested an explicit formula for reliability evaluation of that system in Laplace domain. However, due to the complexity of those formulas, their conversion to the time domain to express system reliability did not carry out. Reference [7] evaluated the reliability of reconfigurable TMR supported with two hot standby spares by the use of stochastic Petri Nets in which imperfect coverage and repair policy has been considered. The proposed model of this paper did not extend TMR to NMR. A new gate describing the TMR system supported by both cold and hot standby spare has been proposed by [23] for dynamic fault trees.

Despite published research works, there has been no work on the reliability formulation of reconfigurable NMR architecture supported with a pool of hot standby spares. Reported works have mainly focused on the reliability evaluation of TMR architecture (a triple modular system) with one/two spares (mainly cold standby spares). Perhaps, because in the industry due to weight and cost limitations the use of systems with more than three main modules and two spares is not beneficial. However, from the theoretical viewpoint and in some applications like pattern recognition and highly reliable systems, we need NMR supported with n spares (n > 3 and n > 2). Therefore, systematic modelling and reliability evaluation of such systems is important. This paper presents a systematic method for constructing Markov reliability model of reconfigurable NMR architecture supported with n hot standby spares and suggests a parametric and explicit formula for reliability evaluation of these type of systems. The results are then compared with the reliability of a simple NMR system exist in the literature. The systematic model and its solution enable designers to have a deep view on reliability behaviour of these systems.

3   Markov Modelling

Markov processes are a special class of stochastic processes. The fundamental assumption is that the behaviour of the system in each state is independent of that of the previous states. The transition from the current system state is determined only by the present state. Before the transition occurs, the time spent in each state follows an exponential distribution. In reliability engineering, this assumption is satisfied if all failures and repairs occur with constant occurrence rates. In reliability analysis, the state space is always binary: (operational and failed), but the time state is usually continuous which means that component failure and repair time are random variable. Thus continuous-time Markov chain is the most commonly used. Markov models are illustrated by state and transition diagrams in which each state is depicted by circle and transition is shown by an arrowed arc. For reliability model, a state is defined to be a particular combination of operating and failed components. Similarly, the state transition reflects the changes which occur within the system state [5]. This section is devoted to the construction of the Markov model of the system for its reliability evaluation through some examples.

3.1 Markov Model of Single Component Systems

Figure 1 shows the reliability model of a single component system. In this figure, it is assumed that the component failure, denoted by, obeys exponential distribution function. Since is small enough, the transition from state "O" to state "F" within occurs as (1).

$$e^{-n\lambda t} = 1 - n\lambda \Delta t + n^2\lambda^2 \Delta t^2 - \cdots \tag{1}$$

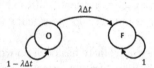

Fig. 1. Reliability Markov model of a single component system

In Fig. 1 the model operates correctly with the probability of at state (O) and fails with the probability of into absorbing state (F).

3.2 Markov Model of a Simple TMR Architecture

TMR architecture has been applied at different hardware levels including gate, chip, computer, sensor, actuator, PLC, etc. There is a considerable amount of research works conducted on its different aspects [5]. Assuming the ideal voter, and the same failure rate for its components, reliability Markov of a TMR system can be created Fig. 2 In this model, no repair is assumed. State "3" represents the initial condition of three working components. State "2" indicates the condition of one failed component. State "F" represents the failure state because a majority of the modules in the system have failed.

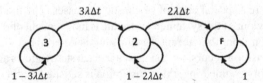

Fig. 2. Reliability Markov model of TMR architecture

Equation (2) is the reliability of TMR architecture, rewritten from previous literature [5].

$$R_{TMR}(t) = 3e^{-2\lambda t} - 2e^{-3\lambda t} \tag{2}$$

3.3 Markov Model of a Reconfigurable TMR Architecture

This section presents a systematic method for creating the Markov model of reconfigurable TMR architecture supported with hot standby spares. This method is explained with a reconfigurable TMR architecture supported with one hot spare. Schematic representation of a reconfigurable TMR architecture supported with n hot standby spare is shown in Fig. 3 The idea of this system is to provide a basic core of three modules arranged in a voting configuration through a switch. The system remains in the basic TMR configuration until a disagreement detector unit determines that faulty modules exist. One approach to fault detection is to compare the output of the voter with individual outputs of the modules. A module that disagrees with the majority value is labelled as a faulty module [24]. Upon the detection of disagreement between the outputs of working modules, the switching mechanism operates appropriately to replace it with one of the existing spares. This replacement is carried out until no spare remains. Therefore, this system tolerates (masks) S + 2 faults where n is the number of spares. The Fault detection unit and the switch are called "switching mechanism" in this paper and its probability of correct functioning is assumed "C". The probability of correct functioning of the switch can be extracted either from its MTBF given in its catalogue or from its historical record.

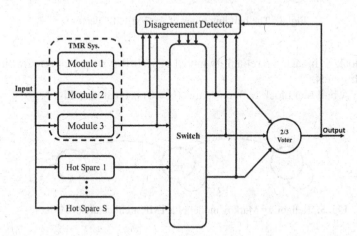

Fig. 3. A Schematic diagram for a reconfigurable TMR architecture supported with n hot spares

To create the Markov reliability model of a reconfigurable TMR, it is assumed that:

- All modules are physically isolated so that a failed module cannot affect other working modules.

- The system starts with no failed modules.
- The simultaneous occurrence of more than one fault such as common cause failures (CCFs) is not allowed.
- No repair is allowed.
- Upon the failure of each module the spare replaces it immediately.
- All modules are performing the same computation with the same inputs.

4   Systematic Model Construction

The proposed method creates the Markov reliability model of a reconfigurable TMR with "S" spares in four steps. In this model, each state is labelled with a vector (a, b) in which "a" represents the number of operational modules and "b" indicates the number of working spares. The "building block" of the model is defined in the form of chain shown in Fig. 4 This building block is made of three states. State (3, b) indicates the primary state of the whole system (three modules of the core and b spares are working correctly). Upon the failure of one of the main modules, the system goes to state (2, b) and the probability of this transition is. Upon the failure of the next module, the system goes to failing state with the transition probability. For more details, readers can see [23].

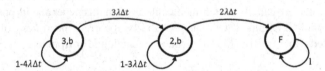

Fig. 4. The building block of the TMR architecture

This block is, in fact, the reliability model of a TMR system supported with a spare pool with b spares.

Step 1: A building block with no spares (b = 0) is created as Fig. 5.

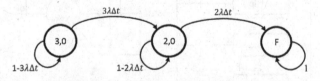

Fig. 5. Reliability Markov model of a TMR architecture (TMR core)

Step 2: Having constructed the model of Fig. 5 another building block with b = 1 is placed above the existing model (previous building block with b = 0). Figure 6 is obtained. Note that in the added building block all forward transitions are attached with coefficient "1−c". This is indicative of failing the switch. For example, It is clear that upon the failure of one main module in the state (3,1) the system will go to state (2,1) with the transient rate because of the inability of its switching.

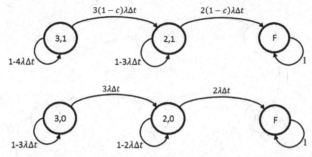

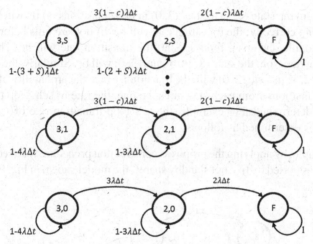

Fig. 6. Reliability Markov model creation of TMR architecture supported with a hot standby spare (Step 2.)

Fig. 7. Reliability Markov model creation of TMR architecture supported with S hot standby spare (Step 3.)

Step 3: A new building block with b = 2 is placed above the model of Fig. 7 and this procedure continues until b = S.

Step 4: In this step, the disjoint building blocks are connected, as follows to create the whole system model:

- All "F" state are merged.
- States (3, b) are connected via state transition with rate.
- States (2, b) are connected via state transition with rate.

Applying these rules to the model of Fig. 7 gives Fig. 8 which is the final model of a TMR architecture with one spare.

Lemma: We can now explain the transition rates of the model from Fig. 8 Starting from the primary state (3, 1) upon the failure of one of the main modules, if the switching mechanism functioning correctly, the system will go to state (2, 1) with the rate. The

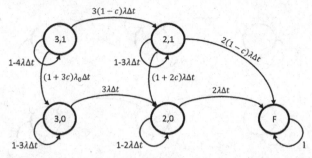

Fig. 8. Reliability Markov model creation of TMR architecture supported with a hot standby spare (Step 4.)

system goes from the state (3, 1) to state (3, 0) in two conditions: a) if switching mechanism functioning correctly; the transition rate will be. b) if spare fails before the failing of the main module and spare replacement; the transition rate will be. Therefore, the entire transition rate from the state (3, 1) to state (3, 0) will be. Similarly, the system goes from the state (2, 1) to state (2, 0) with the transition. Since the probability of all ongoing and ingoing transitions from each state must be one, the rate of self-loop transitions is automatically determined. For example, the self-loop transition rate of state (3, 1), if named x will be determined as follows:

As an example, by applying the proposed construction procedure for a reconfigurable TMR system supported by two hot standby spares, the model shown in Fig. 9 is obtained.

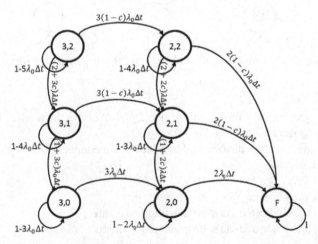

Fig. 9. Reliability Markov model of TMR architecture supported with two hot standby spare

Noted that, the transitions rate from the state (3, 2) to state (3,1) is in which denotes a condition when one of the primary modules has failed and switching mechanism has operated correctly or one of the two spares has been failed before replacement with a transition rate of. In general, the transition rate from the state (3, b) to state (3, b-1) is and similarly, the transition rate from the state (2, b) to state (2, b-1) is $(2c + b) \lambda \, \Delta t$.

The proposed procedure can be easily extended to model an NMR reconfigurable system supported with n hot spares as shown in Fig. 10 In this figure $A = N - 1$, $B = (N + 1)/2$ and $C = (N - 1)/2$.

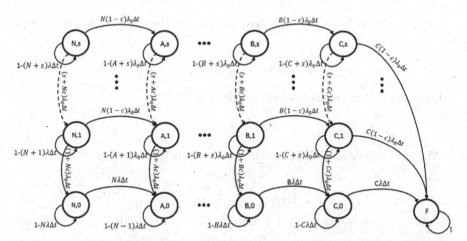

Fig. 10. Reliability Markov model of NMR architecture supported with two hot standby spare

It should be noted that the above-constructed model can be so complex without considering the proposed steps. For example, the example of subsea blowout preventer control systems provided by [8]. The model construction strategy can also be used in any other system and its Markov model (e.g. Markov model of UAV propulsion system [25]). The model can also be incorporated with other models in a complex system through using hierarchical dynamic fault tree [26] or complex basic event [27].

5   Reliability Analysis of Reconfigurable NMR Architecture Supported with a Hot Standby Spare

In this section, the reliability of a reconfigurable TMR architecture supported with a hot standby spare is evaluated from which formula is extracted for its reliability. The achieved formula is then extended to the NMR system. The Markov equations of Fig. 8 can be written as (3).

$$P(t + \Delta t) = M \cdot P(t) \tag{3}$$

Where P is the "states vector" (4) and M is the discrete state transition matrix (5).

$$P(t) = \left[P_{3,1}(t), P_{2,1}(t), P_3(t), P_2(t), P_F(t) \right]^T \tag{4}$$

$$M = \begin{bmatrix} 1-4\lambda\Delta t & 3(1-c)\lambda\Delta t & (1+3c)\lambda\Delta t & 0 & 0 \\ 0 & 1-3\lambda\Delta t & 0 & (1+2c)\lambda\Delta t & 2(1-c)\lambda\Delta t \\ 0 & 0 & 1-3\lambda\Delta t & 3\lambda\Delta t & 0 \\ 0 & 0 & 0 & 1-2\lambda\Delta t & 2\lambda\Delta t \\ 0 & 0 & 0 & 0 & 1 \end{bmatrix} \tag{5}$$

Equation (3) can be recursively solved if is known. The result at times is given by (6).

$$P(n\Delta t) = P^n.P(0) \tag{6}$$

Equation (3) in its continuous form is written as (7).

$$\dot{P}(t) = A.P(0) \tag{7}$$

Where A is the continuous Markov transition matrix in the form of (8).

$$A = \frac{\partial M^T}{\partial \Delta t} = \begin{bmatrix} -4\lambda & 0 & 0 & 0 & 0 \\ 3(1-c)\lambda & -3\lambda & 0 & 0 & 0 \\ (1+3c)\lambda & 0 & -3\lambda & 0 & 0 \\ 0 & (1+2c)\lambda & 3\lambda & -2\lambda & 0 \\ 0 & 2(1-c)\lambda & 0 & 2\lambda & 0 \end{bmatrix} \tag{8}$$

The solution of (7) results in the reliability of the system as (9) and (10).

$$R(t) = P_{3,1}(t) + P_{2,1}(t) + P_3(t) + P_2(t) \tag{9}$$

$$R_{TMR\_1S}(t) = \frac{e^{-4\lambda t}}{2}\left(-6c^2 + 12c\right)$$
$$+ e^{-3\lambda t}\left(6c^2 - 12c - 2\right) + \frac{e^{-2\lambda t}}{2}\left(-6c^2 + 12c + 6\right) \tag{10}$$

If the proposed procedure is used for 5MR and 7MR systems each supported with one spare the following equations are achieved.

$$R_{5MR\_1S}(t) = -\frac{e^{-6\lambda t}}{6}\left(60c^3 - 180c^2 + 180c\right)$$
$$+ \frac{e^{-5\lambda t}}{2}\left(60c^3 - 180c^2 + 180c + 12\right)$$
$$- \frac{e^{-4\lambda t}}{2}\left(60c^3 - 180c^2 + 180c + 30\right)$$
$$+ \frac{e^{-3\lambda t}}{6}\left(60c^3 - 180c^2 + 180c + 60\right) \tag{11}$$

$$R_{7MR_1S}(t) = -\frac{e^{-8\lambda t}}{24}\left(840c^4 - 3360c^3 + 5040c^2 - 3360c\right)$$

$$+ \frac{e^{-7\lambda t}}{6}\left(840c^4 - 3360c^3 + 5040c^2 - 3360c - 140\right)$$

$$- \frac{e^{-6\lambda t}}{4}\left(840c^4 - 3360c^3 + 5040c^2 - 3360c - 280\right)$$

$$+ \frac{e^{-5\lambda t}}{6}\left(840c^4 - 3360c^3 + 5040c^2 - 3360c - 504\right)$$

$$- \frac{e^{-4\lambda t}}{24}\left(840c^4 - 3360c^3 + 5040c^2 - 3360c - 840\right) \tag{12}$$

By extending Eqs. (10), (11) and (12), the following formula is obtained for the reliability of an NMR architecture supported with one hot spare.

$$R_{TMR\_1S}(t) = \sum_{k=(N+1)/2}^{N+1} \frac{(\alpha + \beta(N+1-k))e^{-k\lambda t}}{((N+1)/2)!/\binom{(N+1)/2}{k-(N+1)/2}} \tag{13}$$

In this formula, N is the number of modules and are computed from (14) and (15).

$$\alpha \triangleq \sum_{j=0}^{(N-1)/2} \binom{\frac{N+1}{2}}{j}\left(\prod_{i=\frac{N+1}{2}}^{N} i\right) c^{\left(\frac{N+1}{2}-j\right)}(-1)^{j+1} \tag{14}$$

$$\beta(k) \triangleq \begin{cases} 0 & k = \frac{N+1}{2} \\ \binom{k + \binom{\frac{N+1}{2}}{\frac{N-3}{2}}}{\frac{N+1}{2}}\left(\frac{N+1}{2}\right) & O.W. \end{cases} \tag{15}$$

6 Numerical Results

In this section, (13) is studied in details, and the reliability of NMR architecture supported with a hot standby spare is investigated in terms of system parameters. The reliability behaviour of both simple and reconfigurable TMR systems for, mission time = 400 (h) and various numbers of modules (N = 3, 5 and 7) have been calculated based on (13), and the results are shown in Table 1. As seen, when one spare is added to TMR architecture, the system reliability improves. The table shows that the reliability of a simple 5MR system is less than that of the "TMR architecture supported with one hot standby spare" for all values of "C" (any switching mechanism quality). This means that while the cost a TMR architecture supported with one hot standby spare is less than that of the simple 5MR system, its reliability is higher than that of the 5MR system at the price of some complexity (the extra cost of switching mechanism). The same is valid for reliability results of 5MR architecture supported with one hot standby spare and simple 7MR. This is, in fact, the advantage of reconfigurable architectures: higher reliability is achieved with a lower number of modules at the price of some complexity.

Table 1. Reliability comparison of simple and reconfigurable NMR architecture ($\lambda = 0.001$ at time = 400, N = 3, 5 & 7)

System Type	c = 0.3	c = 0.5	c = 0.8	c = 1
Simple TMR	0.75	0.75	0.75	0.75
TMR + HSP	0.83	0.86	0.88	0.90
Simple 5MR	0.80	0.80	0.80	0.80
5MR + HSP	0.87	0.89	0.90	0.91
Simple 7MR	0.85	0.85	0.85	0.85
7MR + HSP	0.91	0.92	0.92	0.92

For a better understanding of the relationship between system reliability, several modules, probability of "switching mechanism" failure, and failure rate (time), Fig. 11 and 12 are constructed. Figure 11 indicates the reliability behaviour of NMR architecture with a hot standby spare versus "time" and "probability of switch correct functioning" when N = 5 and. Figure 12 shows that by increasing the quality of the switching mechanism, system reliability enhances dramatically as expected. The descending rate of reliability is considered as the quality of the switching mechanism decreases especially of lower values of probability of switch correct functioning. Moreover, the reliability of the system decreases by elapsing the time as expected. Figure 12 indicates the reliability behaviour of the system versus the number of modules and switching mechanism's quality when and mission time 50 (h).

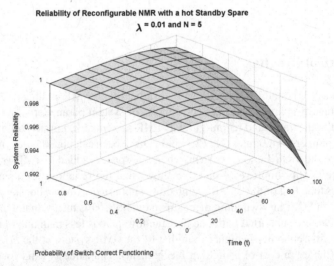

Fig. 11. Reliability of Reconfigurable NMR architecture supported with a hot standby spare (Time vs. Probability of switch failure)

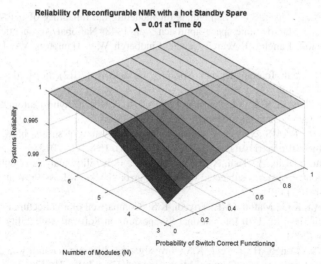

Fig. 12. Reliability of Reconfigurable NMR architecture supported with a hot standby spare (Number of modules vs. Probability of switch failure)

7 Conclusion

Designing fault-tolerant systems with a high level of reliability are one of the ongoing challenges in industries. In this paper, a systematic procedure for construction of the Markov model of a reconfigurable NMR system supported with hot standby spares is proposed, and its reliability is formulated. The relationship between system reliability obtained from the proposed formula and the number of modules, probability of "switching mechanism" failure, and failure rate (time) are then studied. Systematic construction of the Markov model of a system facilitates its extension to large systems and leads to the creation of more error-free and intelligible model. The introduced formula gives a good view of reliability behaviour of the reconfigurable NMR, for system designers, in terms of the number of modules, switch quality, and the failure rate of modules. The result shows that the reliability of a reconfigurable NMR system with a spare is higher than that of an (N + 1) MR system at the price of some complexity due to the reconfiguration mechanism. This interesting result has not been directly addressed in the literature.

References

1. Cathebras, G.: Dependability: a challenge for electrical medical implants. In: IEEE International Conference of Engineering in Medicine and Biology Society (EMBC), Buenos Aires (2010)
2. Yeh, Y.: Triple-triple redundant 777 primary flight computer. In: IEEE Aerospace Applications Conference, Aspen, CO (1996)
3. Latif-Shabgahi, G., Bass, J.M., Bennett, S.: A taxonomy for software voting algorithms used in safety-critical systems. IEEE Trans. Reliab. **53**(3), 319–328 (2004)

4. Butler, R.W., Johnson, S.C.: Techniques for modeling the reliability of fault-tolerant systems with the Markov state-space approach, vol. 1348. National Aeronautics and Space Administration, Langley Research Center, Lindbergh Way, Hampton, VA, United States (1995)
5. Dubrova, E.: Fault-Tolerant Design. Springer, Heidelberg (2012). https://doi.org/10.1007/978-1-4614-2113-9
6. Dugan, J.B., Trivedi, K.S., Smotherman, M.K., Geist, R.M.: The hybrid automated reliability predictor. J. Guidance Control Dyn. 9(3), 319–331 (1986)
7. Liu, Z., et al.: RAMS analysis of hybrid redundancy system of subsea blowout preventer based on stochastic Petri Nets. Int. J. Secur. Appl. 7(4), 159–166 (2013)
8. Cai, B., Liu, Y., Liu, Z., Tian, X., Li, H., Ren, C.: Reliability analysis of subsea blowout preventer control systems subjected to multiple error shocks. J. Loss Prevent. Process Ind. 25(6), 1044–1054 (2012)
9. Popstojanova, K.G., Mathur, A.P., Trivedi, K.S.: Comparison of architecture based software reliability models, In: 12th International Symposium on Software Reliability Engineering, Hong Kong (2001)
10. Distefano, S., Longo, F., Trivedi, K.S.: Investigating dynamic reliability and availability through state-space models. Comput. Math Appl. 64(12), 3701–3716 (2012)
11. Pukite, J., Pukite, P.: Markov Modeling for Reliability, Maintainability, Safety, and Supportability Analyses of Complex Computer Systems, Series on Engineering of Complex Computer Systems. IEEE Press, New York (1998)
12. Butler, R.W.: A primer on architectural level fault tolerance. National Aeronautics and Space Administration, Langley Research Center, Lindbergh Way, Hampton, VA, United States (2008)
13. Butler, R.W., Hayhurst, K.J., Johnson, S.C.: A note about HARP's state trimming method, National Aeronautics and Space Administration, Langley Research Center, Lindbergh Way, Hampton, VA, United States (1998)
14. Mathur, F.P., Avižienis, A.: Reliability analysis and architecture of a hybrid-redundant digital system: generalized triple modular redundancy with self-repair. In: Spring Joint Computer Conference. ACM (1969)
15. Zhang, K., Bedette, G., DeMara, R.F.: Triple Modular Redundancy with Standby (TMRSB) supporting dynamic resource reconfiguration. In: IEEE Autotestcon, Anaheim, CA (2006)
16. Zhe, Z., Daxin, L., Zhengxian, W., Changsong, S.: Research on triple modular redundancy dynamic fault-tolerant system model. In: First International Multi-Symposiums on Computer and Computational Sciences. IMSCCS, Hanzhou, Zhejiang (2006)
17. Walter, M., Gouberman, A., Riedl, M., Schuster, J., Siegle, M.: LARES-A novel approach for describing system reconfigurability in dependability models of fault-tolerant systems. In: European Safety and Reliability Conference, Valencia, Spain (2009)
18. Chellappan, C., Vijayalakshmi, G.: Dependability modeling and analysis of hybrid redundancy systems. Int. J. Qual. Reliab. Manag. 26(1), 76–96 (2009)
19. Chellappan, C., Vijayalakshmi, G.: Dependability analysis of hybrid redundancy systems using fuzzy approach. Int. J. Reliab. Q. Saf. Eng. 17(4), 331–350 (2010)
20. Maire, R.A., Reibman, A.L., Trivedi, K.S.: Transient analysis of acyclic Markov Chains. Perform. Eval. 7(3), 175–194 (1987)
21. Aslansefat, K., Latif-Shabgahi, G.: A new method in drawing reliability markov model of reconfigurable TMR systems with frequency formulations. In: 5th Iranian Conference on Electrical & Electronics Engineering (ICEEE), Gonabad, Iran (2013)
22. Aslansefat, K., Latif-Shabgahi, G.: Systematic methods in Markov reliability modelling of reconfigurable NMR architecture with cold standby spare. In: 16th Iranian Electrical Engineering Students Conference, Kazerun, Iran (2013)

23. Aslansefat, K.: A novel approach for reliability and safety evaluation of control systems with dynamic fault tree. MSc. Thesis, Shahid Beheshti University (2014)
24. Johnson, B.: Design and Analysis of Fault-Tolerant Digital Systems, 6th edn. Addison-Wesley, Boston (1989)
25. Aslansefat, K., Marques, F., Mendonça, R., Barata, J.: A Markov process-based approach for reliability evaluation of the propulsion system in multi-rotor drones. In: Camarinha-Matos, L.M., Almeida, R., Oliveira, J. (eds.) DoCEIS 2019. IAICT, vol. 553, pp. 91–98. Springer, Cham (2019). https://doi.org/10.1007/978-3-030-17771-3_8
26. Aslansefat, K., Latif-Shabgahi, G.R.: A hierarchical approach for dynamic fault trees solution through Semi-Markov process. IEEE Trans. Reliab. (Early Access). https://doi.org/10.1109/tr.2019.2923893
27. Kabir, S., Aslansefat, K., Sorokos, I., Papadopoulos, Y., Gheraibia, Y.: A conceptual framework to incorporate complex basic events in HiP-HOPS. In: Papadopoulos, Y., Aslansefat, K., Katsaros, P., Bozzano, M. (eds.) IMBSA 2019. LNCS, vol. 11842, pp. 109–124. Springer, Cham (2019). https://doi.org/10.1007/978-3-030-32872-6_8

Branching Transitions for Semi-Markov Processes with Application to Safety-Critical Systems

Stefan Kaalen[✉] and Mattias Nyberg

Department of Machine Design,
KTH Royal Institute of Technology, Stockholm, Sweden
{kaalen,matny}@kth.se

Abstract. When developing safety-critical systems, performing dependability analyses such as computing the reliability is of utmost importance. In the safety standard IEC61508, Markov processes are suggested for quantifying the reliability. However, real-world systems can not always be accurately modeled as a Markov process. Semi-Markov Processes (SMPs) generalizes Markov processes to allow for more accurate models. It has been previously suggested that a intuitive modeling approach of semi-Markov processes is to assign a timer to each possible transition. These timers race to first reach zero which triggers the corresponding transition. However, some situations such as non-perfect diagnostic procedures cannot be modeled with these transition timers. As the first, and main contribution, the theory of modeling SMPs with transition timers is extended with branching transitions, i.e. transitions with several possible output states. The second contribution is tool support for dependability analyses of SMPs modeled with branching transitions. A use case example of an automotive steering system modeled as an SMP with transition timers and with branching transitions is considered and analyzed.

Keywords: Semi-Markov process · Transition timers · Branching transitions

1 Introduction

When developing safety-critical systems, it is essential to quantify the reliability of systems and hardware [1]. This becomes apparent when considering current safety standards such as the standard for functional safety of electric, electronic, and programmable electronic safety-related systems, IEC61508 [2]. While important, as systems today are increasingly complex, so is also the difficulty in computing the reliability.

There are several possible methods for computing the reliability of a system. In IEC61508 [2], the methods *fault trees*, *reliability block diagrams*, *Markov chains*, and *stochastic petri nets*, are mentioned. However, both fault trees and

© Springer Nature Switzerland AG 2020
M. Zeller and K. Höfig (Eds.): IMBSA 2020, LNCS 12297, pp. 68–82, 2020.
https://doi.org/10.1007/978-3-030-58920-2_5

reliability block diagrams lack the capability of incorporating temporal properties of systems.

Stochastic Petri Nets SPNs can consider temporal properties [3]. SPNs can be divided into two classes, those that are equivalent to Markov chains and those that are not. For SPNs that are not equivalent to Markov chains, the reliability is usually quantified through *Monte Carlo simulations* [3]. However, for safety-critical systems the required level of reliability is often high and therefore the amount of simulation required can also be too high to in a reasonable time prove the highest levels of reliability [4].

Markov chains, also referred to as *Markov processes*, incorporate temporal properties. The *memoryless* property of Markov processes also makes analytically calculating the reliability easier than for general *stochastic processes*. However, real-world systems do not always exhibit the memoryless property [3,5] as illustrated in the example system presented in Sect. 2. As the complexity of safety-critical systems grows, their likelihood of exhibiting this property also decreases even further.

Semi-Markov Processes (SMPs), as introduced in [6,7], generalizes Markov processes by relaxing the memoryless property. In SMPs, the probability of transitioning from any state i to any state j may depend on the time that has been spent in state i. While performing dependability analyses is more difficult for semi-Markov processes than Markov processes, previous work has presented several different methods and tools for doing this [8–14].

The present paper will consider SMPs modeled with *transition timers* as presented in [11]. The concept of transition timers was introduced as an intuitive approach for modeling SMPs. When a state i of the SMP is entered, a number of timers: one for each possible transition from state i start counting down. The time that each transition timer starts counting down from is given by a random variable and when the first timer reaches zero, the corresponding transition is made.

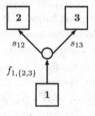

Fig. 1. SMP with one branching transition.

The first, and main contribution of the present paper expands the modeling approach of transition timers for SMPs by introducing the concept of *branching transitions*. Dependability measures of SMP are often computed through their so called *semi-Markov kernel*, and it is therefore also presented what shape the semi-Markov kernel takes for SMPs modeled with branching transitions. A minimalistic example of an SMP modeled with a branching transition is illustrated in Fig. 1. The three-state SMP has a branching transition originating in state 1, with the two possible output states 2 and 3. The function $f_{1,\{2,3\}}$ is the probability density function of the random variable $T_{1,\{2,3\}}$ representing the starting time of the transition timer corresponding to taking the branching transition. The constants s_{12} and s_{13} represents the time-independent probabilities of ending up in states 1 and 2 respectively when the branching transition is made. Generally, branching transitions are transitions originating from one state but with several possible output states. Branching transitions provide an intuitive modeling of when there are time-independent probabilities of reaching different states, a situation which can not be modeled using transition timers without branching transitions.

Branching transitions are useful for modeling several situations for when after a time delay has passed, a probabilistic choice is triggered. One example of when branching transitions are useful is when modeling the diagnostic coverage of a diagnostic test of a system. The diagnostic coverage of a diagnostic test is by [15] given as the probability that a fault is detected given that is it present when initiating the diagnostic test. This situation can be exemplified in Fig. 1 by letting state 1 denote that a fault is present in the system, state 2 denote that the fault has been detected by the diagnostic test, and state 3 denote that the fault was undetected by the diagnostic test. In this scenario, $T_{1,\{2,3\}}$ denotes the time it takes from that the fault becomes present until a diagnostic test has been run. The diagnostic coverage of the test is represented by the probability s_{12} while s_{13} simply is given by $1 - s_{12}$.

The second contribution of the paper is a tool-support for modeling and performing dependability analyses of SMPs with branching transitions. This support for branching transitions has been added to the preexisting Matlab app SMP-tool [16]. SMP-tool can perform several types of analyses, such as computing the reliability of SMPs belonging to the class where each transition timer has a uniform, degenerate, or exponential distribution.

The organisation of the paper is as follows. In Sect. 2 an example of an SMP modeling the reliability of an automotive steering system is presented. In Sect. 3, some preliminaries about SMPs are presented. In Sect. 4, the first, and main contribution, i.e. the concept of branching transitions in the context of SMPs, is presented. Finally, in Sect. 5 the second contribution, i.e. the tool support for performing dependability analyses of SMPs modeled with branching transitions, is presented by applying it to the steering system.

2   Steering System

A simple example system that evolves over time is modeled as an SMP in Fig. 2. The labels of the transitions describe the distributions of transition timers.

The system controls the steering of a road vehicle. The steering can be performed by two different subsystems, the Primary Steering (PS) and the Secondary Steering (SS). PS steers the vehicle by changing the angle of the steering

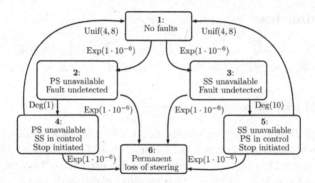

Fig. 2. Model of example system

axes of the vehicle. If there is a failure of PS, SS takes over the steering of the vehicle by applying different levels of braking force to the different wheels. For simplicity, when either one of the subsystems becomes faulty it is always discovered. For PS it takes 1 s to discover the fault and for SS it takes 10 s to discover the fault. This is modeled by two transition timers with degenerate distributions, i.e. with two timers for which the cumulative distribution functions of the times each timers starts counting down from being given by shifted Heaviside step functions. Each subsystem has a constant failure rate of $10^{-6}\,\mathrm{h}^{-1}$, modeled by exponentially distributed transition timers. Finally, it takes a uniform distributed time between 4 s and 8 s for the vehicle to stop once one of the subsystems has been found faulty. Stopping also implies that the vehicle is repaired before the vehicle is started again. The set of states of the model are as follows.

1: Both subsystems works as they should. A transition into state 2 is made when there is a failure of PS. A transition into state 3 is made when there is a failure of SS.

2: Undetected failure of PS. A transition into state 4 is made when the failure is detected. A transition into state 6 is made when there is a failure of SS.

3: Undetected failure of SS. A transition into state 5 is made when the failure is detected. A transition into state 6 is made when there is a failure of SS.

4: Detected failure of PS. A transition into state 1 is made when the vehicle has stopped by the side of the road. A transition into state 6 is made when there is a failure of SS.

5: Detected failure of SS. A transition into state 1 is made when the vehicle has stopped by the side of the road. A transition into state 6 is made when there is a failure of SS.

6: The vehicle has lost all its steering capability.

The reliability of the steering system is now considered as the probability that state 6 has not yet been reached after the system has been in use for a certain amount of time t.

3   Preliminaries

This section introduces the theory of semi-Markov processes as described in among others [8, 9] as well as the theory of transition timers as introduced in [11].

3.1   Semi-Markov Process

In general, let S be the set of states, chosen so that a system of interest is always in exactly one of these states. Assume that the system is observed only in discrete time-points $n = 0, 1, 2, ...$ directly after each transition from one state to another has been made. Let X_n be a random variable describing the state of the system at time-point n, the family of random variables $(X_n, n \in \mathbb{N})$ is then called a discrete-time *stochastic process*. Let U_n be the *sojourn time* in X_n, i.e. the time that is spent in X_n before transitioning into X_{n+1}. Assume now that the system is observed continuously and let $(Z_t, t \in \mathbb{R}_+)$ be the continuous-time stochastic process with state space S where $Z_t = X_{N(t)}$ and

$$N(t) = \begin{cases} 0 & \text{if } U_0 > t \\ \sup\{n \in \mathbb{N}_+ : U_0 + ... + U_{n-1} \leq t\} & \text{if } U_0 \leq t. \end{cases}$$

Let $\mathbb{R}_+$ denote the non-negative real numbers. The continuous-time stochastic process $(Z_t, t \in \mathbb{R}_+)$ is a *Semi-Markov Process* (SMP) [8] if

$$P(X_{n+1} = j, \ U_n \leq t \mid X_n = i, U_{n-1}, ..., \ X_0, U_0)$$
$$= P(X_{n+1} = j, \ U_n \leq t \mid X_n = i). \tag{1}$$

Let the matrix $\mathbf{Q}(t)$ be the *semi-Markov kernel* connected to an SMP, the elements of the semi-Markov kernel are given by

$$Q_{ij}(t) = \begin{cases} P(X_{n+1} = j, \ U_n \leq t \mid X_n = i) & \text{if } i \neq j \\ 0 & \text{if } i = j. \end{cases} \tag{2}$$

The same matrix is in some literature referred to as the Markov renewal matrix [9]. Through the semi-Markov kernel, dependability measures such as the reliability of the SMP can be computed [8, 9].

3.2   Transition Timers

We consider semi-Markov processes modeled using transition timers, as presented in [11]. An independent timer is assigned to each possible transition in the semi-Markov process. When a state i is entered, every timer corresponding to a transition out of the state starts counting down. All the timers count down in the same pace but from different starting times. The starting time for the timer corresponding to the transition to a state j when the process is in state i at time step n, is given by the random variable T_{ij}^n with probability density function

$f_{ij}(t)$. When the first timer in state i reaches zero, the corresponding transition is made. In the present paper, the distribution of the random variables T_{ij}^n will sometimes be referred to as distribution of the corresponding transitions or of the corresponding transition timer. When a semi-Markov process is modeled with transition timers, the semi-Markov kernel takes the form

$$Q_{ij}(t) = \int_0^t f_{ij}(u) \left(\prod_{\substack{k \in S_i \\ k \neq j}} \int_u^\infty f_{ik}(v)dv \right) du, \tag{3}$$

where $S_i \subset S$ is the set of all states that can be reached in one transition from state i. [11].

4 Branching Transitions

To increase the usefulness of SMPs for modeling real world systems, as the first, and main contribution we introduce SMPs with branching transitions. A branching transition is a transition from one state that has several possible output states. Each branching transition has a corresponding transition timer but also a set of probabilities, adding up to 1, corresponding to which of the possible output states that will be entered. Branching transitions provides an intuitive approach for modeling when there are time-independent probabilities for a system to take different transitions.

4.1 Use Case Example

One situation where branching transitions are highly useful is for modeling of diagnostic procedures. As an example, consider again the system modeled in Fig. 2. In the model it is assumed that all faults in the system will eventually be discovered. When looking at systems in the real world this assumption is however not realistic; it is likely that faults will sometimes be missed by the diagnostic procedure, i.e. that the diagnostic coverage is below one.

We assume the diagnostic procedure for the steering system systematically misses 1% of all faults in both the primary and secondary steering. By the use of branching transitions with degenerate distributions, the model given in Fig. 2 can now be updated to incorporate the diagnostic coverage of the diagnostic procedure. The updated model is given in Fig. 3.

4.2 Semi-Markov Kernel for SMPs with Branching Transitions

The reliability of SMPs is usually computed through their semi-Markov kernel $\mathbf{Q}(t)$. An expression for the semi-Markov kernel when branching transitions are allowed is here derived.

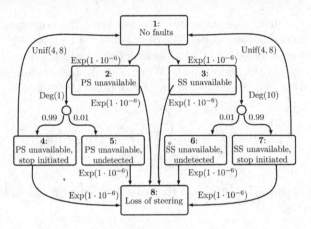

Fig. 3. Model of steering system with diagnostic procedure added, two branching transitions with two output states each have been added to incorporate the diagnostic coverage of discovering faults in PS and SS.

Semi-Markov Kernel for SMPs with Transition Timers. Let T_{ij}^n denote the random variable giving the time the timer for the transition to state j starts counting down from when the SMP is in state i at the time step n. From [11], it holds that when in state i at time step n, the next state is state j if and only if the corresponding transition timer is the first to reach zero, i.e. given $X_n = i$ it holds that $X_{n+1} = j \iff \forall k \in \mathcal{S}_i \ T_{ij}^n \leq T_{ik}^n$. Furthermore, it holds that when in state i at time step n and the next state is state j, the sojourn time in X_n is $U_n = T_{ij}^n$. From this, the following theorem can be derived.

Theorem 1. *Every finite state-space continuous-time stochastic process modeled with transition timers is an SMP.*

Proof. Consider a general finite state-space continuous-time stochastic process modeled with transition timers. It holds that

$$P(X_{n+1} = j, \ U_n \leq t \mid X_n = i, \ U_{n-1}, ..., \ X_0, \ U_0)$$
$$= P(U_n \leq t \mid X_{n+1} = j, \ X_n = i, \ U_{n-1}, ..., \ X_0, \ U_0)$$
$$\times \ P(X_{n+1} = j \mid X_n = i, \ U_{n-1}, ..., \ X_0, \ U_0)$$
$$= P(T_{ij}^n \leq t \mid \forall k \in \mathcal{S}_i : \ T_{ij}^n \leq T_{ik}^n, \ X_n = i, \ U_{n-1}, ..., \ X_0, \ U_0)$$
$$\times \ P(\forall k \in \mathcal{S}_i : \ T_{ij}^n \leq T_{ik}^n \mid X_n = i, \ U_{n-1}, ..., \ X_0, \ U_0)$$
$$= P(T_{ij}^n \leq t, \ \forall k \in \mathcal{S}_i : \ T_{ij}^n \leq T_{ik}^n \mid X_n = i, \ U_{n-1}, ..., \ X_0, \ U_0).$$

Since, per definition, the time each transition timer starts counting down from is independent of all previous states and sojourn times, it now holds that

$$= P(T_{ij}^n \leq t, \ \forall k \in \mathcal{S}_i : \ T_{ij}^n \leq T_{ik}^n \mid X_n = i, \ U_{n-1}, ..., \ X_0, \ U_0)$$
$$= P(T_{ij}^n \leq t, \ \forall k \in \mathcal{S}_i : \ T_{ij}^n \leq T_{ik}^n \mid X_n = i)$$
$$= P(X_{n+1} = j, \ U_n \leq t \mid X_n = i).$$

By the definition of an SMP in Eq. (1), the continuous-time stochastic process is thereby an SMP.   □

Remember that Eq. (3) gives the expression of the non-zero elements in the semi-Markov kernel corresponding to a transition from an arbitrary state i to an arbitrary state j when there are no branching transitions from state i.

Generalized Semi-Markov Kernel to Allow Branching Transitions. Equation (3) will now take a more general form to allow for branching transitions to be present in the model of interest. To find this new expression we consider the example illustrated in Fig. 4a, which is a model where there are three possible states that can be reached by a transition from state i, out of which two are through a branching transition. The squares denote the states of the model while the small circle denotes the branching of the corresponding branching transition. The notation s_{ij} denotes the probability that a transition made through the branching transition from state i is a transition into state j. There are two different notations for starting times of transition timers: $T^n_{i\{j,k\}}$ with probability density function $f_{i,\{j,k\}}(t)$ is associated with a branching transition that has states j and k as possible output states, while T^n_{ij} with probability density function $f_{ij}(t)$ is associated with a non-branching transition. In order to find a general expression for the semi-Markov kernel, without loss of generality, we interpret a non-branching transition as a branching transition with only one possible output state. A visualization of this is given in Fig. 4b.

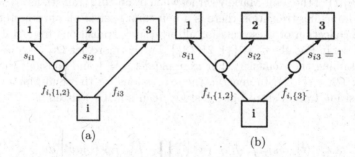

Fig. 4. (a) Simple model including a branching transition. (b) The same model visualized as having two branching transition out of which one only has one possible output state.

Consider the definition of the non-diagonal elements of the semi-Markov kernel presented in Eq. (2). In order to find a general expression for the semi-Markov kernel when branching transitions are allowed, we first try to find Q_{i1} for the model in Fig. 4b.

$$Q_{i1}(t) = P(X_{n+1} = 1, \ U_n \leq t \mid X_n = i)$$
$$= P(X_{n+1} \in \{1,2\}, \ X_{n+1} = 1, \ U_n \leq t \mid X_n = i)$$
$$= P(X_{n+1} = 1 \mid X_{n+1} \in \{1,2\}, \ U_n \leq t, \ X_n = i)$$
$$\times \ P(X_{n+1} \in \{1,2\}, \ U_n \leq t \mid X_n = i).$$

By noting that $s_{i1} = P(X_{n+1} = 1 \mid X_{n+1} \in \{1,2\})$ and that which of the possible output states of a branching transition that is entered is time independent, it holds that

$$Q_{i1}(t) = P(X_{n+1} = 1 \mid X_{n+1} \in \{1,2\}, \ X_n = i)$$
$$\times \ P(X_{n+1} \in \{1,2\}, \ U_n \leq t \mid X_n = i)$$
$$= s_{i1}P(X_{n+1} \in \{1,2\}, \ U_n \leq t \mid X_n = i)$$
$$= s_{i1}P(U_n \leq t \mid X_{n+1} \in \{1,2\}, \ X_n = i)P(X_{n+1} \in \{1,2\} \mid X_n = i)$$
$$= s_{i1}P(T^n_{i,\{1.2\}} \leq t \mid T^n_{i,\{1.2\}} < T^n_{i,\{3\}})P(T^n_{i,\{1.2\}} < T^n_{i,\{3\}})$$
$$= s_{i1}P(T^n_{i,\{1.2\}} \leq t, \ T^n_{i,\{1.2\}} < T^n_{i,\{3\}}).$$

Finally, since $T^n_{i,\{1.2\}}$ and $T^n_{i,\{3\}}$ have the probability density functions $f_{i,\{1,2\}}$ and $f_{i,\{3\}}$ respectively, it holds that

$$Q_{i1}(t) = s_{i1} \int_0^t f_{i,\{1,2\}}(u) \int_u^\infty f_{i,\{3\}}(v) dv \ du. \tag{4}$$

We now generalize in order to find a general expression for an arbitrary element $Q_{ij}(t)$ of the semi-Markov kernel when branching transitions are allowed. For each branching transition there is a non-empty set of all output states. Let Ω_i be the collection of these sets for all branching transitions from state i, i.e. for the model in Fig. 4b: $\Omega_i = \{\{1,2\}, \{3\}\}$. Furthermore, let $\Omega_{ij} \in \Omega_i$ be the set in Ω_i containing the element j. For example, let $j = 1$ and consider the model in Fig. 4b: $\Omega_{i1} = \{1,2\}$. In general, the expressions for the semi-Markov kernel for a transition from a state i into a state j can now be written as

$$Q_{ij}(t) = s_{ij} \int_0^t f_{i,\Omega_{ij}}(u) \left(\prod_{\substack{\mathcal{K} \in \Omega_i \\ \mathcal{K} \neq \Omega_{ij}}} \int_u^\infty f_{i,\mathcal{K}}(v) dv \right) du. \tag{5}$$

The following theorem generalize Theorem 1 to hold for continuous-time stochastic processes modeled with transition timers and branching transitions.

Theorem 2. *Every finite state-space continuous-time stochastic process modeled with transition timers and branching transitions is an SMP.*

Proof. Consider a general finite state-space continuous-time stochastic process modeled with transition timer and branching transitions. By interpreting all non-branching transitions as branching transitions with only one output state, as is exemplified in Fig. 4b, it holds that

$$P(X_{n+1} = j,\ U_n \le t \mid X_n = i,\ U_{n-1}, ...,\ X_0,\ U_0)$$
$$= P(X_{n+1} \in \Omega_{ij},\ X_{n+1} = j,\ U_n \le t \mid X_n = i,\ U_{n-1}, ...,\ X_0,\ U_0)$$
$$= P(X_{n+1} = j \mid X_{n+1} \in \Omega_{ij},\ U_n \le t,\ X_n = i,\ U_{n-1}, ...,\ X_0,\ U_0)$$
$$\times\ P(X_{n+1} \in \Omega_{ij},\ U_n \le t \mid X_n = i,\ U_{n-1}, ...,\ X_0,\ U_0).$$

By Theorem 1 and the fact that which of the possible output states of each branching transition that is entered is independent of all previous states and sojourn times, it now holds that

$$P(X_{n+1} = j,\ U_n \le t \mid X_n = i,\ U_{n-1}, ...,\ X_0,\ U_0)$$
$$= P(X_{n+1} = j \mid X_{n+1} \in \Omega_{ij},\ U_n \le t,\ X_n = i)P(X_{n+1} \in \Omega_{ij},\ U_n \le t \mid X_n = i)$$
$$= P(X_{n+1} = j,\ U_n \le t \mid X_n = i).$$

By the definition of an SMP in Eq. (1), the continuous-time stochastic process is thereby an SMP. □

The theorem will in the upcoming section be used to see how elements of the semi-Markov kernel for SMPs modeled with branching transitions can be found through elements of associated SMPs modeled without branching transitions.

Connection to Associated SMPs Without Branching Transitions. Now consider an SMP without branching transitions, associated with each state i of an SMP with branching timers. The associated SMP is given through having the output states of each branching transition from state i combined into one single state. An illustration of this for the models in Fig. 4 is given in Fig. 5. It follows directly from Eq. 2 that for the model in Fig. 5 it holds that

$$Q_{i,\{1,2\}}(t) = \int_0^t f_{i,\{1,2\}}(u) \int_u^\infty f_{i,\{3\}}(v)dv\ du. \tag{6}$$

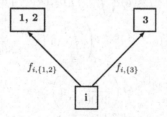

Fig. 5. Simple model where states 1 and 2 has been combined into the state "1, 2".

We now compare Eq. (4) and Eq. (6), the relationship between them is given by

$$Q_{i1}(t) = s_{i1}Q_{i,\{1,2\}}(t). \tag{7}$$

In general, we can compare Eqs. (3) and (5) and obtain the following theorem.

Theorem 3. *Consider a SMP modeled with transition timers and branching transitions with the transition from state i to state j being through a branching transition. It holds that*

$$Q_{ij}(t) = s_{ij}Q_{i\Omega_{ij}}, \tag{8}$$

where $Q_{i,\Omega_{ij}}$ are elements of the semi-Markov kernel of the associated SMP given by combining the output states of each branching transition from state i into a single state.

4.3 Semi-Markov Kernel of Steering System

To exemplify how to calculate the semi-Markov kernel from (5), consider again the model in Fig. 3 and more specifically at the transitions out of state 2. Let $\delta(t)$ denote the Dirac delta function, the elements of the semi-Markov kernel are then calculated as follows:

$$Q_{24}(t) = s_{24} \int_0^t f_{2,\Omega_{24}}(u) \left(\int_u^\infty f_{28}(v)dv \right) du$$

$$= 0.99 \int_0^t \delta \left(u - \frac{1}{3600} \right) \left(e^{-10^{-6}u} \right) du$$

$$= 0.99 \, \Theta \left(t - \frac{1}{3600} \right) e^{-10^{-6}\frac{1}{3600}}$$

$$Q_{25}(t) = s_{25} \int_0^t f_{2,\Omega_{25}}(u) \left(\int_u^\infty f_{28}(v)dv \right) du$$

$$= 0.01 \, \Theta \left(t - \frac{1}{3600} \right) e^{-10^{-6}\frac{1}{3600}}$$

$$Q_{28}(t) = s_{28} \int_0^t f_{28}(u) \left(\int_u^\infty f_{2,\Omega_{24}}(v)dv \right) du$$

$$= 1 \int_0^t 10^{-6} e^{-10^{-6}u} \left(\int_u^\infty \delta \left(v - \frac{1}{3600} \right) dv \right) du$$

$$= \int_0^t 10^{-6} e^{-10^{-6}u} \Theta \left(\frac{1}{3600} - u \right) du$$

$$= \Theta \left(t - \frac{1}{3600} \right) \int_0^{1/3600} 10^{-6} e^{-10^{-6}u} \, du$$

$$+ \, \dot{\Theta} \left(\frac{1}{3600} - t \right) \int_0^t 10^{-6} e^{-10^{-6}u} \, du$$

$$= 1 - e^{-10^{-6}} + \Theta \left(t - \frac{1}{3600} \right) \left(e^{-10^{-6}t} - e^{-10^{-6}\frac{1}{3600}} \right).$$

Clearly, calculating the semi-Markov kernel by hand can become lengthy. Therefore, there is also tool support both for calculating the semi-Markov kernel of
SMPs modeled with transition timers and branching transition, and for performing dependability analysis of the processes based the semi-Markov kernel. This
tool-support will be presented in the following section.

5   Tool Support for SMPs with Branching Transitions

The second contribution of the paper is a tool support for performing dependability analysis of SMPs with branching transitions. This support for branching
transitions has been added to the preexisting Matlab app SMP-tool [16]. SMP-
tool is an app for performing several different analyses of SMPs modeled in
Stateflow. We will here look specifically at computing reliability, which arguably
is one of the most important steps of performing a dependability analysis of
safety-critical systems. SMP-tool can compute the reliability for all SMPs where
each transition timer has a uniform, degenerate, or exponential distribution,
combined with any finite number of branching transitions.

We will now use SMP-tool to compute the reliability of the steering system
modeled in Fig. 3, which has two branching transitions, presented in this paper.
Fig. 6 illustrates how the steering system looks when modeled in Stateflow.

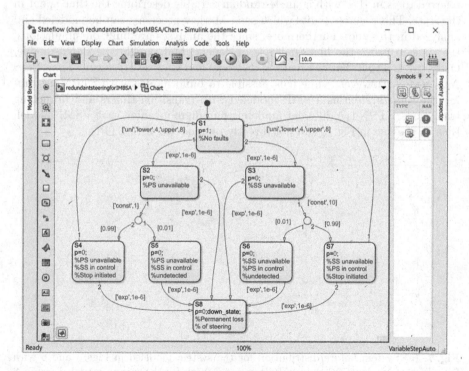

Fig. 6. Steering system modeled in Stateflow.

The reliability will be computed for several different time points in the span from 1 to 100000 h. Since the reliability is so close to zero in this interval, we will visualize the result by presenting the value of the *system failure distribution*, $F_T(t)$, given by $F_T(t) = 1 - R(t)$ instead of presenting the value of the reliability itself. The result of using SMP-tool for computing the system failure distribution for a few different time points is presented in Fig. 7a. Linear interpolation has been applied in order to connect the values between the different time points. For comparison, Fig. 7b show the corresponding plot for when the diagnostic coverage was not considered, i.e. for the model in Fig. 2. Clearly, the addition of incorporating the diagnostic coverage into the model affects the system failure distribution, and thereby reliability, heavily. Assuming a system lifetime of 45000 h, the model without branching transitions yields a reliability of $1 - 2.9 \cdot 10^{-10}$ over the systems lifetime. With the addition of branching transitions, allowing a more realistic model where the diagnostic coverage of the system is considered, the reliability takes the very different value of the reliability of $1 - 2.0 \cdot 10^{-5}$.

There are several preexisting tools capable of performing analyses of models similar to the ones SMP-tool can handle. The UPPAAL Statistical Model Checking (SMC) branch of the tool environment UPPAAL [13] can be used for analysis of some semi-Markov processes modeled as stochastic timed automatas [17]. However, UPPAAL SMC associates each state, or location as they are referred to as in [17], with a single random variable describing the time spent in the state. This severely limits which semi-Markov processes can be modeled and analyzed in this tool. Furthermore, since the analyses are built on simulations, the time to prove the highest levels of dependability might me unreasonable. ORIS [14] is a tool that can be used to model and analyze *Stochastic Time Petri Nets* STPN. However, while it is possible to build models with STPN describing the same system as a SMP modeled with transition timers and branching transitions, STPN is a different modeling paradigm meaning that a SMP model, such as the one in Fig. 3, can not directly be modeled with STPN.

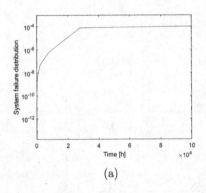

(a)

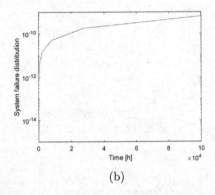

(b)

Fig. 7. (a) System failure distribution for the system modeled in Figs. 3 and 6 with branching transitions. (b) System failure distribution for the system modeled in Fig. 2 without branching transitions.

6   Conclusions

When developing safety-critical systems, it is essential to quantify the reliability of systems and hardware. In order to do so it has in previous literature been suggested using SMPs [8,9]. SMPs generalize Markov processes, and allow for more accurate modeling of real world systems. An intuitive approach for modeling SMPs is through transition timers [11]. While providing an intuitive modeling approach for SMPs, transition timers can not model SMPs with time-independent probabilities of taking different transitions.

The present paper has therefore, as its first, and main contribution proposed an extension to the modeling approach of transition timers. The extension is to allow branching transitions. A branching transition is a transition originating in one state, but which have several possible output states. Each of these possible output states has a time-independent probability of being the next state in the process if a transition through the branching transition is made.

The second contribution of the paper is a tool-support for SMPs modeled with branching transitions. The support for branching transitions has been added to the preexisting Matlab app SMP-tool [16]. SMP-tool can analyse every SMP modeled with branching transitions belonging to the class where each transition timer has a uniform, degenerate, or exponential distribution.

The introduction of branching transitions creates a whole new possibility to accurately model real-world systems as SMPs. Specifically, the concept of branching transitions enables modeling of diagnostic tests, which are often found in real-world safety-critical systems. Through SMP-tool, dependability analyses, such as computing the reliability of these SMPs, can now be performed.

Acknowledgments. The authors acknowledge the following agencies and projects for financial support: FFI, the Swedish strategic vehicle research and innovation programme through the AVerT project (reference number 2018-02727), and the European H2020 - ECSEL PRYSTINE (grant agreement number 783190). The work was performed with the support of Scania CV AB. This work was also partially supported by the Wallenberg AI, Autonomous Systems and Software Program (WASP) funded by Knut and Alice Wallenberg Foundation.

References

1. Trivedi, K.S., Bobbio, A.: Reliability and Availability Engineering: Modeling, Analysis, and Applications. Cambridge University Press, Cambridge (2017)
2. International Electrotechnical Commission: Functional Safety of Electrical/Electronic/Programmable Electronic Safety-related Systems (IEC61508) (2010)
3. Marsan, M.A.: Stochastic Petri nets: an elementary introduction. In: Rozenberg, G. (ed.) APN 1988. LNCS, vol. 424, pp. 1–29. Springer, Heidelberg (1990). https://doi.org/10.1007/3-540-52494-0_23
4. Zio, E.: The Monte Carlo Simulation Method for System Reliability and Risk Analysis, 1st edn. Springer, London (2013). https://doi.org/10.1007/978-1-4471-4588-2

5. Limnios, N. : Dependability analysis of semi-Markov systems. In: Reliability Engineering and System Safety, vol. 55, pp. 203–207. Elsevier (1997)

6. Levy, P.: Processus semi-Markoviens. In: Proceedings of the International Congress of Mathematicians, Amsterdam, pp. 416–426 (1954)

7. Smith, W.: Regenerative stochastic processes. Proc. Roy. Soc. A **232**(1188), 6–31 (1955)

8. Limnios, N., Oprişan, G.: Semi-Markov Processes and Reliability. Springer, New York (2001). https://doi.org/10.1007/978-1-4612-0161-8

9. Grabski, F.: Semi-Markov Processes: Applications in System Reliability and Maintenance. Elsevier Inc., Amsterdam (2015)

10. Nyberg, M. : Safety analysis of autonomous driving using semi-Markov processes. In: Proceedings of the 28th International European Safety and Reliability Conference, pp. 781–788 (2018)

11. Kaalen, S., Nyberg, M., Bondesson, C.: Tool-supported dependability analysis of semi-Markov processes with application to autonomous driving. In: 4th International Conference on System Reliability and Safety (ICSRS), Rome, pp. 126–135 (2019)

12. https://sharpe.pratt.duke.edu/

13. http://www.uppaal.org/

14. https://www.oris-tool.org/

15. Rausand, M.: Reliability of Safety-Critical Systems: Theory and Applications. Wiley, Hoboken (2014)

16. http://www.kth.se/itm/smptool

17. David, A., Larsen, K.G., Legay, A., Mikučionis, M., Poulsen, D.B.: UPPAAL SMC tutorial. Int. J. Softw. Tools Technol. Transf. **17**(4), 397–415 (2015). https://doi.org/10.1007/s10009-014-0361-y

Optimal Scheduling of Preventive Maintenance for Safety Instrumented Systems Based on Mixed-Integer Programming

Anas Abdelkarim[ID] and Ping Zhang[✉]

Institute of Automatic Control, Faculty of Electrical and Computer Engineering,
Technische Universität Kaiserslautern, 67663 Kaiserslautern, Germany
abelkari@rhrk.uni-kl.de, pzhang@eit.uni-kl.de

Abstract. Preventive maintenance is essential to guarantee the reliability of the safety instrumented systems in the process industry. The safety integrity level of the safety instrumented systems is evaluated based on the probability of failure on demand, which is significantly influenced by preventive maintenance. In this paper, we give an approach to optimize the schedule of the preventive maintenance for the safety instrumented systems, which considers not only the time instants but also the sequence of the maintenance schedule. The basic idea is to discretize the continuous-time Markov model from the viewpoint of maintenance and then reformulate the problem as a mixed-integer programming problem. Examples are given to illustrate the proposed approach.

Keywords: Safety instrumented systems · Probability of failure on demand · Preventive maintenance · Markov model · Mixed-integer programming

1 Introduction

Safety instrumented systems (SIS) consist of sensors, logic solver and final elements which are added to an industrial process to preclude the risk or extenuate consequences of an accident [1–3]. The international norm IEC 61511 provides guidelines for the design, operation and maintenance of the SIS [3, 4]. The safety integrity level is an important index that describes the reliability of the SIS and is determined by the probability of failure on demand (PFD) [4, 5]. Several approaches can be applied to model the reliability of SIS, for instance, reliability block diagrams, fault tree analysis, Petri nets and Markov models [6].

Preventive maintenance (PM) is one of the main measures to enhance the reliability of SIS. In many SIS, two kinds of maintenance tests are available, namely, main tests and partial tests [5]. The scheduling of PM tests requires to specify the time instants and the sequence of the tests over a specified period. Different PM plans impact the PFD and thus the reliability of SIS.

© Springer Nature Switzerland AG 2020
M. Zeller and K. Höfig (Eds.): IMBSA 2020, LNCS 12297, pp. 83–96, 2020.
https://doi.org/10.1007/978-3-030-58920-2_6

Machleidt has modelled the SIS as a stochastic and deterministic automaton. Then, an optimization problem is formulated to minimize PFD by finding optimal time instants for a predefined sequence of PM tests and solved using a heuristic nonlinear optimization method (Nelder-Mead method) [7]. However, the method may converge to non-stationary points [8]. Martynova and Zhang [9] have established for the first time the connection between the optimal scheduling problem of SIS with the optimal control problem of switched systems with state jumps. They apply the gradient method proposed in [10] to solve the optimization problem, which converges to a minimal value. Yet the approach in [9] can only find an optimal switching time instants for a predefined sequence. In this paper, we aim to find not only the optimal time instants but also the optimal sequence of the preventive maintenance.

Switched systems are a class of hybrid systems that have been much investigated in the control community in recent years [11–13]. A detailed survey on optimal control of switched systems are presented in [14]. For switched systems with state jumps, several approaches are available to find the optimal switching time instants for a predefined switching sequence. In [11], the switching time instants are determined implicitly by numerical calculation to compute a region on state spate such that the switching instants should occur only if the state belongs to this region. Gradient method [10] and Ant Colony Optimization algorithm method [15] can find the explicit optimal switching time instants.

On the other hand, there are few practical algorithms to find both optimal switching time instants and sequence. The master-slave procedure proposed by [16] iterates between two stages. In the first stage (i.e., slave procedure), the optimal switching time instants are determined under the assumption of a known switching sequence. In the second stage (i.e., master procedure), an optimal switching sequence is determined under the assumption of known switching time instants. The solution obtained by this approach depends strongly on the initial values and may sometimes achieve only a suboptimal solution.

The switching table procedure [16,17] is another approach that is based on the construction of switching tables which specify when the switching shall occur and what the next subsystem shall be. The method is not applicable for our optimization problem, because the tables are basically partitioned regions of the state space ($\mathbb{R}^n$) for the subsystems. But in our case, there is only one subsystem, as between two neighbouring state jumps the system state evolves according to the same state equation. Therefore, the partition of the state space can not be carried out making the method not applicable.

The approach presented in [18] has been extended by Kirches et al. to consider states jumps [19], where their framework involves finding both the optimal switching time instants and the sequence for non-linear, non-autonomous switched dynamic systems. The basic idea is to combine all subsystems into one equation by introducing binary variables in order to produce a mixed-integer optimal control problem. Then the differential non-nonlinear dynamics are approximated using adaptive collocation method (see section five in [19] for more details). The resulted optimization problem is then solved by a nonlinear optimization solver, e.g., IPOPT.

The state jumps in [19] are introduced as jumps occur due to switching from subsystem dynamics to another one. However, in our optimization problem, the state jumps occur due to external events on the system that undergoes only one dynamics, which means we can not directly formulate the problem as a mixed-integer optimization problem as in [19]. Therefore, we propose to integrate the state jumps directly into the system difference equations as explained in Sect. 3. Then, we can treat the problem as a mixed-integer problem as in [18] and [19]. In addition, because the system dynamics are linear, the discretization is done by solving the differential equations instead of using adaptive collocation method.

The paper is organized as follows. In Sect. 2, the Markov model of SIS is introduced and the optimization problem is formulated. In Sect. 3, the optimization problem is reformulated as a mixed-integer optimal problem and then solved. Numerical examples in Sect. 4 are provided to illustrate the proposed approach.

2 Preliminary

In this section, we briefly review the multi-phase continuous Markov model of SIS, the definition of PFD and formulate the optimization problem.

2.1 Modelling of the SIS and PM Tests

For the sake of clarity, we consider SIS with only one channel of the 1oo1-architecture. As shown by Machleidt [7], the failures of SIS can be divided into safe failures (SF) and dangerous failures. Depending on the detectability, the dangerous failures can be further classified into non-detectable failures (DN), failures detectable by a diagnosis system (DD), failures detectable by both main test or partial test (DUAB) and failures detectable only by main test (DUA). The state transition diagram of the SIS is shown in Fig. 1. The OK state is the state that the SIS is entirely functional and capable to give the safety function. The SF state represents the safe failures, which may cause an unnecessary shutdown of the plant and economic loss but have no influence on the PFD. The DR state is the state in which a dangerous failure is detected and the functionality of the SIS is not yet restored. The SIS is prevented from providing the safety function, when it is in the DR, DUA, DUAB or DN state.

The SIS can be modelled by [7,9]

$$\frac{dp(t)}{dt} = Qp(t),$$

$$= \begin{bmatrix} q_{11} & \mu_{cms} & \mu_{md} & 0 & 0 & 0 \\ \lambda_s & -\mu_{cms} & 0 & 0 & 0 & 0 \\ \lambda_{dd} & 0 & -\mu_{md} & 0 & 0 & 0 \\ \lambda_{duab} & 0 & 0 & 0 & 0 & 0 \\ \lambda_{dua} & 0 & 0 & 0 & 0 & 0 \\ \lambda_{dn} & 0 & 0 & 0 & 0 & 0 \end{bmatrix} \begin{bmatrix} p_1(t) \\ p_2(t) \\ p_3(t) \\ p_4(t) \\ p_5(t) \\ p_6(t) \end{bmatrix}, \tag{1}$$

$$q_{11} = -\lambda_s - \lambda_{dd} - \lambda_{duab} - \lambda_{dua} - \lambda_{dn},$$

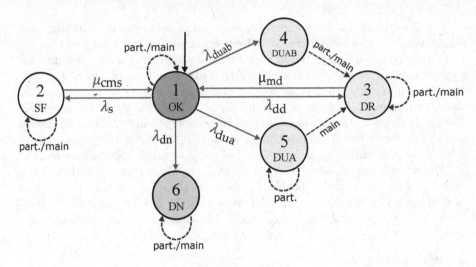

Fig. 1. State transition diagram of a 1oo1 SIS [9]

where $p_1, \cdots, p_6$ denote, respectively, the probability that the SIS is in the OK state, SF, DD, DUAB, DUA and DN, Q is constant matrix, λ_s is the failure rate of safe failures, $\lambda_{dd}, \lambda_{duab}, \lambda_{dua}, \lambda_{dn}$ are, respectively, DD failure rate, DUAB failure rate, DUA failure rate and DN failure rate, μ_{cms} is the repair rate when a safe failure is recognized and μ_{md} is the repair rate when a DD failure is recognized.

The PM tests can be divided into two types based on the depth of the test: main tests and partial tests. For instance, a complete functional test is the main test. In comparison, a partial stroke test is a partial test. The PM test causes a jump in the state vector in (1) immediately after applying the test. The jump can be described by [9]

$$p(t_i^+) = Mp(t_i^-), \qquad i = 1, 2, \cdots, n, \tag{2}$$

where t_i^- and t_i^+ represent, respectively, the time instants immediately before and after i-th maintenance test, n is the total number of the PM tests over a finite time period and M is a matrix that describes the effect of PM test,

$$M = \begin{cases} M_A, & \text{in case of main test} \\ M_B, & \text{in case of partial test} \end{cases} \tag{3}$$

where

$$M_A = \begin{bmatrix} 1 & 0 & 0 & 0 & 0 & 0 \\ 0 & 1 & 0 & 0 & 0 & 0 \\ 0 & 0 & 1 & 1 & 1 & 0 \\ 0 & 0 & 0 & 0 & 0 & 0 \\ 0 & 0 & 0 & 0 & 0 & 0 \\ 0 & 0 & 0 & 0 & 0 & 1 \end{bmatrix}, \quad M_B = \begin{bmatrix} 1 & 0 & 0 & 0 & 0 & 0 \\ 0 & 1 & 0 & 0 & 0 & 0 \\ 0 & 0 & 1 & 1 & 0 & 0 \\ 0 & 0 & 0 & 0 & 0 & 0 \\ 0 & 0 & 0 & 0 & 1 & 0 \\ 0 & 0 & 0 & 0 & 0 & 1 \end{bmatrix}. \tag{4}$$

2.2   The Probability of Failure on Demand (PFD)

The PFD value refers to the probability that the SIS has a dangerous failure and can not respond further in case that an accident happens. It is calculated by

$$PFD = p_3(t) + p_4(t) + p_5(t) + p_6(t).   \tag{5}$$

The average value of the PFD over the life cycle can be calculated by

$$PFD_{avg} = \frac{1}{t_f - t_0} \int_{t_0}^{t_f} PFD(t)dt,   \tag{6}$$

where t_0 and t_f are, respectively, the initial time and the end time of the life cycle.

2.3   The Optimization Problem Formulation

According to the international norm IEC 61511, the safety integrity level of the SIS is evaluated by PFD_{avg} in (6). The smaller PFD_{avg} is, the more reliable is the SIS. The main purpose is to schedule PM tests over the life cycle to minimize the value of PFD_{avg} by selecting both the optimal sequence of the tests (i.e, the order of main and partial tests) and the optimal time instants to apply the corresponding PM tests.

Let us assume there are n_f number of main tests and n_p number of partial tests to be applied over the life cycle. The optimization problem of minimization of PFD_{avg} can be formulated as

$$\min_{t_{Aj}, t_{Bz}} \quad PFD_{avg}   \tag{7a}$$

$$\text{s.t.} \quad \frac{dp(t)}{dt} = Qp(t), \qquad\qquad\qquad t \in [t_0, t_f]   \tag{7b}$$

$$p(t_{Aj}^+) = M_A p(t_{Aj}^-), \quad t_{Aj} \in [t_0, t_f], \ j = 1, \cdots, n_f   \tag{7c}$$

$$p(t_{Bz}^+) = M_B p(t_{Bz}^-), \quad t_{Bz} \in [t_0, t_f], \ z = 1, \cdots, n_p   \tag{7d}$$

where t_{Aj} and t_{Bz} are the time instants that the full and the partial tests occur. Note that the switching sequence is not explicitly formulated as decision variables in (7a)–(7d), rather embedded in the time instants. For example, if we consider one main test and one partial test to be applied and if the solution of the optimization problem gives t_{A1} value higher than t_{B1}, we can conclude that the order is {partial test, main test}.

3   The Solution

In this section, we describe the basic idea of the proposed approach.

3.1   Discretization of the Optimization Problem

In the industrial practice, the PM tests are usually planned in hours or days. Therefore, we assume that the sampling time (h) is 1 h. In terms of the cost function (7a), it is a definite integral and it, therefore, can be approximated using a numerical method such as rectangle, trapezoidal or Simpson's method. For purposes of clarification, we have considered the rectangular method for discretization. As a result, the cost function can be described as

$$J = PFD_{avg}$$
$$\approx \frac{1}{N} \sum_{k=0}^{N-1} (p_3(k) + p_4(k) + p_5(k) + p_6(k)), \tag{8}$$

where $N = \lceil t_f/h \rceil$ represents the total number of the samples in the horizon with $\lceil \ \rceil$ being the ceiling function. Observe that a smaller sampling time h leads to a larger N.

On the other hand, the differential equation in (7b) is linear; hence, it can be discretized without any approximation as

$$p(k+1) = Q_d p(k), \tag{9}$$

where $p(k) = p(kh)$, $Q_d = e^{Qh}$, h is the sampling time and k only holds for time steps that does not belongs to switching periods. By assuming that the PM tests can take place only as multiples of the sampling time, when a PM test is applied at a time k_i, the state vector $p(k_i)$ will jump to $Mp(k_i)$. By substituting the updated state vector $Mp(k_i)$ in (9), the states at next time step, $p(k_i + 1)$, after doing the PM test is described by

$$p(k_i + 1) = Q_d(Mp(k_i)), \qquad i = 1, 2, \cdots, n, \tag{10}$$

where M is either M_A or M_B depending on the type of PM test as shown in (3) and $n = n_f + n_p$.

Based on (9) and (10), there are three modes during the entire dynamic, namely, in normal mode without maintenance described by (9), main test mode or partial test modes described by (10). By introducing binary variables, it is possible to combine all modes in one difference equation. As a result, the dynamics (7b)–(7d) can be equivalently described by

$$p(k+1) = \gamma(k)(Q_d p(k)) + \alpha(k)(Q_d(M_A p(k)) + \\ \beta(k)(Q_d(M_B p(k)) \tag{11}$$

where $k = 0, 1, \cdots, N-1$ and $\alpha(k)$, $\beta(k)$ and $\gamma(k)$ are binary variables that take value either 0 or 1. The binary variables are indicators of the active mode at time instant k. Therefore, at any time k, only one binary variable has the value of one and the other two binary variables are zero.

Based on (8)–(11), the optimization problem (7a)–(7d) can be reformulated as

$$\min_{\alpha(k),\beta(k),\gamma(k)} \frac{1}{N} \sum_{k=0}^{N-1} (p_3(k) + p_4(k) + p_5(k) + p_6(k)) \tag{12a}$$

$$\text{s.t.} \quad p(k+1) = \gamma(k)Q_d p(k) + \tag{12b}$$
$$\alpha(k)Q_d M_A p(k) + \beta(k)Q_d M_B p(k),$$

$$\sum_{k=0}^{N-1} \alpha(k) \leq n_p, \qquad\qquad \alpha(k) \in \{0,1\} \tag{12c}$$

$$\sum_{k=0}^{N-1} \beta(k) \leq n_f, \qquad\qquad \beta(k) \in \{0,1\} \tag{12d}$$

$$\alpha(k) + \beta(k) + \gamma(k) = 1, \qquad k = 0, 1, \cdots, N-1 \tag{12e}$$

where α, β and γ are binary sequences. The number of the partial tests and main tests are, respectively, specified in the relaxed constraints (12c)–(12d). The constraint in (12e) guarantees that only one mode is active at any time k. This optimization problem is a mixed-integer programming due to the fact that the decision variables involve both binary and continuous variables.

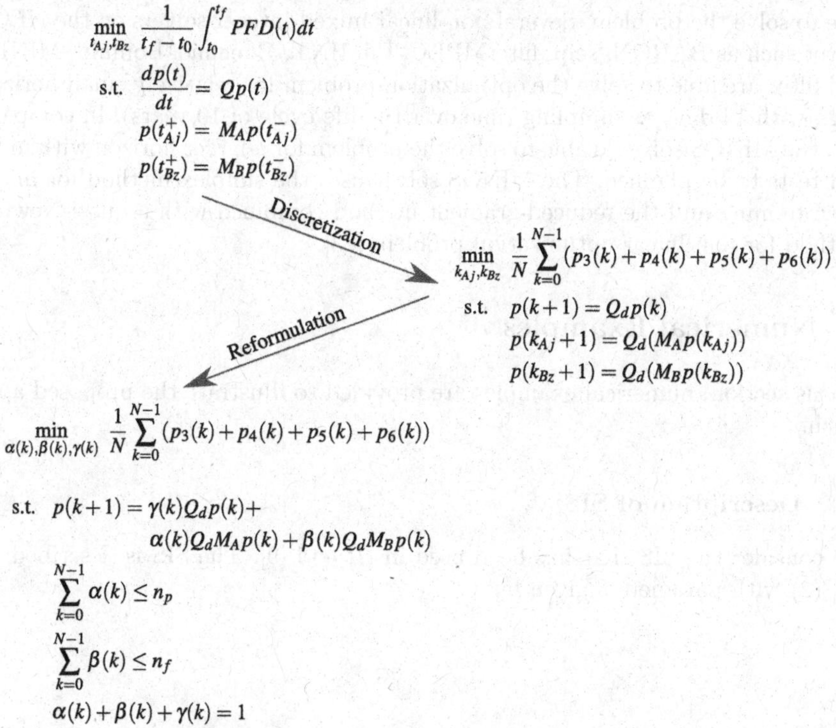

$$\min_{t_{Aj},t_{Bz}} \frac{1}{t_f - t_0} \int_{t_0}^{t_f} PFD(t)dt$$

$$\text{s.t.} \quad \frac{dp(t)}{dt} = Qp(t)$$
$$p(t_{Aj}^+) = M_A p(t_{Aj}^-)$$
$$p(t_{Bz}^+) = M_B p(t_{Bz}^-)$$

Discretization

$$\min_{k_{Aj},k_{Bz}} \frac{1}{N} \sum_{k=0}^{N-1} (p_3(k) + p_4(k) + p_5(k) + p_6(k))$$

$$\text{s.t.} \quad p(k+1) = Q_d p(k)$$
$$p(k_{Aj}+1) = Q_d(M_A p(k_{Aj}))$$
$$p(k_{Bz}+1) = Q_d(M_B p(k_{Bz}))$$

Reformulation

$$\min_{\alpha(k),\beta(k),\gamma(k)} \frac{1}{N} \sum_{k=0}^{N-1} (p_3(k) + p_4(k) + p_5(k) + p_6(k))$$

$$\text{s.t.} \quad p(k+1) = \gamma(k)Q_d p(k) +$$
$$\alpha(k)Q_d M_A p(k) + \beta(k)Q_d M_B p(k)$$

$$\sum_{k=0}^{N-1} \alpha(k) \leq n_p$$

$$\sum_{k=0}^{N-1} \beta(k) \leq n_f$$

$$\alpha(k) + \beta(k) + \gamma(k) = 1$$

Fig. 2. Illustration of the proposed approach

Solving the optimization problem (12a)–(12e) will give an optimal solution $\alpha^*(k)$, $\beta^*(k)$ and $\gamma^*(k)$, $k = 0, 1, \cdots, N - 1$. The schedule of the PM tests can be extracted from $\alpha^*(k)$ and $\beta^*(k)$. To sum up, the proposed approach involves two steps: discretization of the continuous model and then using the binary variables to reformulate the problem as a mixed-integer programming problem as illustrated in Fig. 2.

3.2 Numerical Solution to the Optimization Problem

After the reformulation of optimization problem (12a)–(12e), a solver can be applied to get an optimal solution. Due to the variety of mixed-integer solvers based on different algorithms, higher-level algebraic modelling languages (i.e. AMPL, GAMS, MPS and YALMIP) are used as interface environments between the optimization problem and the solvers, which provide flexibility in using different solvers with the same code. The AMPL is chosen as environment to describe our optimization problem due to its features, for instance, its syntax is similar to the mathematical notation of optimization problems and it is compatible with most solvers supported by the free NEOS Server [20–22]. Furthermore, the AMPL software can detect the proper solver for the defined problem. It has chosen MINOS (Modular In-core Nonlinear Optimization System) solver for our optimization problem (12a)–(12e). For the final implementation, we have used the solvers available on the NEOS server that accept the AMPL as input interface to solve the problem. Several non-linear mixed-integer solvers on the NEOS server such as BARON, scip, filterMPEC, FilMINT, Couenne, Bonmin, MINLP and filter are able to solve the optimization problem for relatively small horizon (e.g., with 14 days as sampling time over the life cycle of 10 years). In comparison, the MINOS solver is able to solve the problem for a larger horizon with more PM tests to be planned. The MINOS solver uses the simplex method for linear programming and the reduced-gradient method combined with a quasi-Newton method for non-linear optimization problem [23].

4 Numerical Examples

In this section, numerical examples are provided to illustrate the proposed approach.

4.1 Description of SIS

We consider the SIS that has been used in [7] and [9]. The SIS is described by (1)–(2) with parameters given by

$$dc = \frac{\lambda_{dd}}{\lambda_d}$$
$$\lambda_d = \lambda_{dd} + \lambda_{duab} + \lambda_{dua} + \lambda_{dn}$$
$$\lambda_{dd} = dc \cdot \lambda_d$$
$$\lambda_{duab} = tcb \cdot (1 - dc) \cdot \lambda_d \qquad (13)$$
$$\lambda_{dua} = (tca - tcb) \cdot (1 - dc) \cdot \lambda_d$$
$$\lambda_{dn} = (1 - tca) \cdot (1 - dc) \cdot \lambda_d$$

where dc, tca, tcb denote, respectively, the diagnostic coverage factor, test coverage of main test and test coverage of partial test. The concrete values in (13) are shown in Table 1, where h^{-1} refers to per hour.

Table 1. Parameters of the SIS

Parameter	Value	Parameter	Value
λ_s (h^{-1})	3×10^{-7}	λ_d (h^{-1})	3×10^{-8}
μ_{cms} (h^{-1})	5×10^{-3}	μ_{md} (h^{-1})	1×10^{-3}
dc	0.40	tca	0.80
tcb	0.48		

Therefore, the matrix Q in (1) is

$$\mathbf{Q} = \begin{bmatrix} -3.30 \times 10^{-7} & 5 \times 10^{-3} & 1 \times 10^{-3} & 0 & 0 & 0 \\ 3.00 \times 10^{-7} & -5 \times 10^{-3} & 0 & 0 & 0 & 0 \\ 1.20 \times 10^{-8} & 0 & -1 \times 10^{-3} & 0 & 0 & 0 \\ 8.64 \times 10^{-9} & 0 & 0 & 0 & 0 & 0 \\ 5.76 \times 10^{-9} & 0 & 0 & 0 & 0 & 0 \\ 3.60 \times 10^{-9} & 0 & 0 & 0 & 0 & 0 \end{bmatrix}. \qquad (14)$$

Under sampling time $h = 1$ h, the matrix Q_d in (9) is

$$\mathbf{Q}_d = \begin{bmatrix} 1 & 5.000 \times 10^{-3} & 9.995 \times 10^{-4} & 0 & 0 & 0 \\ 2.993 \times 10^{-7} & 9.950 \times 10^{-1} & 1.497 \times 10^{-10} & 0 & 0 & 0 \\ 1.199 \times 10^{-8} & 2.994 \times 10^{-11} & 9.990 \times 10^{-1} & 0 & 0 & 0 \\ 8.640 \times 10^{-9} & 2.156 \times 10^{-11} & 4.319 \times 10^{-12} & 1 & 0 & 0 \\ 5.760 \times 10^{-9} & 1.438 \times 10^{-11} & 2.879 \times 10^{-12} & 0 & 1 & 0 \\ 3.600 \times 10^{-9} & 8.985 \times 10^{-12} & 1.799 \times 10^{-12} & 0 & 0 & 1 \end{bmatrix}. \qquad (15)$$

At the very beginning (i.e., $t = t_0$), the SIS is in the failure free state (i.e., OK state). Hence,

$$p(0) = [1 \ 0 \ 0 \ 0 \ 0 \ 0]^T.$$

4.2　PM Schedule for 1 Main Test and 2 Partial Tests

In this example, we considered scheduling of 3 PM tests for the SIS described in Sect. 4.1, over the life cycle of 10 years, which includes 1 main test and 2 partial tests. Hence, the parameters of the optimization problem in (12a)–(12e) are $n_f = 1$, $n_p = 2$ and $N = 87,600$. The mixed-integer optimization problem is solved using the MINOS on the free NEOS server and the results are shown in the Table 2.

By checking the values of α^* and β^* over the horizon, we find the main test presented by α^* occurs at $k = 43,301$. The partial tests resented by β^* occur at $k = 21,652$ and 64,951. Map k values to continuous time by

$$t = t_0 + \frac{k}{N}(t_f - t_0). \tag{16}$$

After mapping k to years, the main test occurs at 4.943 year and the partial tests occur at 2.472 year and 7.414 year. Hence, optimal switching time instants and sequence, and the corresponding PFD_{avg} value are

$$\sigma^* = \{\sigma_1^*, \sigma_2^*, \sigma_3^*\}$$
$$= \{(\text{partial}, 2.472), (\text{main}, 4.943), (\text{partial}, 7.414)\} \tag{17}$$
$$PFD_{avg} = 3.996 \times 10^{-4}.$$

Table 2. The optimal solution $\alpha^*(k)$, $\beta^*(k)$ and $\gamma^*(k)$ to the optimization problem (12a)–(12e) obtained by the MINOS solver

k	$\alpha^*(k)$	$\beta^*(k)$	$\gamma^*(k)$
0	0	0	1
⋮	⋮	⋮	⋮
21651	0	0	1
21652	0	1	0
21653	0	0	1
⋮	⋮	⋮	⋮
43300	0	0	1
43301	1	0	0
43302	0	0	1
⋮	⋮	⋮	⋮
64950	0	0	1
64951	0	1	0
64952	0	0	1
⋮	⋮	⋮	⋮
87599	0	0	1

In terms of computational cost, it takes on average about 3.5 min. Recall that, if the switching sequence is pre-specified, the method given in [9] can find optimal switching time instants. As there are 1 main test and 2 partial tests, there are only 3 possible switching sequences, i.e., B-B-A, B-A-B and A-B-B, where A denotes main test and B denotes partial test. Combining the enumeration approach with the method in [9], it is also possible to get an optimal schedule including an optimal switching sequence and optimal switching time instants. For the purpose of validation, we compare the optimal solution (17) obtained by the proposed approach with the results obtained by applying [9] to all possible switching sequences.

Table 3 shows the optimal switching time instants for these three switching sequences obtained with the method of [9]. As can be seen from Table 3, the switching sequence B-A-B gives the minimal performance index (i.e., achieves the minimal value of PFD_{avg}). Thus, the switching sequence B-A-B is the optimal switching sequence. The optimal switching time instants under the switching sequence B-A-B (see the row highlighted in the table) are

$$t_1 = 2.471, \qquad t_2 = 4.943, \qquad t_3 = 7.414. \tag{18}$$

By comparing (17) with (18), we can see that the optimal time instants in (17) and (18) are same for the first 3 digits precision. That means, the optimal solution (17) got by the approach proposed in Sect. 3 can find an optimal solution of the scheduling problem. Note that the proposed approach needs to solve only one optimization problem, while the method of [9] needs to solve an optimization problem for each possible sequence to get the optimal solution.

Table 3. Optimal switching time instants for different switching sequences obtained with the method of [9].

Switching sequence	t_1 year	t_2 year	t_3 year	PFD_{avg}
B-A-B	2.471	4.943	7.414	3.996×10^{-4}
A-B-B	3.707	5.767	7.826	4.150×10^{-4}
B-B-A	2.060	4.119	6.179	4.149×10^{-4}

4.3   PM Schedule for 3 Main Tests and 5 Partial Tests

To investigate the ability of the proposed approach to scheduling more PM tests, we consider scheduling for the SIS described in Sect. 4.1 with 8 tests, namely 3 main tests and 5 partial tests over 3 different lengths of life cycles: 5, 10 and 15 years. The results are shown in Table 4. The sampling time is 1 h and time units in the table are in years.

Table 4 shows an optimal switching sequence and an optimal time instants found by the approach proposed in Sect. 3. The MINOS solver is able to find an

Table 4. Optimal PM schedule for the SIS with 3 main tests and 5 partial tests over different length of life cycle (A: main test, B: partial test)

Optimal PM schedule	Life cycle 5 years	Life cycle 10 years	Life cycle 15 years
σ_1^*	(B, 0.612)	(B, 0.800)	(B, 1.864)
σ_2^*	(A, 1.223)	(A, 2.185)	(A, 3.723)
σ_3^*	(B, 1.834)	(B, 2.935)	(B, 5.820)
σ_4^*	(A, 2.445)	(B, 3.939)	(B, 7.444)
σ_5^*	(B, 2.814)	(A, 4.944)	(A, 8.649)
σ_6^*	(B, 3.234)	(B, 6.276)	(B, 9.889)
σ_7^*	(A, 3.829)	(B, 7.607)	(A, 11.128)
σ_8^*	(B, 4.359)	(A, 8.747)	(B, 13.007)
PFD_{avg}	1.556×10^{-4}	2.886×10^{-4}	4.251×10^{-4}

optimal solution for all cases. Note that if the enumeration approach combined with the approach in [9] is considered, the number of the possible sequences is 56. However, the method in [9] becomes cumbersome to use because the first and second derivatives of the cost function must be calculated for every sequence. Moreover, the number of possible sequences increases exponentially with the increase in the number of main tests and partial tests.

The resulting $PFD(t)$ of the 1oo1 SIS over 15 years life cycle is shown in Fig. 3. The PFD_{avg} got by the proposed approach is 4.251×10^{-4}.

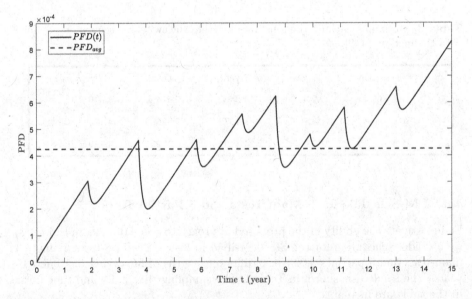

Fig. 3. $PFD(t)$ (solid line) and PFD_{avg} (dashed line) of the 1oo1 SIS with 3 main tests and 5 partial tests over 15 years life cycle

5   Conclusions

In this paper, we give an approach to minimize the average PFD for safety instrumented system (SIS) by optimizing the schedule of main tests and partial tests of the preventive maintenance. The proposed approach is able to optimize both the switching sequence and time instants. The basic idea is to present the state jumps as sub-dynamics described by difference equations and then to combine all sub-dynamics in one difference equation using binary variables. After that, the optimization problem is reformulated as a mixed-integer optimization problem. AMPL can be used as a describing language to input the reformulated optimization problem to the MINOS solver available on the free NEOS server. It is an efficient approach in terms of computational cost. This approach can be extended easily to consider more than two types of maintenance tests. For the SIS with complex architectures (e.g., 2oo3), the matrices Q and M as well as the state vector $p(t)$ in the SIS model (1)–(2) need to be adapted. The next work is to extend this approach to minimize the costs of preventive maintenance or the number of PM tests while satisfying the requirements on the average PFD.

References

1. Torres-Echeverria, A.C.: Modelling and optimization of safety instrumented systems based on dependability and cost measures. Ph.D. thesis, University of Sheffield (2009)
2. Gruhn, P., Cheddie, H.: Safety shutdown systems: design, analysis, and justification. Instrument Society of America (ISA), Research Triangle Park, NC (1998)
3. Catelani, M., Ciani, L., Luongo, V.: A simplified procedure for the analysis of safety instrumented systems in the process industry application. Microelectron. Reliab. **51**(9–11), 1503–1507 (2011)
4. Mechri, W., Simon, C., BenOthman, K.: Switching Markov chains for a holistic modeling of SIS unavailability. Reliab. Eng. Syst. Saf. **133**, 212–222 (2015)
5. Innal, F., Lundteigen, M.A., Liu, Y., Barros, A.: PFDavg generalized formulas for SIS subject to partial and full periodic tests based on multi-phase Markov models. Reliab. Eng. Syst. Saf. **150**, 160–170 (2016)
6. Liu, Y., Rausand, M.: Reliability assessment of safety instrumented systems subject to different demand modes. J. Loss Prevent. Process Ind. **24**(1), 49–56 (2011)
7. Machleidt, K.: Preventive maintenance of safety-related systems-modeling, analysis, and optimization. Ph.D. thesis, University of Kaiserslautern, Department of Electrical and Computer Engineering (2016)
8. McKinnon, K.I.: Convergence of the Nelder-Mead simplex method to a nonstationary point. SIAM J. Optimiz. **9**(1), 148–158 (1998)
9. Martynova, D., Zhang, P.: Optimization of maintenance schedule for safety instrumented systems. IFAC-PapersOnLine **50**(1), 12484–12489 (2017)
10. Xu, X., Antsaklis, P.J.: Optimal control of hybrid autonomous systems with state jumps. In: Proceedings of the 2003 American Control Conference, Denver, USA, pp. 5191–5196 (2003)
11. Giua, A., Seatzu, C., Van Der Mee, C.: Optimal control of autonomous linear systems switched with a pre-assigned finite sequence. In: Proceedings of the 2001 IEEE International Symposium on Intelligent Control, Mexico City, Mexico, pp. 144–149 (2001)

12. Analysis and design of hybrid systems (chap). In: The Control Systems Handbook: Control System Advanced Methods, p. 31. CRC Press (2018)
13. De Marchi, A.: On the mixed-integer linear-quadratic optimal control with switching cost. IEEE Control Syst. Lett. **3**(4), 990–995 (2019)
14. Zhu, F., Antsaklis, P.J.: Optimal control of hybrid switched systems: a brief survey. Discrete Event Dyn. Syst. **25**(3), 345–364 (2014). https://doi.org/10.1007/s10626-014-0187-5
15. Majdoub, N., Sakly, A., Sakly, M.: ACO-based optimization of switching instants for autonomous switched systems with state jumps. IFAC Proc. Vol. **43**(8), 449–454 (2010)
16. Seatzu, C., Corona, D., Giua, A., Bemporad, A.: Optimal control of continuous-time switched affine systems. IEEE Trans. Autom. Control **51**(5), 726–741 (2006)
17. Bemporad, A., Giua, A., Seatzu, C.: Synthesis of state-feedback optimal controllers for continuous-time switched linear systems. In: Proceedings of the 41st IEEE Conference on Decision and Control, Las Vegas, USA, vol. 3, pp. 3182–3187 (2002)
18. Bock, H.G., Kirches, C., Meyer, A., Potschka, A.: Numerical solution of optimal control problems with explicit and implicit switches. Optimiz. Methods Softw. **33**(3), 450–474 (2018)
19. Kirches, C., Kostina, E., Meyer, A., Schlöder, M.: Numerical solution of optimal control problems with switches, switching costs and jumps. Optimiz. Online J. **6888**, 1–30 (2018)
20. Fourer, R., Gay, D.M., Kernighan, B.W.: AMPL A Modeling Language for Mathematical Programming. Thomson (2002)
21. Kirches, C., Leyffer, S.: TACO a toolkit for AMPL control optimization. Math. Program. Comput. **5**(3), 227–265 (2013)
22. NEOS Solver Statistics. https://neos-server.org/neos/report.html. Accessed 20 May 2020
23. Murtagh, B.A., Saunders, M.A.: MINOS 5.51 user's guide. Technical report, Stanford University, Systems Optimization Lab (2003)

Dependability Analysis Processes

Counterexample Interpretation
for Contract-Based Design

Arut Prakash Kaleeswaran[1,2]([⊠]), Arne Nordmann[1], Thomas Vogel[2],
and Lars Grunske[2]

[1] Bosch Corporate Sector Research, 71272 Renningen, Germany
{ArutPrakash.Kaleeswaran,Arne.Nordmann}@de.bosch.com
[2] Humboldt-Universität zu Berlin, Berlin, Germany
{Thomas.Vogel,Grunske}@informatik.hu-berlin.de

Abstract. Contract-based design (CBD) is an emerging paradigm for
complex systems, specifying the input-output behavior of a component
by defining what the component guarantees, provided its environment
satisfies the given assumptions. Under certain circumstances, it is possible to verify the decomposition of contracts to conclude the correctness
of the top-level system requirements. Verification is performed by using
model checkers. If the decomposition of the contract is found to be incorrect, a model checker generates a counterexample. However, the challenging task is to understand the counterexample, which usually is lengthy,
cryptic, and verbose. In this paper, we propose an approach to derive an
understandable error explanation for counterexamples in CBD. In addition, we highlight the erroneous variables and erroneous states in the
counterexample, which reduces the effort to identify errors. Therefore,
our approach supports error comprehension of the original counterexample. Our approach is evaluated based on two industrial use cases, the
Bosch Electronic Power Steering (EPS) and a redundant sensor system.

Keywords: Contract-based design · Counterexample comprehension

1 Introduction

When software-intensive systems are used in safety-critical domains such as automotive and avionics, their malfunction might lead to severe damages or even
loss of lives. Thus, safety is of paramount importance and systems have to be
developed according to safety standards such as IEC 61508 or ISO 26262. These
standards require safety methods such as Failure Mode and Effects Analysis
(FMEA), Fault Tree Analysis (FTA), or Hazard and Operability (HAZOP) that
analyze the safety of a system based on a model of the system [14,15,28,30].

In previous work, we presented Model-Based Safety Analysis (MBSA) methods for FMEA [24], FTA [25], and HAZOP [18] by combining and linking safety
analysis with Model-Based System Development (MBSD). These methods help
in analyzing safety goals: If safety goals are violated, engineers derive safety

M. Zeller and K. Höfig (Eds.): IMBSA 2020, LNCS 12297, pp. 99–114, 2020.
https://doi.org/10.1007/978-3-030-58920-2_7

requirements to satisfy these goals. However, the analysis to identify the faults is performed manually by engineers, which should be ideally automated. In recent years, formal methods have been developed to analyze and verify complex systems [33], and as such, for instance, formal verification would have revealed the exposed defects in Ariane-5, Mars Pathfinder, Intel's Pentium II processor, and the Therac-25 therapy radiation machine [1].

One example of a formal method is *model checking* [1,11], where a *model checker* verifies whether a provided *property/specification* φ is satisfied by a given state-based *system model* K, that is, $K \vDash \varphi$. Otherwise, if φ is not satisfied by K, a model checker generates a *counterexample* describing an execution path in K that leads from the initial system state to a state that violates φ [1], whereas each state consists of variables (atomic propositions) with their values. Engineers can use the counterexample to find the fault in K that causes the violation of φ. According to Clarke [9, p. 3], "It is impossible to overestimate the importance of the counterexample feature. The counterexamples are invaluable in debugging complex systems. Some people use model checking just for this feature."

Nevertheless, a counterexample is only the symptom of a fault, and understanding a counterexample to actually identify a fault in the system model is complicated, error-prone, and time-consuming because of the following problems: **(P1)** a counterexample is cryptic and can be lengthy [26], **(P2)** not all the states in a counterexample are relevant to an error [4], **(P3)** not all the variables in a state are related to the violation [4], **(P4)** the debugging of a system model using a counterexample is performed manually [2,26], and **(P5)** a counterexample does not explicitly highlight the source of the error that is hidden in the model [2]. Thus, an automated method for explaining counterexamples that assists engineers in localizing faults in their models is highly desirable [21].

Contract-based design (CBD) is an emerging paradigm for designing complex systems using components and contracts [3]. The components are defined by a component diagram, and each of them is associated with a contract that precisely specifies the expected behavior of the component by assumptions and guarantees [8]. If a component is refined to sub-components, its contract is also refined and assigned to its sub-components. Thus, all of the sub-components should satisfy the expected behavior of the parent component. This corresponds to the correctness and consistency of the refined contracts and can be verified by a model checker, which is known as a *refinement check*.

In this paper, we present an approach that supports engineers in comprehending a counterexample and locating the fault in a CBD that does not pass the refinement check. The contribution of our approach is the automated identification of *(i)* the *erroneous specification* as those parts of a CBD specification that cause the violation of the refinement, *(ii)* the *erroneous states*, that is, those states in a counterexample that are relevant to an error, *(iii)* the *erroneous variables* as those variables in a counterexample that are related to the violation, and *(iv)* the *erroneous component* that causes the violation and particularly, whether its assumptions or guarantees are erroneous. As the *erroneous states* distinguish relevant and irrelevant states in a counterexample, the length of a counterexample to be investigated by engineers is reduced. The *erroneous specification* and *variables* support engineers in relating the CBD specification with the counterexample by focusing on the erroneous parts. Finally, the *erroneous component* helps engineers with identifying the hidden error in the component model of a CBD. Thus, our approach highlights the erroneous states, specification, variables, and component rather than showing the raw specification and counterexample to engineers, which aims for reducing the complexity, error-proneness, and costs of debugging, and supporting error comprehension.

For this purpose, our approach takes a CBD, translates the component model to a system model (K), specifically a Kripke Structure (KS), and the contracts to a refinement check formula defined in Linear Temporal Logic (LTL) [31], and verifies the refinement of contracts using the NuSMV [7] model checker. If the refinement is violated, the resulting counterexample and the violated LTL specification is processed. First, to identify the *erroneous specification*, we extend the work of Narizzano et al. [27]. It identifies inconsistent LTL sub-specifications from the whole violated LTL specification. Second, to identify the *erroneous states* in the counterexample, for which we adapt the idea of Barbon et al. [2], where the full system behavior of a Labeled Transition System (LTS) is simulated. Adapting the work of Barbon et al. for KS, we face two challenges: **(Ch1)** We specify the behavior of a system by contracts (LTL specifications) in contrast to an LTS. Thus, we cannot simulate the behavior in terms of contracts. **(Ch2)** To simulate the full system behavior, all of the possible initial states needs to be collected, which is not possible due to limitations of NuSMV. To overcome **Ch1**, once we find the *erroneous specification*, we remove the erroneous specification from the complete LTL specification and translate the remaining specification to the system model KS that can be simulated by NuSMV. To address **Ch2**, we consider each state from the counterexample as an initial state and simulate the behavior for all such states. Further, by comparing the counterexample trace with the simulation trace, the *erroneous states* in the counterexample are identified. Third, to identify the *erroneous variable* in the counterexample, the variables that belong to *erroneous specification* are extracted and highlighted in the counterexample. Fourth, to identify the component to which the *erroneous specification* belongs and whether the assumptions or guarantees of the component's contract are erroneous, we use information from the refinement check and the *erroneous variables*. We evaluate the proposed approach by using two industrial use cases. To the best of our knowledge, the presented approach is the first one to identify the *erroneous specification*, *erroneous states* and *erroneous variables* from counterexamples in CBD.

2   Contract-Based Design and Motivating Example

Contract-Based Design (CBD) exploits the contracts for compositional reasoning, step-wise refinement, and reuse of components that are already pre-designed or designed independently [8]. CBD consists of a component model and contracts; particularly, a contract C is a pair of assumptions α and guarantees β, thus $C = (\alpha, \beta)$. According to Kaiser et al. [17, p. 70], "the assumption specifies how the context of the component, i.e., the environment from the point of

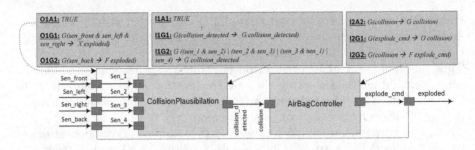

Fig. 1. CBD with its component model and contracts of the airbag system.

view of the component, should behave. Only if the assumption holds, then the component will behave as guaranteed". To illustrate CBD and our approach, we model and use the airbag system from Ratiu et al. [32] as a running example. The corresponding CBD with its component model and contracts are shown in Fig. 1. The input of the airbag system is the detection signal taken from four sensors: *sen_front*, *sen_left*, *sen_right*, and *sen_back*, and the output signal *exploded* activates the airbag system. The system consists of two sub-components: *CollisionPlausibilation* and *AirBagController*. *CollisionPlausibilation* detects the collision or crash from the input sensor signal. The *AirBagController* processes the output from *CollisionPlausibilation* and controls the activation of the airbag.

In Fig. 1, a contract of a component is labeled by $O_N A_N$ and $I_N G_N$, whereas O and I indicate whether the component is an outer or an inner one, A means assumption (α), G means guarantee (β), and the number N is used for enumeration. The contract of the top-level component (in this case, the system) has two guarantees. **O1G1**: whenever the detection signal is given by all of the sensors *sen_front*, *sen_left*, and *sen_right*, then the *exploded* signal will be activated in the next time step. **O1G2**: whenever the detection signal is given by *sen_back*, then the *exploded* signal will be activated in a future time step.

Considering the contracts of a parent/outer component $C_T = (\alpha, \beta)$ and a sub-/inner component $C_S = (\alpha_S, \beta_S)$, the refinement relations between C_T and C_S are $\alpha \subseteq \alpha_S$ and $\beta_S \subseteq \beta$ [17]. In the airbag system, α is $O_N A_N$, α_S is $I_N A_N$, β is $O_N G_N$, and β_S is $I_N G_N$. Cimatti and Tonetta [8, Section 4.D] describe the formulae to verify the correctness of a refinement, which is also used with minor modifications in [32]. These *refinement check formulae* R are shown in Eqs. (1) and (2), in which the *wire* construct connects the input and output ports of the components. R is restricted to the standard propositional LTL in order to be able to perform verification by standard model checking [8].

$$(\alpha \wedge \underbrace{\bigwedge_{1 \leq j \leq n, j \neq i} (\alpha_j \implies \beta_j)) \wedge wire}_{antecedent} \implies \underbrace{\alpha_i}_{consequent} \tag{1}$$

$$\underbrace{\alpha \wedge ((\alpha_1 \implies \beta_1) \wedge \ldots \wedge (\alpha_n \implies \beta_n)) \wedge wire}_{antecedent} \implies \underbrace{\beta}_{consequent} \tag{2}$$

Equation (1) is to verify whether the assumption of each sub-component (α_i) holds true whenever the contracts of all of the other sub-components ($\alpha_j \implies \beta_j$) and the assumption of the parent component (α) holds. Equation (2) is to verify whether the guarantee of the parent component (β) holds true whenever the contracts of all n sub-components ($\alpha_n \implies \beta_n$) and the assumption of parent component (α) holds. In the case that α_i or β fails to hold, R is violated and the verification by a model checker returns a counterexample. Applying R to the airbag systems results in the following formulae, whereas Eqs. 3a and 3b instantiate Eq. (1), and Eq. 4 instantiates Eq. 2.

$$(O1A1 \wedge (I2A1 \implies I2G1 \wedge I2G2) \wedge wire) \implies I1A1 \tag{3a}$$

$$(O1A1 \wedge (I1A1 \implies I1G1 \wedge I1G2) \wedge wire) \implies I2A1 \tag{3b}$$

$$(O1A1 \wedge (I1A1 \implies I1G1 \wedge I1G2) \wedge$$
$$(I2A1 \implies I2G1 \wedge I2G2) \wedge wire) \implies (O1G1 \wedge O1G2) \tag{4}$$

Equation (3a) verifies whether the assumption of *CollisionPlausibilation* ($I1A1$) holds true, whenever the contract of the *AirBagController* and the assumption of the system ($O1A1$) hold. Similarly, Eq. (3b) verifies the assumption of the *AirBagController* ($I2A1$). Finally, Eq. (4) verifies whether the system guarantees ($O1G1$ and $O1G2$) hold true, whenever the contracts of *CollisionPlausibilation* and *AirBagController* and the system's assumption ($O1A1$) hold.

3   Approach

To reduce the complexity, error-proneness, and costs of debugging, and thus to support error comprehension when checking a refinement in a CBD, our approach highlights relevant parts of the CBD and counterexample rather than showing the raw CBD and counterexample. For this purpose, our approach processes a CBD and a counterexample in several steps as shown in Fig. 2.

Step1 comprises the modeling of a CBD and the verification of the refinement formulae R for this CBD (cf. Sect. 2) using the NuSMV model checker. If any formula of R is violated, the refinement check fails so that NuSMV generates a counterexample. This indicates that there must be a fault in the CBD. Using the CBD encoded in a NuSMV file (FSMV), the violated formula/specification R, and the counterexample, *Step2* finds the erroneous (sub-)specification E_{spec} from R, which consequently identifies as well the correct (sub-)specification C_{spec}. This step is based on the work of Narizzano et al. [27]. To enable simulation of the system behavior in terms of the LTL-based C_{spec}, we translate C_{spec} to a Kripke structure and combine this structure with the Kripke structure of FSMV, which results in the NuSVM model SMV_{new}. This step adapts the work of Barbon et al. [2] by addressing challenge Ch1 (cf. Sect. 1). Simulating the SMV_{new} model, *Step4* generates traces of correct behavior, which are then compared to the counterexample trace. This comparison identifies the *erroneous states* E_{state}

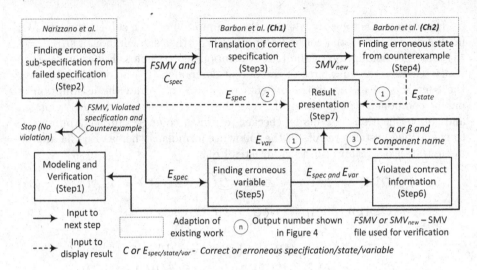

Fig. 2. Overview of the approach.

in the counterexample. This step is based on the work of Barbon et al. [2] by addressing challenge Ch2 (cf. Sect. 1). From the erroneous specification E_{spec}, *Step5* extracts the variables as they are related to the violation of R, thus being the *erroneous variables* E_{var}. Based on E_{spec} and E_{var}, *Step6* identifies the component with its contract that causes the violation, and particularly whether the assumptions or guarantees of the contract are erroneous. Finally, *Step7* collects all of the results from the other steps to highlight the erroneous specification E_{spec}, states E_{state}, variables E_{var}, component in the CBD and counterexample, thus to display the result of our approach. The highlighted elements support an engineer in understanding the counterexample and finding the fault in the CBD. Then, the engineer can correct the CBD by remodeling the CBD and re-verifying the refinement (Step1). In the following, we discuss each step in detail.

3.1 Step 1: Modeling and Verification

This step comprises the modeling of a CBD and verification of the refinement for the CBD. We use FASTEN [32] to specify the component model and contracts. FASTEN is an extensible platform for modeling and model checking safety-critical systems. Specifically, it translates the component model to a system model (K) being a Kripke structure (KS), and the contracts to an LTL specification (φ) based on the refinement formulae R (see the generic Eqs. (1) and (2)). The output of the translation is an SMV file ($FSMV$), which is then used by the NuSMV model checker for verification, that is, to perform the refinement check in terms of the correctness of R. If one of the formulae in R is violated, NuSMV generates a *concrete counterexample* (C_C).

For the airbag system in Fig. 1, FASTEN creates the formulae of Eqs. 3 and 4, which instantiate the generic Eqs. (1) and (2), respectively. Verifying this specification, a C_C is generated for violating Eq. (4) due to the inconsistency between the guarantees $O1GA$ and $I2G2$. This is because the variable $exploded\_cmd$ in $I2G2$ holds true for a future time step but $exploded$ in $O1G1$ holds true immediately for next time step.

Algorithm 1. Algorithm to identify the erroneous specification.

INPUT: R - violated specification and C - concrete counterexample
OUTPUT: E_{spec} - erroneous sub-specification and C_{spec} - correct sub-specification

1: E_{spec}, global list1
2: C_{spec}, global list2
3: **function** FINDINCONSISTENCY(R, C)
4:     $(antecedent, consequent) \leftarrow$ SPLIT(R)
5:     **if** SIZEOF($consequent$) $== 1$ **then**
6:         $E_{spec} \leftarrow consequent$
7:     **else**
8:         **for** $n \leftarrow 0$ to SIZEOF($consequent$) -1 **do**
9:             $consequent \leftarrow consequent \setminus consequent(n)$
10:             $C_{new} \leftarrow$ RUNNUSMV($antecedent +$ " $\implies$ " $+ consequent$)
11:             **if** $C_{new}.equals(C)$ **then**
12:                 $C_{spec} \leftarrow C_{spec} \cup consequent(n)$
13:                 $n \leftarrow n - 1$
14:             **else**
15:                 $E_{spec} \leftarrow E_{spec} \cup consequent(n)$
16:                 $consequent \leftarrow consequent \cup consequent(n)$

3.2   Step 2: Identifying the Erroneous Specification

Using $FSMV$, C_C, and the violated specification R from *Step 1*, this step identifies the violated (*erroneous specification E_{spec}*) and correct sub-specifications (*correct specification C_{spec}*) from R, whereas a sub-specification can be one of the assumptions α or guarantees β of the contracts. For this purpose, we adapt the work of Narizzano et al. [27], which identifies inconsistency between functional requirements, to contracts as shown in Algorithm 1. The algorithm performs two tasks: *(Task1)* Split the violated R, and *(Task2)* identify C_{spec} and E_{spec} in R. Referring to Eq. (5), φ fails whenever the *antecedent* holds *true* and the *consequent* holds *false*. Applying the same rule to Eqs. (1) and (2): if one of the R fails, a counterexample is generated for the violated *consequent*. Thus, **Line** 4 performs *Task1* by splitting R into two lists: *antecedent* and *consequent*.

$$\varphi ::= p \implies q \text{ is false iff } p = true \text{ and } q = false \qquad (5)$$

Task2 identifies E_{spec} and C_{spec} in the *consequent* list. This is achieved by removing one consequent at a time, and repeat the verification to see which consequent makes the formula fail. If the removed consequent belongs to E_{spec}, the counterexample generated during the verification will differ from C_C. On the other hand, if the counterexample is same as C_C, it is considered as C_{spec}. In detail, if the size of the *consequent* list is one (line 5), then there is only one consequent that is then added to the E_{spec} list. In this case, *Task2* is finished. Otherwise, the iterative approach is performed from line 8 to line 16. In the following, we refer to each sub-specification in the *consequent* list as *consequent(n)*, where n is the number of the sub-specification. In line 9, *consequent(n)* is removed from the *consequent* list and verification is performed by running NuSMV in line 10. For verification, the *antecedent*, $\implies$, and the *consequent* list are concatenated as a propositional LTL property. The generated counterexample is assigned to C_{new} (line 10) and compared with C_C (line 11). If $C_{new} \equiv C_C$, *consequent(n)* is added to the C_{spec} list (line 12) and n is subtracted by one in line 13. Otherwise, when $C_{new} \neq C_C$, *consequent(n)* is added to the E_{spec} list (line 15) and *consequent(n)* is added back to the *consequent* list (line 16).

For the airbag system, we know from *Step1* that Eq. (4) is the violated R. The *antecedent* of this equation is $(O1A1 \land (I1A1 \implies I1G1 \land I1G2) \land (I2A1 \implies I2G1 \land I2G2))$ and the *consequent* is $(O1G1 \land O1G2)$. The guarantee $O1G2$ is added to C_{spec} as it is consistent with the *antecedent*, while the guarantee $O1G1$ is added to E_{spec} since it is inconsistent with guarantee $I2G2$.

3.3   Step 3: Translating the LTL Specification to a System Model (K)

This step is required to apply the idea by Barbon et al. [2] to identify the erroneous states in the counterexample using simulation of the correct behavior, which is done in the subsequent step. In our case, the behavior of the system is only implicitly modeled in the form of contracts (φ), and not explicitly as a system model (K). Thus, we cannot simulate the behavior directly (cf. challenge Ch1 in Sect. 1). To overcome this challenge, we translate φ to K.

LTL2SMV [10] is an independent component of NuSMV, which takes an LTL specification as input and produces a corresponding system model in SMV format as output. We take $FSMV$, the *consequent*, and C_{spec} from *Step 2* as input, combine the *consequent* and C_{spec} along with *implies* as the LTL specification $\varphi_{new} :=$ *consequent* $\implies C_{spec}$. Then, φ_{new} is provided as input to LTL2SMV that will generate a new SMV file ($SMV_{LTL2SMV}$) consisting of K corresponding to φ_{new}. Finally, $SMV_{LTL2SMV}$ is integrated with $FSMV$, i.e., $SMV_{new} = prod(SMV_{LTL2SMV}, FSMV)$.

During the generation of $SMV_{LTL2SMV}$, additional variables are generated by LTL2SMV. Therefore, verification is performed once again with SMV_{new} and the counterexample C_M is generated. Due to space constraints, $SMV_{LTL2SMV}$ and additional variables that are generated by LTL2SMV are not shown in this paper. If additional variables are removed from the counterexample (C_M), then C_M is same as the concrete counterexample, i.e., $C_M \equiv C_C$.

3.4   Step 4: Identifying Erroneous States in the Counterexample

In this step, we identify the *erroneous* (E_{state}) and *correct states* (C_{state}) in the counterexample. For this purpose, this step takes C_M and SMV_{new} from *Step2* as its input. Using the approach by Barbon et al. [2], we face challenge **Ch2** (cf. Sect. 1) since it is not feasible to simulate the full system behavior due to limitations in NuSMV. Particularly, we are not interested in all possible initial states I but just the states from the counterexample in order to simulate them. Therefore we use all states with their variables and values of the counterexample as initial states I.

Thus, to identify E_{state} and C_{state} in the counterexample, each state from the counterexample is taken as an initial state. Behavior of the system is simulated for every initial state, and each state from the simulation trace is compared with the counterexample trace. If a state from the counterexample is found in the simulation trace, then we consider it as C_{state}. If the simulation trace is empty, we consider the selected initial state as E_{state}.

This approach is defined in detail in Algorithm 2. From `line` 4 to `line` 12, we iterate over all initial states I to get the simulation trace for each of these states. The number n of initial states is equal to the number of states in the counterexample C_M. Provided every initial state from I, that is, $I(n)$, and SMV_{new} as input to NuSMV, the simulation trace S_{trace} is generated (`line` 5). If the simulation trace is empty, NuSMV returns the message "the set of initial state is EMPTY" (see ⑤ in Fig. 3). In `line` 6, we check whether S_{trace} is empty. If this is the case, we add the *state label* of the selected $C_M(n)$ to the E_{state} list (`line` 7). Otherwise, from `line` 9 to `line` 12, we iterate over all states in the S_{trace} and $C_M(n)$ to compare each state from S_{trace} with every state in C_M (`line` 11). If any of the state from S_{trace} is found in C_M, the *state label* is added to the C_{state} list (`line` 12).

Algorithm 2. Algorithm for erroneous state identification

INPUT: SMV_{new} - SMV file integrating $SMV_{LTL2SMV}$ and $FSMV$, C_M - counterexample generated by using SMV_{new}, I -initial states
OUTPUT: E_{state} - erroneous state and C_{state} - correct state in the counterexample

```
1:  E_state, global list1
2:  C_state, global list2
3:  function FINDERRORSTATE(C_M, SMV_new, I)
4:      for n ← 0 to SIZEOF(I) −1 do
5:          S_trace ← RUNNUSMV(SMV_new, I(n))
6:          if ISEMPTY(S_trace) then
7:              E_state ← E_state ∪ C_M(n).stateLabel
8:          else
9:              for j ← 0 to SIZEOF(S_trace) −1 do
10:                 for k ← 0 to SIZEOF(C_M) −1 do
11:                     if S_trace(j).equals(C_M(k)) then
12:                         C_state ← C_state ∪ C_M(i).stateLabel
```

For our running example, the counterexample C_M shown in Fig. 3 is generated because the variable *exploded_cmd* from guarantee *I2G2* holds true for future time step but *exploded* from guarantee *O1G1* holds true immediately for next time step. Selecting *State 1.1* as $I(n)$ from C_M, we get S_{trace} (S1) and (S2). Comparing S_{trace} with C_M, {*State 1.2, State 1.3, State 1.5*} are found as E_{state} and {*State 1.1, State 1.4*} are found as C_{state}. In Fig. 3, the states marked with (E) resulted from empty traces due to the NuSMV result (S3), while the states marked with (C) match with the simulation trace (S1) or (S2).

3.5 Step 5: Identifying Erroneous Variables in the Counterexample

A system is also defined in terms of variables. By finding the *erroneous variables* E_{var} in the counterexample, we isolate the correct variables. Thus, we can focus on highlighting E_{var} to support error comprehension and debugging since these variables are related to the violation of the refinement formulae. To identify E_{var}, we use E_{spec} obtained in *Step2*. In general, an LTL specification consists of temporal operators, mathematical symbols, variables, and values of variables. Removing temporal operators, mathematical symbols, and values from a specification, the variables can be identified. The same principle is applied to E_{spec}, which is an LTL specification, to identify E_{var}. For the airbag system, the guarantee *O1G1*, that is, $G(sen\_front \ \& \ sen\_left \ \& \ sen\_right \implies X \ exploded)$ is identified as E_{spec}. Removing the temporal operators, mathematical symbols, and values, we obtain *sen_front, sen_left, sen_right*, and *exploded* as E_{var}.

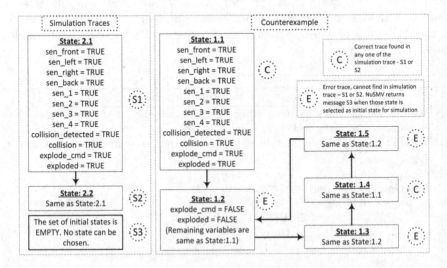

Fig. 3. Simulation and Counterexample traces.

3.6   Step 6: Identifying Violated Contract Details

In this step, we identify whether the erroneous specification E_{spec} belongs to an assumption or guarantee, along with the respective component of the system. E_{spec} found in *Step2* belongs to a contract, that is, it will be either an assumption or a guarantee. It is possible to recognize whether the identified E_{spec} belongs to one or the other based on Eqs. (1) and (2). In Eq. (1), the *consequent* contains only the assumptions of sub-components, whereas in Eq. (2), the *consequent* contains only guarantee of the top-component. Furthermore, the respective component can be identified by name from E_{var}. During the generation of *FSMV*, FASTEN avoids duplicate variable names by prefixing the variable names of a sub-component with the name of the sub-component, wheres the variable names of the parent component remain unchanged. However, the top-component name is used as the *Module* name in *FSMV*. Thus, we can use the variable names from E_{var} to identify the related components by name.

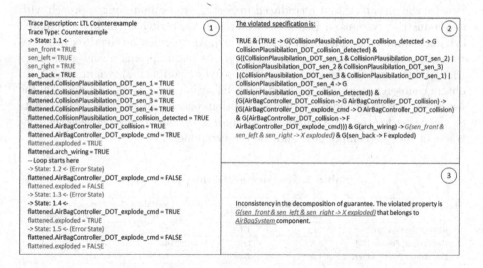

Fig. 4. Result of our approach for the airbag system.

In the airbag system, Eq. (4) is violated (see *Step1*), which is formulated using Eq. (2). Thus, we know that the erroneous specification belongs to a *guarantee*. The E_{var} found in *Step5* are *sen_front, sen_left, sen_right,* and *exploded.* These are not prefixed by a component name so that the respective component is the parent component, being the "AirBagSystem".

3.7   Step 7: Presentation of Results

As shown in Fig. 2, the outcome of individual steps of our approach are used to support error comprehension by presenting three types of error information to an engineer: ① E_{state} and E_{var} in the counterexample found by *Step4* and *Step5*, ② E_{spec} in R found by *Step2*, and ③ Violated contract information found by *Step2* and *Step6*. This information is highlighted when showing the counterexample and failed specification to an engineer as exemplified by Fig. 4 for the airbag system. Particularly, E_{var} (i. e., {*sen_front, sen_left, sen_right, exploded*}) and E_{state} (i. e., {*State 1.2, State 1.3, State 1.5*}) are highlighted in the complete counterexample to distinguish erroneous variables and states from non-erroneous variables and states ①. Similarly, the E_{spec} as the erroneous sub-specification is highlighted in the failed specification R ②. Information about the violated contract ③ consists of three elements: (i) that E_{spec} in R belongs to a *guarantee*, (ii) the concrete formulae of E_{spec} being *O1G1*, i. e., $G(sen\_front \ \& \ sen\_left \ \& \ sen\_right \implies X \ exploded)$, and (iii) that E_{spec} belongs to the "AirBagSystem" component.

4   Evaluation

Besides the airbag system introduced in Sect. 2, we evaluate our approach with two industrial systems: a Bosch electronic power steering for highly-automated driving [5] and a redundant sensor system [22]. An overview on the three use cases with the number of components, specifications (assumptions α and guarantees β), variables, and the size of the resulting counterexample is shown in Table 1. To obtain counterexamples for evaluation, specification errors were introduced in the use cases, that is, we modify either assumptions or guarantees of sub-components or vice versa for the top-component to cause an inconsistency between the contracts of the sub-components and the top-component.

Table 1. Overview of the three use cases

#	System	Component parent/sub	Specifications α/β	Variables (i/o ports)	States in counterexample
1	Airbag System [32]	1/2	3/6	12	5
2	Redundant Sensor [22]	1/6	7/9	42	4
3	Electronic Power Steering [5]	1/8	9/24	26	5

Table 2. Evaluation results for the three use cases

#	System	Variables/E_{var} (i/o ports)	States/E_{state} in counterexample	Run-time (sec.)	
				NuSMV	NuXMV
1	Airbag System [32]	12/4	5/3	1.528	1.622
2	Redundant Sensor [22]	42/2	4/1	109.347	110.973
3	Electronic Power Steering [5]	26/2	5/3	57.003	65.226

Redundant Sensor System. This system is an industrial use case developed by the European Space Agency project FoReVer[1]. It monitors the sensor outcomes to detect and possibly isolate failures to keep the output value reliable. It has 1 parent component, 6 sub-components, 7 assumptions, and 9 guarantees.

Electronic Power Steering (EPS). The EPS system is an industrial product from Bosch for highly-automated driving (HAD) vehicles. To cope with the availability demands of HAD, the system has two redundant channels: primary and secondary channel communication. The output from each channel is *master, slave,* or *passive* mode. The mode transition switches from *master* to *slave,* and *master* or *slave* to *passive.* The nominal behavior of the system is that either one of the channel should be *master* and the other one should be *slave*; in this case the system provides torque to motor for steering. The EPS system has 1 parent component, 8 sub-components, 9 assumptions, and 24 guarantees.

Results. Looking at Fig. 4, the complete information labeled with ① and ② but without the highlighted parts is returned by NuSMV. It is cryptic and does not give any explicit error information or explanation, which makes error understanding even harder. To overcome this issue and to improve the error understanding and usability, the *erroneous states, variables, specification* and *violated contract information* are highlighted and presented to engineers. This helps the engineers in debugging to identify the cause of error.

The results provided in Table 2 indicate that our approach can help engineers in identifying the error in the counterexample compared to analyzing the concrete and complete counterexample given by a model checker. For the redundant sensor system, the number of *erroneous states* found in the counterexample is 1. Therefore, an engineer can focus on this single state to identify the error instead of understanding 4 states in the counterexample. In addition, the approach also highlights that only 2 variables are responsible for the violation. Therefore, the user can focus only on 2 variables while ignoring all other 42 variables. Similarly for EPS, out of 5 total states in the counterexample, 3 are *erroneous states* and from 26 variables, 2 variables are found to be *erroneous variables.* This shows that our approach is able to reduce number of states and particularly of variables that need to be understood and investigated to find the error.

Implementation. The seven steps described in Sect. 3 are developed as a script in Java that runs NuSMV in batch mode and triggers LTL2SMV. NuXMV [6] is used as an alternative to NuSMV, to evaluate the performance of verification (Table 2), although our goal was not to improve the run-time of model checking.

Constraints of our Approach. During the evaluation, we identified some constraints for the application of our approach. If a port or variable is declared but its behavior is not defined by contracts, it affects the generated simulation traces and the result is not reliable. Further, our approach cannot be applied if a specification is inconsistent by itself. For example, $G(A \implies \neg A)$ is inconsistent by itself and our approach cannot handle such a scenario.

---

[1] https://es-static.fbk.eu/projects/forever/.

5   Related Work

The main motivation of this work is to identify the *erroneous specification, states*, and *variables* from the violated specification and counterexample. Existing work addresses the identification of *erroneous specification* and *states*.

The approach by Langenfeld et al. [20] verifies inconsistencies for real-time requirements and is evaluated with industrial use cases. Crapo et al. [13] and Moitra et al. [23] use the Requirements Analysis Engine (RAE) of ASSERT that accept formal requirements in an easily understandable syntax by making use of a domain ontology. Further, RAE of ASSERT analyze an incomplete set of requirements and localizes the error by identifying the responsible requirements with an error marker. For finding *erroneous states* or traces in a counterexample, Jin et al. [16] presented an enhanced error trace that explicitly distinguishes fated and free segments. Fated segments show unavoidable progress towards the error while free segments show the choices that, when avoided, might have prevented the error. Hence, demarcation into segments highlight the critical events.

Pakonen et al. [29] presented a method that assists with identifying the root of the failure in both the model and the specification, by animating the model of the function block diagram as well as the LTL property. The counterexample visualization and explanation from Pakonen et al.addresses both aspects: finding the root cause of failure in the model and finding the failure in the trace.

6   Conclusion and Future Work

To the best of our knowledge, the presented approach is the first one to identify the *erroneous specification, states* and *variables* from counterexamples in CBD. The presented approach aids in finding erroneous specification in the provided contracts, and erroneous states in the counterexample, which improves error comprehension and usability aspects of CBD. Our approach is evaluated with one example and two industrial systems of different size and complexity. This shows that the approach scales up to the size of an industrial product.

> "*Researchers in and educators in formal methods, we should strive to make our notations and tools accessible to non-experts.*"— Edmund Clarke [12, p. 638]

There are several open points and options to enhance the presented approach. Currently, the result is presented separately from the component model. In the future, the result will be lifted back to original component model, where it can be integrated and linked to model elements. The presented approach can identify the *erroneous specification* but not the specification or contract which is inconsistent with the *erroneous specification*. Finding the inconsistent specification along with the *erroneous specification*, improves error comprehension. While this paper supports error comprehension and understanding of counterexamples for experts, future work will focus on supporting interpretation of counterexamples for non-experts, e. g., through natural language like format by using domain terminology supported by ontologies as sketched in earlier work [19].

References

1. Baier, C., Katoen, J.: Principles of Model Checking. MIT Press, Cambridge (2008)
2. Barbon, G., Leroy, V., Salaun, G.: Debugging of behavioural models using counterexample analysis. IEEE Trans. Softw. Eng. 1–14 (2019). https://ieeexplore.ieee.org/abstract/document/8708934
3. Benveniste, A., Caillaud, B., Passerone, R.: A generic model of contracts for embedded systems. CoRR abs/0706.1456 (2007)
4. van den Berg, L., Strooper, P.A., Johnston, W.: An automated approach for the interpretation of counter-examples. ENTCS **174**(4), 19–35 (2007)
5. Bozzano, M., Munk, P., Schweizer, M., Tonetta, S., Vozárová, V.: Model-based safety analysis of mode transitions. In: Proceedings of SAFECOMP (2020, in press)
6. Cavada, R., et al.: The NUXMV symbolic model checker. In: Biere, A., Bloem, R. (eds.) CAV 2014. LNCS, vol. 8559, pp. 334–342. Springer, Cham (2014). https://doi.org/10.1007/978-3-319-08867-9_22
7. Cimatti, A., et al.: NuSMV 2: an opensource tool for symbolic model checking. In: Brinksma, E., Larsen, K.G. (eds.) CAV 2002. LNCS, vol. 2404, pp. 359–364. Springer, Heidelberg (2002). https://doi.org/10.1007/3-540-45657-0_29
8. Cimatti, A., Tonetta, S.: A property-based proof system for contract-based design. In: 38th Euromicro Conference on Software Engineering and Advanced Applications, SEAA 2012, pp. 21–28 (2012)
9. Clarke, E.M.: The birth of model checking. In: 25 Years of Model Checking - History, Achievements, Perspectives, pp. 1–26 (2008)
10. Clarke, E.M., Grumberg, O., Hamaguchi, K.: Another look at LTL model checking. Formal Methods Syst. Des. **10**(1), 47–71 (1997). https://doi.org/10.1023/A:1008615614281
11. Clarke, E.M., Grumberg, O., Peled, D.A.: Model Checking. MIT Press, Cambridge (2001)
12. Clarke, E.M., Wing, J.M.: Formal methods: state of the art and future directions. ACM Comput. Surv. **28**(4), 626–643 (1996)
13. Crapo, A.W., Moitra, A.: Using OWL ontologies as a domain-specific language for capturing requirements for formal analysis and test case generation. In: 13th IEEE International Conference on Semantic Computing, ICSC, pp. 361–366 (2019)
14. Fenelon, P., McDermid, J.A.: An integrated tool set for software safety analysis. J. Syst. Softw. **21**(3), 279–290 (1993)
15. Grunske, L.: Towards an integration of standard component-based safety evaluation techniques with SaveCCM. In: Hofmeister, C., Crnkovic, I., Reussner, R. (eds.) QoSA 2006. LNCS, vol. 4214, pp. 199–213. Springer, Heidelberg (2006). https://doi.org/10.1007/11921998_17
16. Jin, H.S., Ravi, K., Somenzi, F.: Fate and free will in error traces. Int. J. Softw. Tools Technol. Transf. **6**(2), 102–116 (2004). https://doi.org/10.1007/s10009-004-0146-9
17. Kaiser, B., Weber, R., Oertel, M., Böde, E., Nejad, B.M., Zander, J.: Contract-based design of embedded systems integrating nominal behavior and safety. CSIMQ **4**, 66–91 (2015)
18. Kaleeswaran, A.P., Munk, P., Sarkic, S., Vogel, T., Nordmann, A.: A domain specific language to support HAZOP studies of SysML models. In: Papadopoulos, Y., Aslansefat, K., Katsaros, P., Bozzano, M. (eds.) IMBSA 2019. LNCS, vol. 11842, pp. 47–62. Springer, Cham (2019). https://doi.org/10.1007/978-3-030-32872-6_4

19. Kaleeswaran, A.P., Nordmann, A., ul Mehdi, A.: Towards integrating ontologies into verification for autonomous driving. In: ISWC 2019 Satellite Tracks (Posters & Demonstrations, Industry, and Outrageous Ideas), pp. 319–320 (2019)
20. Langenfeld, V., Dietsch, D., Westphal, B., Hoenicke, J., Post, A.: Scalable analysis of real-time requirements. In: 27th IEEE International Requirements Engineering Conference, RE, pp. 234–244 (2019)
21. Leue, S., Tabaei Befrouei, M.: Counterexample explanation by anomaly detection. In: Donaldson, A., Parker, D. (eds.) SPIN 2012. LNCS, vol. 7385, pp. 24–42. Springer, Heidelberg (2012). https://doi.org/10.1007/978-3-642-31759-0_5
22. Marcantonio, D., Tonetta, S.: Redundant Sensors (2014). https://es-static.fbk.eu/tools/ocra/download/RedundantSensors.pdf
23. Moitra, A., et al.: Automating requirements analysis and test case generation. Requir. Eng. **24**(3), 341–364 (2019). https://doi.org/10.1007/s00766-019-00316-x
24. Munk, P., et al.: Semi-automatic safety analysis and optimization. In: 55th ACM/ESDA/IEEE Design Automation Conference (DAC) (2018)
25. Munk, P., Nordmann, A.: Model-based safety assessment with SysML and component fault trees: application and lessons learned. Softw. Syst. Model. **19**, 889–910 (2020). https://doi.org/10.1007/s10270-020-00782-w
26. Muram, F.U., Tran, H., Zdun, U.: Counterexample analysis for supporting containment checking of business process models. In: Reichert, M., Reijers, H. (eds.) BPM 2015. LNBIP, vol. 256, pp. 515–528. Springer, Cham (2016). https://doi.org/10.1007/978-3-319-42887-1_41
27. Narizzano, M., Pulina, L., Tacchella, A., Vuotto, S.: Property specification patterns at work: verification and inconsistency explanation. Innov. Syst. Softw. Eng. **15**(3–4), 307–323 (2019). https://doi.org/10.1007/s11334-019-00339-1
28. Ortmeier, F., Thums, A., Schellhorn, G., Reif, W.: Combining formal methods and safety analysis – the ForMoSA approach. In: Ehrig, H., et al. (eds.) Integration of Software Specification Techniques for Applications in Engineering. LNCS, vol. 3147, pp. 474–493. Springer, Heidelberg (2004). https://doi.org/10.1007/978-3-540-27863-4_26
29. Pakonen, A., Buzhinsky, I., Vyatkin, V.: Counterexample visualization and explanation for function block diagrams. In: INDIN, pp. 747–753 (2018)
30. Papadopoulos, Y., McDermid, J., Sasse, R., Heiner, G.: Analysis and synthesis of the behaviour of complex programmable electronic systems in conditions of failure. Reliab. Eng. Syst. Saf. **71**(3), 229–247 (2001)
31. Pnueli, A.: The temporal logic of programs. In: 18th Annual Symposium on Foundations of Computer Science, pp. 46–57 (1977)
32. Ratiu, D., Gario, M., Schoenhaar, H.: FASTEN: an open extensible framework to experiment with formal specification approaches: using language engineering to develop a multi-paradigm specification environment for NuSMV. In: FormaliSE@ICSE, pp. 41–50. IEEE/ACM (2019)
33. Sharvia, S., Papadopoulos, Y.: Integrating model checking with hip-hops in model-based safety analysis. Reliab. Eng. Syst. Saf. **135**, 64–80 (2015)

Property-Based Fault Injection: A Novel Approach to Model-Based Fault Injection for Safety Critical Systems

Athira Varma Jayakumar$^{(\boxtimes)}$ and Carl Elks

Electrical and Computer Engineering Department, Virginia Commonwealth University,
Richmond, VA, USA
{jayakumarav,crelks}@vcu.edu

Abstract. With the recent popularity of model-based design and verification (MBDE), fault injection testing at the functional model level is gaining significant interest. The reason for this interest is it aids in detecting design errors and incorrect requirements on fault detection and tolerance features, very early in the development lifecycle. This is evidenced by the fact that functional safety standards like IEC 61508 and ISO 26262 identify fault injection testing as a highly recommended technique for SIL-3 and SIL-4. The main challenges to date with model-based fault injection are lack of completeness in the fault injection space, semi-manual integration and insertion of fault injection modules into the models and manual identification of fault activation conditions. The work presented in this paper describes a novel model-based fault injection technique that is *property-based* and applies formal model checking verification methods at the functional model level of design thereby guaranteeing a near-exhaustive state, input and fault space coverage. This method also introduces the usage of properties and model checking capabilities to automate the identification of fault activation conditions for all the faults within the fault space. We describe the workflow and implementation of the property-based Fault injection using Simulink Design Verifier and its application on the functional model of a representative safety-critical system.

Keywords: Fault injection · Fault tolerance assessment · Model-based fault injection · Safety-critical systems · Model-checking

1 Introduction

With technology advancements in semiconductor electronics, communication networks, system-on-chip architectures we have been witnessing continuing high density integration of CPS technology. At the same time we are seeing an increase in software intensive systems for critical applications that take advantage of the capabilities of today's highly integrated devices. To identify and understand potential failures and their consequences, the use of systematic approaches for assuring digital system safety (dependability) is gaining acceptance across many industries from process control, nuclear, automotive, to aerospace. These systematic approaches include methods like safety case analysis

© Springer Nature Switzerland AG 2020
M. Zeller and K. Höfig (Eds.): IMBSA 2020, LNCS 12297, pp. 115–129, 2020.
https://doi.org/10.1007/978-3-030-58920-2_8

methodologies, STPA, STAMP, and formal design assurance methods [1]. Almost all of these systematic approaches require some form of analysis or study of failures, faults, and losses within a system context. Dependability evaluation involves the study of failures and errors and their potential impact on system attributes such as reliability, safety and security. This is evidenced by the fact that functional safety standards like IEC 61508 and ISO 26262 identify fault injection testing as a highly recommended validation technique for SILs 3 and 4.

Fault Injection (FI) is defined as a dependability evaluation technique based on the realization of formal controlled validation experiments in which system behavior is observed while faults are explicitly induced in the system by the deliberate introduction (injection) of faults [2]. At a broad stance, contemporary fault injection approaches fall into 3 categories; physical fault injection, simulation-based fault injection, and SWIFI (Software Implemented Fault Injection). While all of these contemporary approaches to fault injection are needed for assuring dependability and safety case arguments, we suggest a new class of fault injection should be defined by the dependability community – *model based fault injection*. With the recent popularity of model-based design and development (MBDE) and testing, fault injection testing at the functional model level is gaining significant interest. The reason for this interest is it aids in detecting design flaws, omissions and incorrect requirements that impact hazard mitigation very early in the lifecycle development process.

The work presented in this paper describes a model-based fault injection framework that is implemented in the Mathworks Simulink environment. The innovation of the work is that the fault injection technique is *property based* and applies formal model checking at the functional model level of design thereby guaranteeing a near-exhaustive state, input and fault space coverage. This work is noteworthy in that it links fault injection to properties (safety, functional, and liveness) that are vital for making safety case arguments in the presence of hazards, failures and faults. This work also solves the challenge of manually identifying fault activation conditions during fault injection by employing model checking tool to automate it. Our fault injection framework implements a comprehensive insertion of fault modules throughout the system functional model thus enabling an exhaustive fault location coverage.

2 Background and Challenges

Fault injection is often characterized by its statistical nature, meaning that statistical models are used to govern the fault injection experiment [3]. The classical fault injection approach involves iteratively conducting a set of tests (called trials) to inject faults into the system and observing the response of the system. As such, the fault space often involves the dimensions injection time (t), fault location (l), fault type (f_m) as sampled from fault classes, fault value (v) and fault duration (Δ). An extremely important metric for assessment of safety-critical systems is fault coverage, C which denotes the conditional probability that the system detects or corrects a fault given that a fault is present in the system. Due to the multi-variable nature of the statistical experiments, fault injection experiments without a-priori knowledge of what types of fault to inject, where to inject, and at what time to inject becomes very combinatorically challenging, which can lead to very large numbers of fault injection experiments. System safety and reliability are highly sensitive to fault coverage and therefore high levels of fault coverage estimation is often required for such systems [4]. Another major challenge with simulation-based FI is the manual identification of fault activation conditions which is very essential for conducting effective fault injections and avoiding no-response faults. The Property-based FI proposed in this paper is capable of addressing these challenges.

3 Related Work

In the last decade, FI community has started gaining interest on the application of formal methods to fault injection and to the analysis of fault tolerance mechanisms. Few works that extend formal verification techniques like model checking, assertion based verification and symbolic analysis to fault injection are discussed below. Scott et al. [5] present a methodology called ABVFI which is fault injection based on assertion based verification, that checks for critical properties at the hardware level by embedding assertion statements into the hardware design (RTL). Krautz et al. [6] used formal verification to exhaustively measure the fault coverage of a VHDL design. Symbolic simulation of sequential circuits is performed by creating Binary Decision Diagrams of the circuit's state space. Leveugle [7] introduced the new approach of combining property with mutation of the circuits to conduct fault injection experiments on circuits. Critical properties are checked for any violations in the mutated circuits thereby helping in identifying the undesirable effects of multiple faults in the circuit. Daniel et al. [8] were the first to demonstrate the effectiveness of symbolic fault injection on a SIHFT application in Java platform. This approach involved the injection of symbolic faults during the symbolic execution of the software. Another work by Vedder et al. [9] that combines property-based testing with fault injection enables automatic generation of testcases from specified system properties and verifying them in the presence of faults. Most of these works combining fault injection with formal verification are targeted for hardware design level. Whereas this study is targeted to analyze the feasibility and effectiveness of formal verification for fault injection in a model-based design environment.

Few works like [10] and [11] have proven the usage of model checking and fault injection to automate FMEA and deviation analysis on Behavior Tree models and NuSMV models respectively. xSAP tool [12] offers a platform to formally conduct faults/safety analysis, but necessitates the system model to be represented in NuSMV. We extend on these works by introducing the use of exhaustive model checking for fault injection and fault behavior analysis on executable functional models in Simulink capable of progressing into code generation. These Simulink behavioral models are deterministic functional/logical models with no probabilistic aspects. While studies [13] and [14] describe the usage of Design Verifier model checker to formally prove safety properties in the presence of faults introduced in the functional models, we go beyond these works by addressing the practical problem of identifying fault activation conditions during fault injection. Faults even though triggered may not be activated if other input/state conditions are not satisfied. Inactivated faults could cause the model checker to falsely validate the safety properties. This practical problem is systematically addressed using model checking in this paper. In addition, while other studies including [13] and [14] selectively introduce failure modes in the model to capture the various ways in which the system components malfunction, our work implements exhaustive fault saboteur insertion, thus allowing for an exhaustive fault behavior analysis by the model checker. An automation script that is part of our FI framework facilitates insertion of fault saboteurs throughout all signal lines within the model, thus ensuring complete fault location coverage. The framework also enables an extensive and diverse fault model selection that consists of permanent, transient and delay faults [15].

4 Property-Based Fault Injection

The conceptual idea of property proof based fault injection is shown in Fig. 2. The basic premise of our approach is to use the power of *model checking* to overcome some of the challenges associated with classical fault injection methods – namely the burden of executing large numbers of FI combinatorial experiments and finding fault activation conditions. This approach is complementary to classical fault injection methods in that it identifies potential problems as early as possible in the design process. Model checking is a formal verification technique that mathematically verifies the validity of critical properties of a model of a system through systematic state exploration. Unlike testing, where the input and expected output vectors have to be fed into the system, there is no need to feed in input sequences for model checking. It is a verification procedure that involves an *exhaustive search* of the state and input space of the design to ensure that a system always satisfies specific property under given constraints.

Fig. 1. Classical fault injection vs property based fault injection

To understand the difference between property-based FI and classical statistical-based FI, we consider the FI experiment space exploration achieved with each of these methods as shown in Fig. 1. Classical FI experiment covers a single point within the FI experiment space of the system, per experimental trial. As such, with classical FI there are always points in the FI experiment space (input/fault/state space points) that are not covered, which could overlook a faulty part of the design to go unnoticed. In contrast, fault injection based on property proving works at the property level. Given a safety property and a functional model, property based FI exhaustively searches the entire fault, input and state space for safety property violations, by covering all possible faults in all possible input and state conditions – for that given property.

Referring to Fig. 2, the fault tolerance properties and fault activation conditions are specified in a formal language accepted by the chosen model-checker. Fault tolerance property denotes critical system behavior or safety property that needs to be met by the system outputs in the presence of faults. Fault activation conditions specify the input/state sequences that cause the injected fault to manifest as error and propagate within the system design. To activate a fault, the necessary input/state preconditions are specified as constraints/assumptions to the model checker. Under the given preconditions, the model-checker systematically explores the state, input and fault space of the system functional model and mathematically verifies that a fault from the representative fault space does not violate the fault tolerance property for any given state and input sequence. While maintaining the assumptions, if any violation of the property is encountered, the model checker falsifies the property and generates a counterexample showing the input and fault vector that caused the safety property to fail.

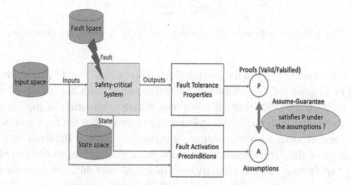

Fig. 2. Fault injection with property proving

We define property based fault injection as: *Let system functional model be represented as five-tuple $M = \langle I, O, S, S_0, T \rangle$, where I-set of inputs, O-set of outputs, S-set of states, $S_0 \subseteq S$ – set of initial states, T-S X S - set of transitions.*

We say a fault tolerance property P_{FT} for the model M is satisfied if every state reachable from the initial state s_0 (by following all possible transition relations within T) in the Model M satisfies the fault tolerance property P_{FT}, in the presence of fault f_i taken from the fault space F and the fault activation assumptions A_{fa}.

$$M \vDash P_{FT} \quad If \quad All \ Reachable_T (s_0) \vDash P_{FT} \quad | \quad f_i \ and \ A_{fa} = true \qquad (1)$$

Else

$$M \nvDash P_{FT} \quad If \quad Any \ Reachable_T (s_0) \nvDash P_{FT} \quad | \quad f_i \ and \ A_{fa} = true \qquad (2)$$

where $s_0 \in S_0, f_i \in F$ and $A_{fa} = $ Fault activation conditions as assumptions.

Figure 3 shows the efficacy of the property based fault injection approach in terms of the coverage of the fault, input and state space. Referring to Fig. 3, the left side enumerates the assumptions made by the model checker during model checking based

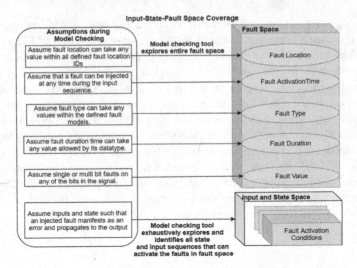

Fig. 3. Property based fault injection - fault-input-state space coverage

on the constraints we specify in the model. During property-based FI, the model checker is allowed to assume the fault location control signal to take any value from the list of defined fault location IDs thus ensuring a complete exploration of the fault location dimension within the fault space. Model checker assumes that the fault can be injected at any time instant during an input/state sequence and for any duration (as permitted by the datatype of the Fault duration control signal). This causes the model checker to completely explore the entire fault activation time and fault duration dimensions of the fault space to find property violation. Model checker explores and covers all fault types within the defined fault model list with constraints to consider only the defined fault models in the fault injection framework. Model checker is allowed to assume single or multi bit faults on any of the bits in the signal thus causing the model checker to completely explore and cover the fault value dimension of the fault space. Thereby, the model checker exhaustively explores the entire input and state space and identifies all possible input and state sequences that can activate the considered faults in the fault space. In this manner, each fault tolerance or safety property verification completely covers the corresponding fault activation space from within the entire input and state space.

5 Implementation of Property-Based FI Using Simulink Design Verifier

We implement the proposed property-based Fault injection technique on Simulink behavioral models using Simulink Design Verifier (SDV) property prover tool [16]. The workflow for realizing the Property based Fault injection in Simulink is given below in Fig. 4. There are few preparation steps (steps 1, 2 and 3) to be performed before starting the property proving within Simulink Design Verifier (DV).

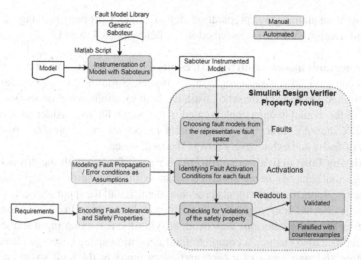

Fig. 4. Property based fault injection workflow

1. **Instrumentation of Model with Saboteurs** - The process starts with an automated insertion of a generic saboteur into all signals in the given test model. This automated saboteur insertion framework is described in detail in [15]. In the model-based context, a 'Saboteur' can be defined as a special module added between signal drivers and receivers in the model-based design, which when activated alters the value or timing characteristics of the signals, thereby simulating faults for Fault Injection [17]. The saboteur in the considered FI framework [15] is a generic one and supports multiple fault models. The saboteur instrumented model generated in this process is further used for the property based fault injection process.

2. **Modeling Fault propagation/Error conditions as assumptions** – With the automatic exhaustive saboteur insertion within the model, we end up with a very large set of fault locations within the model. Thus manually finding the activation condition for each fault location could be an extremely time-consuming process. It would require a complete analysis of the model and identifying all possible input scenarios that can activate the faults – which is infeasible for system models commensurate of practical system scales. The approach we employ to solve this problem is to use the model checking tool to automatically identify the fault activation conditions (e.g. the input conditions) for any given fault. In this method, instead of manually exploring the entire input space to identify and specify the input conditions to activate the faults, the tester has to specify the state/output condition that indicates an error or system failure as an assumption that becomes true after a fault is injected. The error propagation scenario is modeled as an assumption using Simulink Design Verifier blocks.

3. **Encoding Fault Tolerance and Safety Properties** - Finally, the fault tolerance properties derived from the safety requirements of the system that needs to be validated have to be modeled using the proof objective blocks in Simulink DV library.

After completing all the above preparation steps 1, 2 and 3, property proving is executed in Simulink Design Verifier as described in the below steps 4, 5 and 6.

4. **Choosing fault models from the representative fault space** - When property proving is initiated on the saboteur inserted model, Simulink DV selects fault locations/signals from the entire set of available fault locations and chooses fault models from all the available ones implemented in the Saboteurs to consider for fault injection. DV model checker proves the safety properties in the presence of different kinds of faults and exhaustively covers the fault space.

5. **Identifying fault activation conditions for each fault** - With the erroneous/fault propagation behavior being specified as an assumption in the model, the Design Verifier explores the entire input space and identifies all the input sequences that can cause the injected fault to manifest as an error and propagate. In addition to relieving the tester from the laborious task of identifying the activation input sequences for each fault, it also ensures a complete fault activation space coverage (from within the input and state space) for each and every faults in the fault space and avoids no-response faults.

6. **Checking for Violations of the safety property** - Finally, the safety properties modeled as proof objectives are proven to be valid or false. Validated properties would mean that the fault tolerance functionality is capable of tolerating all the specified faults (from considered fault space). If the property falsifies, a counterexample is generated which clearly shows the location, duration, type, value and time of injection of the fault that bypassed the tolerance functionality or safety feature.

6 Application of Property Based Fault Injection

Property-based fault injection technique was applied to verify "the fail-stop/fail-fast" semantics and fault tolerant features of a safety-critical digital I&C architecture called *SymPLe* [18] developed for Nuclear Power Plant applications. Referring Fig. 5, SymPLe architecture is an FPGA based architecture comprised of three basic control hierarchies: the global sequencer, local sequencers or tasks, and a complete set of Function Blocks (FB) per task lane. In SymPLe, all executions occur in task lanes. These are independent processing stations where function blocks organized as function block programs are executed. Functions blocks assigned to a task lane are scheduled via a deterministic sequence of task executions. Functions blocks receive data, operate on that data per intended functionality, and provide results in their output registers. The global sequencer is concerned with scheduling of task lanes and the marshaling of data I/O in the architecture. The local sequencers' function is to locally coordinate the triggering of a task lane and marshal data to function blocks while executing. Function Blocks (FB) are the elementary "program or computation" units that SymPLe architecture employs for its program organization or application building.

Fault detection and tolerance mechanisms in SymPLe architecture are implemented at several levels, however, in this case study we evaluated the fault handling mechanisms at the Function Block level. Among several fault detection techniques, hardware redundancy is one of the main fault tolerance strategies implemented at the function block

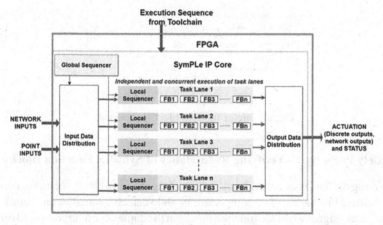

Fig. 5. SymPLe architecture

level. As shown in Fig. 6, each FB is constructed as a duplex system as a means of detecting single and multi-event upsets. The inputs, outputs and states of the duplicated function blocks are compared to report data mismatch/State error that happens due to any kind of faults within the individual FBs. The individual function blocks in the duplex structure are each designed to detect errors in SymPLe's control flow execution and data path execution. An execution error is an error that violates the execution semantics of SymPLe computational model like input register read overflow, output register write overflow, execution timeout and so on. Prolonged execution of a function block could be a sign of malfunction within the function blocks due to transient or permanent physical faults. This execution error is detected and reported using the execution timeout feature of the function block controller. In addition, computation errors that affect logic and arithmetic operations like datatype error, underflow, overflow, division by zero etc. are also detected within the function blocks. Described below are two use case examples of applying the property-based fault injection technique to verify the safety properties related to hardware redundancy and execution timeout feature of the function block array consisting of 32 different function blocks in the SymPLe architecture.

The application of the property-based fault injection method on SymPLe architecture is facilitated by an automated fault injection framework developed in Simulink. This model-based FI framework facilitates FI process on a Simulink model by enabling fault injection control within the functional model and automating saboteur insertion throughout the model. A generic saboteur that implements a diverse set of fault models including 'Single/Multi Bit Flip', 'Stuck at 0', 'Stuck at 1', 'Floating', and Delay faults are automatically inserted on all signal lines within the test model by a Matlab script. The Saboteurs are designed using basic Simulink blocks and encapsulated in a masked subsystem. More details on the Saboteur implementation, fault model and the algorithm of the saboteur insertion script can be found in [15].

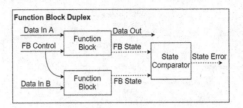

Fig. 6. Duplex function block architecture

6.1 Safety Property 1 - Verifying Redundancy of SymPLe Function Blocks

For verifying the hardware redundancy feature of the function block, the critical property to be considered is that the state comparator module detects anomalies and sends a high on 'state_error' signal when the function blocks in the duplex configuration hold different states. The property for verifying the hardware redundancy feature of the 'ADD' function block in SymPLe architecture is modeled as shown in Fig. 7. The mismatch property states that: *"A difference between the states of the ADD1 and ADD2 function blocks, implies that the 'state_error' signal is true"*.

$$\textbf{Prop: } (ADD1\_State \neq ADD2\_State) \rightarrow (state\_error = true) \tag{3}$$

The fault injected in function blocks gets activated when erroneous values propagate to the outputs of the function blocks causing a mismatch between the two function blocks. For each fault location, different preconditions are applicable to ensure the fault is activated and actually propagates far enough to cause a failure at the output. To direct the model checker to consider input conditions that can activate the faults, an assumption condition as stated below is modeled as shown in Fig. 7.

"There is mismatch between the states (which comprises of the inputs read into FBs and FB outputs) of the ADD1 and ADD2 function blocks, within 5 clock cycles after a fault is injected".

$$\textbf{Assumption: } (\textbf{\textit{Fault Injected}}) \rightarrow (ADD1\_State \neq ADD2\_State \textbf{ within 5 cycles}) \tag{4}$$

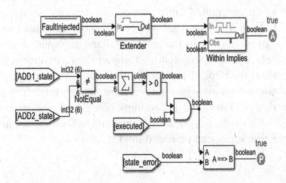

Fig. 7. Property for proving hardware redundancy of Function Blocks

With this assumption in place, the Design verifier explores the entire input space and finds all possible input sequences that can activate a specific fault in the model. Another important assumption that is made is that the *"redundant data inputs to the two function blocks are always equal"*. ***Assumption: DataInA = DataInB***. This is to ensure that the state mismatch between the duplex function blocks is not caused due to the mismatch of inputs to the function blocks, but instead caused due to faults injected within one of the function blocks. Assumptions on the fault injection control signals help to constrain the fault space to a representative set of fault locations and fault models during the FI experiment. The fault location is assumed to be lying within a range of values. The fault type is constrained to take only the defined fault models. Fault injection time, duration, and value parameters are unconstrained thus allowing DV to validate the property by exploring or considering all possible parameter values.

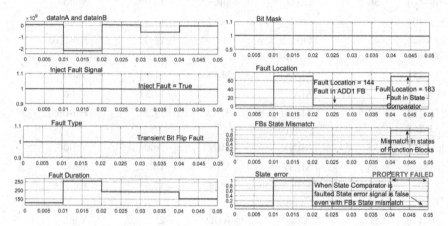

Fig. 8. Counterexample for failed property

The summary of the FI campaign on 6 different function blocks (FBs) are provided in Table 1. The results indicate that faults injected on any of the FBs in the duplex configuration satisfied the safety property as it always resulted in state mismatch error being detected by the system by pulling the 'state_error' signal high. But any transient/permanent faults within the State Comparators in the FBs caused the safety property to be violated with a counterexample as shown in Fig. 8. The counterexample shows a scenario where two separate faults are injected in the function block one after the other. First, a transient bit flip fault is injected in one of the function blocks (ADD1) (fault location ID = 144) leading to output mismatch between the two redundant FBs ADD1 and ADD2 in the next cycle, followed by another transient bit flip fault injected in the State Comparator block. This second fault in State comparator (fault location ID = 183) causes 'state_error' signal to remain false even when there is a mismatch between the redundant FB state/outputs. Thus, the State Comparators were identified as the single point of failures within the FB design. These results are reasonable with hindsight, as state comparators are a vital circuit in the SymPLe function block architecture. The state comparator fault tolerance capabilities were overlooked in the design. The data in

Table 1 shows an increase in the property validation time with an increase in the number of fault locations considered for each experiment.

Table 1. Property-based fault injection campaign results: SymPLe FB redundancy feature

Fault location IDs	No. of locations	Faults injected in module	Function block	Time taken (mins)	Proof validity
485–520	36	AND1	AND	15.3	Valid
449–484	36	AND2	AND	16.00	Valid
489–520, 521–528	40	AND1 & State Comparator	AND	17.3	Falsified
405–440	36	OR1	OR	14.09	Valid
369–404	36	OR2	OR	14.37	Valid
409–440, 441–448	40	OR1 & State Comparator	OR	16.06	Falsified
220–252	33	MAX1	MAX	11.17	Valid
187–219	33	MAX2	MAX	11.51	Valid
221–252, 253–260	40	MAX1 & State Comparator	MAX	17.25	Falsified
36–70	35	MIN1	MIN	16.01	Valid
1–35	35	MIN2	MIN	15.12	Valid
37–70, 71–78	42	MIN1 & State Comparator	MIN	17.53	Falsified
129–178	50	ADD1	ADD	26.16	Valid
79–128	50	ADD2	ADD	26.24	Valid
144–178, 179–186	43	ADD1 & State Comparator	ADD	15.43	Falsified
311–360	50	SUB1	SUB	26.36	Valid
261–310	50	SUB2	SUB	28.51	Valid
326–360, 361–368	43	SUB1 & State Comparator	SUB	19.3	Falsified

6.2   Safety Property 2 – Verifying Execution Timeout of Function Blocks

Another critical safety feature within SymPLe architecture is its detection of malfunction of the system by detecting a prolonged function block execution. The function block execution is expected to timeout, send an error and restart the task, when the execution of a function block extends beyond 50 cycles. The critical property that is expected to hold true is that: *"When 'execute' signal is detected high for 50 cycles, the 'error' signal and timeout bit in the error code shall be set to true indicating the timeout error detection."*

$$\text{Prop: ('execute' = true for 50 cycles)} \rightarrow \text{('error' = true) and} \tag{5}$$
$$\text{('Timeout' bit in error code = true).}$$

This property is modeled as shown in Fig. 9. To verify this property, a fault has to be injected that can cause function block execution to timeout and cause an error. This error condition is modeled as an assumption as given in Fig. 9. It states that: *"Once 'execute' signal has gone high and execution has started, for the next 50 cycles execution is not completed and 'executed' signal does not become high".*

$$\text{Assumption: ('execute' = true)} \rightarrow \text{('executed'} \neq \text{true for 50 cycles).} \tag{6}$$

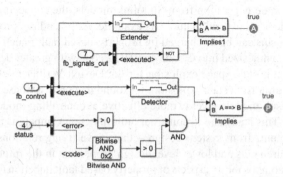

Fig. 9. Property for execution timeout functionality verification

This assumption causes Design Verifier to explore the design and identify all possible faults and input conditions to activate these faults. One direct example of a fault that can cause timeout error is the 'stuck at 0' fault (in bit 0) on the boolean 'executed' signal output from the function blocks. Similarly, there could be several faults that can create a delay in execution. This example also depicts the complete automation of fault and input space exploration by Design Verifier with minimal specification from the tester on the error scenario and fault tolerance property. The time-out property was validated true, indicating that a prolonged execution of function block extending beyond 50 cycles was detected and signaled as an error. The property proving experiment, for a single fault type (stuck-at-0) and all fault locations in a single function block took ~50 min to complete the time-out property verification.

7   Discussions and Future Work

As device geometries and clock speeds shrink, physical faults affecting the operation of devices are becoming a bottleneck to the dependability of safety-critical cyber physical systems. This paper introduces and develops a novel fault injection framework that utilizes the benefits of model checking and model-based design to achieve an efficient exploration of representative fault space, input and state space to attain near exhaustive fault injection on functional models of safety-critical systems. The proposed method overcomes some of the deficiencies of traditional fault injection methods such as coverage of the fault injection experiment space and identifying fault activation conditions for each fault in the fault space. The property-based fault injection framework we developed provides an algorithmic/automated means to identify the fault activation conditions for all faults in the representative fault space using model checking. The time savings achieved with Property-based Fault Injection as compared to traditional simulation based fault injection is orders of magnitude more efficient. Our experiments with Simulink Design verifier and results (in Table 1) indicate that Property based fault injection method was very efficient with respect to exhaustive single fault location injection for our case studies (e.g. ~30 s/fault).

The limitations of Property based fault injection is that it works at the functional level of system development, that is, pre-software and hardware development. In the age of automatic code generation from Simulink models, the connection from models to executable code is robust and mature. As example, fault handling properties of error detection mechanisms can be discharged by property-based fault injection at the model level and then be synthesized into C code or VHDL code with greater design assurance. Another limitation is state space explosion for the Design Verifier model checker. All model checkers suffer from state explosion; we found that property based fault injection conducted at the sub-module level is more effective at controlling model checker state explosion issues. This leads one to construct fault injection campaigns based on "composability" arguments from system design – that is, verifying relations between high level system requirements and lower level design properties. In the future, we intend to investigate these composability aspects of property based fault injection derived from the traceability of system requirements. We also plan to extend the proposed property based fault injection framework with respect to hardware-level fault injection to investigate equivalence. Finally, we will examine the utility of the property based fault injection to assist in system level hazards analysis and failure modes and effects analysis on functional models of safety-critical applications.

References

1. Leveson, N.G., Fleming, C.H., Spencer, M., Thomas, J., Wilkinson, C.: Safety assessment of complex, software-intensive systems. SAE Int. J. Aerosp. 5(2012-01–2134), 233–244 (2012)
2. Elks, C.R., et al.: Application of a fault injection based dependability assessment process to a commercial safety critical nuclear reactor protection system. In: 2010 IEEE/IFIP International Conference on Dependable Systems Networks (DSN), pp. 425–430, June 2010
3. Yu, Y., Bastien, B., Johnson, B.W.: A state of research review on fault injection techniques and a case study. In: Proceedings of Annual Reliability and Maintainability Symposium, Alexandria, VA, USA, pp. 386–392. IEEE (2005)
4. Elks, C.R., George, N.J., Reynolds, M.A., Miklo, M., Berger, C.: Development of a fault injection-based dependability assessment methodology for digital and I&C systems. United States Nuclear Regulatory Commission, Office of Nuclear Regulatory Research, NUREG/CR-7151 (2012)
5. Bingham, S., Lach, J.: Enhanced fault coverage analysis using ABVFI. In: Workshop on Dependable and Secure Nanocomputing, Charlottesville, p. 6, June 2009

6. Krautz, U., Pflanz, M., Jacobi, C., Tast, H.W., Weber, K., Vierhaus, H.T.: Evaluating coverage of error detection logic for soft errors using formal methods. In: Proceedings of the Design Automation Test in Europe Conference **1**, 1–6 (2006)
7. Leveugle, R.: A new approach for early dependability evaluation based on formal property checking and controlled mutations. In: 11th IEEE International On-Line Testing Symposium, pp. 260–265, July 2005
8. Larsson, D., Hähnle, R.: Symbolic fault injection. In: International Verification Workshop (VERIFY), vol. 259 (2007)
9. Vedder, B., Arts, T., Vinter, J., Jonsson, M.: Combining fault-injection with property-based testing. In: Proceedings of International Workshop on Engineering Simulations for Cyber-Physical Systems, Dresden, Germany, pp. 1–8, November 2013
10. Grunske, L., Winter, K., Yatapanage, N., Zafar, S., Lindsay, P.A.: Experience with fault injection experiments for FMEA. Softw. Pract Exp. **41**(11), 1233–1258 (2011)
11. Heimdahl, M.P.E., Choi, Y., Whalen, M.: Deviation analysis through model checking. In: Proceedings 17th IEEE International Conference on Automated Software Engineering, Edinburgh, UK, pp. 37–46 (2002)
12. Fondazione Bruno Kessler and Embedded Systems Unit. xsap - - The xSAP safety analysis platform. https://xsap.fbk.eu/. Accessed 13 July 2020
13. Joshi, A., Heimdahl, M.P.E.: Model-based safety analysis of Simulink models using SCADE design verifier. In: Winther, R., Gran, B.A., Dahll, G. (eds.) SAFECOMP 2005. LNCS, vol. 3688, pp. 122–135. Springer, Heidelberg (2005). https://doi.org/10.1007/11563228_10
14. Güdemann, M., Ortmeier, F., Reif, W.: Using Deductive Cause-Consequence Analysis (DCCA) with SCADE. In: Saglietti, F., Oster, N. (eds.) SAFECOMP 2007. LNCS, vol. 4680, pp. 465–478. Springer, Heidelberg (2007). https://doi.org/10.1007/978-3-540-75101-4_44
15. Jayakumar, A.V.: Systematic model-based design assurance and property-based fault injection for safety critical digital systems. Virginia Commonwealth University (2020)
16. Mathworks: Simulink® Design Verifier Reference, September 2018. https://www.mathworks.com/help/releases/R2018b/pdf_doc/sldv/sldv_ref.pdf
17. Shafik, R.A., Rosinger, P., Al-Hashimi, B.M.: SystemC-based minimum intrusive fault injection technique with improved fault representation. In: 2008 14th IEEE International On-Line Testing Symposium, Rhodes, Greece, pp. 99–104, July 2008
18. Elks, C., Gibson, M., Hite, R., Gautham, S., Jayakumar, A.V., Deloglos, C., Tantawy, A.: Achieving verifiable and high integrity instrumentation and control systems through complexity awareness and constrained design. USDOE Office of Nuclear Energy (NE), 15–8044, July 2019

Failure Mode Reasoning in Model Based Safety Analysis

Hamid Jahanian[1]([⊠]), David Parker[2], Marc Zeller[3], Annabelle McIver[1], and Yiannis Papadopoulos[2]

[1] Macquarie University, Sydney, Australia
hamid.jahanian@hdr.mq.edu.au, annabelle.mciver@mq.edu.au
[2] University of Hull, Hull, UK
{d.j.parker,y.i.papadopoulos}@hull.ac.uk
[3] Siemens AG, Munich, Germany
marc.zeller@siemens.com

Abstract. Failure Mode Reasoning (FMR) is a novel approach for analyzing failure in a Safety Instrumented System (SIS). The method uses an automatic analysis of an SIS program to calculate potential failures in parts of the SIS. In this paper we use a case study from the power industry to demonstrate how FMR can be utilized in conjunction with other model-based safety analysis methods, such as HiP-HOPS and CFT, in order to achieve a comprehensive safety analysis of SIS. In this case study, FMR covers the analysis of SIS inputs while HiP-HOPS/CFT models the faults of logic solver and final elements. The SIS program is analyzed by FMR and the results are exported to HiP-HOPS/CFT via automated interfaces. The final outcome is the collective list of SIS failure modes along with their reliability measures. We present and review the results from both qualitative and quantitative perspectives.

Keywords: FMR · HiP-HOPS · CFT · FTA

1 Introduction

In the process industry, Safety Instrumented Systems (SIS) are mechanisms that protect major hazard facilities against process-related accidents [5]. Failure of SISs can result in catastrophic consequences such as loss of life and environmental damages. An SIS consists of hardware components and a software program. Failure Mode Reasoning (FMR) was introduced for calculating failure modes of SIS components based on an analysis of its program [8]. Through a backward reasoning process on the SIS program, FMR calculates the SIS input failure modes that can result in a given undesired state at its output. Once the failure modes are identified, the probability of failure can be calculated too.

Hierarchically Performed Hazard Origin & Propagation Studies (HiP-HOPS) [11] and Component Fault Trees (CFT) [9] are two model-based dependability analysis techniques that can analyze failure modes of a system based on the

© Springer Nature Switzerland AG 2020
M. Zeller and K. Höfig (Eds.): IMBSA 2020, LNCS 12297, pp. 130–145, 2020.
https://doi.org/10.1007/978-3-030-58920-2_9

failure behavior of its components. The failure models of components are combined to synthesize a system-level fault tree, which is then solved to generate qualitative and quantitative results.

FMR was created to address a shortcoming in safety analyses in the process industry: the impact of SIS program. In this paper we demonstrate how other methods can achieve comprehensive failure analyses by employing FMR for an automatic analysis of the program. HiP-HOPS, for instance, offers automated synthesis and analysis of fault trees and FMEAs and state sensitive analysis of sequences, and it is also enriched with bio-inspired algorithms [12]. However, the method still requires a first-pass manual annotation of failures, which is a challenging task when dealing with SIS programs. Likewise, CFT can benefit from an automated analysis of SIS programs conducted by FMR. In two independent experiments, we will integrate FMR with HiP-HOPS and CFT to analyze a case study from the power industry. Through qualitative and quantitative results we will show how such integrations can improve overall safety analysis.

The rest of this paper is organized as follows: Sect. 2 provides an introduction to the underlying concepts of FMR and SIS failure analysis. Section 3 defines the case study and the method. Section 4 outlines the process of SIS input analysis in FMR. Sections 5 and 6 demonstrate the results of integrating FMR with HiP-HOPS and CFT. Section 7 discusses the challenges and achievements of the project, and Sect. 8 wraps up the paper with a concluding note.

2   SIS and FMR

A typical SIS consists of three main subsystems: sensors that measure the process conditions (e.g. pressure and temperature), logic solver (e.g. a CPU) that processes the program, and final elements (e.g. valves) that isolate the plant from a hazard when needed. The safety function achieved by a combination of sensors, logic solver and final elements to protect against a specific hazard is referred to as Safety Instrumented Function (SIF) [5].

As a layer of protection, the reliability of a SIF is commonly measured by its Probability of Failure on Demand (PFD): $PFD_{SIF} = PFD_s + PFD_{ls} + PFD_{fe}$; with PFD_s, PFD_{ls} and PFD_{fe} being the PFD of sensors, logic solver and final elements respectively, and PFD_{SIF} the aggregated PFD of SIF [5]. The PFD is calculated by using the failure rates of SIS components. A SIS component may fail in one of the following forms: Dangerous Detected (DD), Dangerous Undetected (DU), Safe Detected (SD) and Safe Undetected (SU) [5]. A dangerous failure is a failure that prevents SIF from responding to a demand when a real hazard exists, and safe failure is the one that may result in a safety action being initiated by the SIF when there is no real hazard (i.e. Spurious Trip). The DU, DD, SU and SD elements are measured by failure rates λ_{DU}, λ_{DD}, λ_{SU} and λ_{SD}. For a single component, the relationship between λ_{DU} and the average PFD is expressed by $PFD_{avg} = \lambda_{DU}\tau/2$, in which τ is the Mission Time over which the average PFD is calculated. Other formulas are given by various sources to relate failure rates to the PFD and Spurious Trip Rate (STR) for general K-out-of-N (KooN) combinations [3,6,7,14].

Well established methods, such as Fault Tree Analysis (FTA) [2,17] already exist in the industry for analyzing failure. FTA is a deductive method for failure analysis whereby a failure model, the fault tree, is analyzed to find the causes of a given undesired event. A fault tree is a graphical representation of failure, and it consists of events and logical gates that interconnect those events. The main outcome of an FTA is a set of minimal cut sets (MCS). An MCS is the smallest conjunction of a set of basic events that, together, can lead to the occurrence of the top event. Logically, MCSs represent AND combinations of basic events, and top event the OR combination of MCSs. Having the failure models and rates of occurrence for basic events one can calculate MCSs and the top event [1,14,17].

With the growing complexity of industrial systems and availability of technology, FTA research has shifted towards modularization of models and automation of methods. HiP-HOPS and CFT are two examples of modular analysis of generic systems [10,13], as opposed to FMR which specializes in SIS programs.

SIS programs are typically developed in graphical editors and in the form of Function Block Diagrams (FBD) [4]. An FBD consists of standard Function Blocks (FBs) and their interconnections – variables. Figure 1 includes a simplified picture of some FBs and their interconnections. As a more specific example, $y = (x_1 + x_2)/2$ is an average value FB with output variable y and input variables x_1 and x_2, which can connect this FB to other FBs in the program. Each FB, by itself, is fixed and known, but the function of the overall program depends on the selection of its constituting FBs and the way these FBs interact. Subsequently, the failure behavior of FBs can be defined independently, whereas the failure behavior of the program is identified based on its application-specific configuration. This is the underlying idea of FMR. In an automated process, the SIS program is scanned from its output towards its inputs as local failure behaviors are analyzed around each FB. The results of local analyses are then combined and simplified into a "failure modes short list," which is also used for calculating SIS reliability measures [8].

FMR is based on a failure mode calculus. A failure mode is a manner in which the reported value of a variable in an SIS program deviates from its intended state; with the intended state being what the variable would read if SIS inputs were not affected by faults. Assuming that the SIS program is systematically correct, an undesired state at SIS output can only be caused by the propagation of input deviations through the program. FMR calculates the failure modes corresponding to such deviations by backward analysis of the program. The basic failure modes in FMR are expressed by $\dot{h}$ and $\dot{l}$ for real-valued variables, and $\dot{t}$ and $\dot{f}$ for Boolean variables. Here, $\dot{h}$ is for *false high*, $\dot{l}$ for *false low*, $\dot{t}$ for *false True* and $\dot{f}$ for *false False*. As an example, for the average value FB, $(\hat{y} = \dot{h}) \Rightarrow (\hat{x_1} = \dot{h} \vee \hat{x_2} = \dot{h})$ means if output y is reading too high either input x_1 or x_2 must be too high. FMR combines such local reasoning statements, eliminates the intermediate variables, and produces a final, minimal statement comprising only SIS inputs and outputs.

FMR completes the SIS safety analysis by incorporating the functionally most important part of the system – the program, and it does this by analyzing the actual program rather than a synthesized model. The process is automated and thus it saves time and effort, and offers accuracy and certainty.

3   Definition of the Case

Consider a gas-fired boiler with a high pressure drum for generating super-heat steam. The level and pressure in the drum are measured by three level transmitters and two pressure transmitters. Pressure measurement is used to modify the level readings: drum pressure can vary between 1 and 100 bars, causing wide-range changes to water density and thus to the level measurement. An SIS program uses thermodynamic calculations to correct the level readings based on pressure. Corrected level signals are compared to a preset threshold value, and if 2 out of 3 channels read extreme low, a trip is initiated at the outputs of the SIS logic solver to close the gas valves. Failing to shut the gas valves can result in excessive drum pressure, boiler tube rupture and eventually boiler explosion.

As shown in Fig. 1, level transmitters L1–L3 and pressure transmitters P1–P2 are read in through analog input (AIs). The output of SIS program is connected to gas valves via output modules (DOs) and interposing relays. The gas skid consists of a main isolation valve (MGIV) and two sets of double-block-and-vent valves for the main burner (MBV1, MBV2, MVV) and ignition burner (IBV1, IBV2, IVV). During normal plant operation, MGIV and the block valves are open and the vent valves are closed. If a hazardous situation is detected, block valves should close and vent valves should open. MGIV is not considered a safety actuator and only closes during scheduled plant outages.

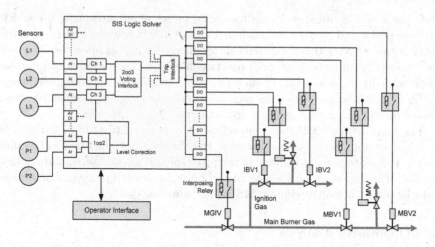

Fig. 1. SIS configuration

The boiler is in its safe state (off) if both the main burner and ignition burners are shut. The following key failure states are defined:

– The SIS is in a DU failure state if the level measurement fails to detect low drum level, or if the logic solver is not capable of responding to a detected low level, or if either the main burner valves (MBV1, MBV2) or ignition burner valves (IBV1, IBV2) are incapable of blocking the supply gas.

– The SIS will spuriously trip the boiler if MGIV, MBV1, MBV2, IBV1 or IBV2 closes when no real hazard exists. This may be due to a random failure of one of these valves or the failure of one of their upstream interposing relays, DO modules, CPU, AI modules or sensors.

To avoid the risk of extreme low drum level, the SIS program is designed to initiate a trip if any 2 out of 3 combination between low level and/or sensor fault is detected. Deviation between level signals alerts the operator but does not initiate a trip. Furthermore, pressure sensor P1 has priority over P2: if P1 is not detected faulty, the output of the 1oo2 block equals P1.

Our objective in this case study is to analyze the SIF both qualitatively and quantitatively. We would like to determine the minimum combinations of component failures that can lead to SIS DU or ST failure. We would also like to calculate the likelihood of individual combinations and the aggregated PFD and STR. In the next three sections we will explain how we molded the SIS in FMR, HiP-HOPS and CFT. Independent from our case study models, we also created a reference fault tree in Isograph's FaultTree+ tool (www.isograph.com), of which no picture is shown here. The model was created to help us compare and evaluate the results of our analysis against one same, independent reference.

4   Modeling SIS Inputs in FMR

This case study is based on a medium-scale power plant project where an SIS program performed 34 SIFs and included almost 100 hardwired inputs, 25 hardwired outputs and 250 software signals exchanged with an operator interface. The program comprised over 2170 function blocks with thousands of interconnections. A by-hand analysis of such programs would certainly be a challenge. Yet, in a typical large-scale power generation unit these figures may be five times greater, making a manual analysis almost impossible.

The input to the FMR tool is an offline copy of the entire SIS program. The analyst does not even need to know what the SIS program consists of. They only need to nominate a single variable in the program and the undesired state of that variable. The tool starts at the nominated point, traces the program backwards, and calculates the corresponding SIS input failure modes.

4.1   Qualitative Analysis

We are interested in both DU and ST failure modes at the SIF output; i.e. at the final output of the Trip Interlock block in Fig. 1. The SIS is configured in a de-energize to trip setup. That is, a *False* signal at the SIS output triggers a safety action and trips the plant. Thus, DU failure occurs when a real hazard exists but the SIS output is left *True*. Assuming that the SIS program is correct, a DU failure can only be due to the failure of SIS inputs in detecting the hazard. ST failure, on the other hand, occurs when the SIS output is set to *False* due to safe failure of SIS inputs. In the FMR terminology, we are interested in SIF output being t (for DU) and f (for ST).

Table 1. FM short list for SIF output DU failure

1	L1: healthy & higher	L3: healthy & higher		
2	L1: healthy & higher	L2: healthy & higher		
3	L2: healthy & higher	L3: healthy & higher		
4	L1: healthy	L2: healthy	P1: healthy & higher	
5	L1: healthy	L3: healthy	P1: healthy & higher	
6	L2: healthy	L3: healthy	P1: healthy & higher	
7	L1: healthy	L2: healthy	P2: healthy & higher	P1: faulty
8	L1: healthy	L3: healthy	P2: healthy & higher	P1: faulty
9	L2: healthy	L3: healthy	P2: healthy & higher	P1: faulty

Table 2. FM short list for SIF output ST

1	L1: healthy & lower	L2: healthy & lower		
2	L2: healthy & lower	L3: healthy & lower		
3	L1: healthy & lower	L3: healthy & lower		
4	L1: faulty	L2: healthy & lower		
5	L1: faulty	L3: healthy & lower		
6	L1: healthy & lower	L2: faulty		
7	L2: faulty	L3: healthy & lower		
8	L1: faulty	L2: faulty		
9	L2: healthy & lower	L3: faulty		
10	L1: healthy & lower	L3: faulty		
11	L1: faulty	L3: faulty		
12	L2: faulty	L3: faulty		
13	L1: healthy	L2: faulty	P1: healthy & lower	
14	L1: healthy	L3: faulty	P1: healthy & lower	
15	L1: faulty	L2: healthy	P1: healthy & lower	
16	L2: healthy	L3: faulty	P1: healthy & lower	
17	L1: healthy	L2: healthy	P1: healthy & lower	
18	L1: faulty	L3: healthy	P1: healthy & lower	
19	L2: faulty	L3: healthy	P1: healthy & lower	
20	L1: healthy	L3: healthy	P1: healthy & lower	
21	L2: healthy	L3: healthy	P1: healthy & lower	
22	L1: healthy	L2: faulty	P2: healthy & lower	P1: faulty
23	L1: healthy	L3: faulty	P2: healthy & lower	P1: faulty
24	L1: faulty	L2: healthy	P2: healthy & lower	P1: faulty
25	L2: healthy	L3: faulty	P2: healthy & lower	P1: faulty
26	L1: healthy	L2: healthy	P2: healthy & lower	P1: faulty
27	L1: faulty	L3: healthy	P2: healthy & lower	P1: faulty
28	L2: faulty	L3: healthy	P2: healthy & lower	P1: faulty
29	L1: healthy	L3: healthy	P2: healthy & lower	P1: faulty
30	L2: healthy	L3: healthy	P2: healthy & lower	P1: faulty

A copy of the SIS program was imported to FMR, and the tag number and failure states of the SIF output were nominated. The tool analyzed the program and generated FM (failure mode) short lists shown in Tables 1 and 2.

Each row in Tables 1 and 2 represents an AND combination of input FMs that can result in the given output FM. A quick comparison with the description of the SIS program we described in Sect. 3 shows that FMR has identified failure modes as expected. In analyses where unexpected FMs are detected, engineers can use the information to correct or modify the program.

4.2   Quantitative Analysis

In the second stage, FMR performs a quantitative analysis to determine the probability of occurrence of failure. The FMR tool uses its internal project database to store failure data. In this database, each FM is described by a failure type and a likelihood value. The failure type can be "Fixed" probability, failure-repair "Rate" or "Dormant". The likelihood value indicates the probability of failure (i.e. unavailability) or the frequency of occurrence (in a time interval).

A Fixed probability model is used when the occurrence of a basic event is expressed independently from time and the repair process. The unavailability (q) of a component with fixed probability value of p will be: $q = p$.

The Rate model is suitable for repairable elements. These are the components for which the occurrence of a fault is detected and for which repair and restoration procedures are in place. The only time that the component is unavailable will be the time that it is under repair. The time interval is known as MTTR (Mean Time To Restoration) and the unavailability of such components will be [14]:

$$q(t) = \lambda(1 - e^{-(\lambda+\mu)t})/(\lambda + \mu) \tag{1}$$

with λ being the failure rate and $\mu = 1/MTTR$ the repair rate. These rates are often expressed *per hour*. For a steady-state estimation of Eq. 1, t is assigned the constant value of Risk Assessment Time, often equal to Mission Time.

A Dormant model is used when a basic event represents the undetected fault of a component that undergoes periodic proof testing. Here we use [14]:

$$q = 1 - (1 - e^{-\lambda\tau})/(\lambda\tau) \tag{2}$$

The failure rates and models used in this project are listed below:

– A sensor being healthy & higher (or healthy & lower): $\lambda_{DU} = \lambda_{SU} = 50\ FIT^1$, $\tau = 2\ years$, and the event is modeled as Dormant. Reading high (or low) values without having an indication of fault is an undetected fault. This is why the Dormant model is selected for this type of failure. Depending on the direction of fault, the failure mode can be considered dangerous or safe. In this case study higher readings lead to DU failures and lower readings lead to ST; due to the intended functionality of the SIF.

---

^{1} $1\ FIT = 1\ in\ 10^9\ h$.

- A sensor having a detected fault: $\lambda_{DD} = \lambda_{SD} = 250\ FIT$, $MTTR = 8\,h$, and the event is modeled as failure-repair Rate.
- A sensor being healthy: $q = 0.999$, modeled as a Fixed probability value. It is assumed that a transmitter is healthy for 99.9% of time.

Basic events with fixed probability values cannot be expressed in frequency form. For the Rate and Dormant models, the frequency of a basic event will be:

$$w = \lambda(1 - q) \tag{3}$$

Collective calculation of probability in FMR is similar to quantitative analysis of MCSs and top events in FTA. An MCS consists of one or several basic events, similar to one row in Tables 1 and 2. With Q_{MCS} and W_{MCS} being the unavailability and frequency of an MCS with n basic events:

$$Q_{MCS} = \prod_{i=1}^{n} q_i \quad \text{and} \quad W_{MCS} = \sum_{i=1}^{n} w_i \prod_{\substack{j=1 \\ j \neq i}}^{n} q_j \tag{4}$$

The top event of a fault tree is an OR combination of its MCSs. The unavailability and frequency of the top event are approximated by:[2]

$$Q_{TE} = (\prod_{i=1}^{c} q_i)(1 - \prod_{k=1}^{m}(1 - Q_k)) \quad \text{and} \quad W_{TE} = \sum_{i=1}^{m} W_i \prod_{\substack{j=1 \\ j \neq i}}^{m}(1 - Q_j) \tag{5}$$

Here, q_i is the unavailability of a basic event that is common between all MCSs, c the number of common basic events, Q_k the unavailability of the kth MCS excluding the common basic events, Q_j the unavailability of the jth MCS, W_i the frequency of the ith MCS, and m the number of constituting MCSs.

Using Eqs. 4 and 5, FMR generated the following results for our case study. The results were verified by replicating the models in FaultTree+, which showed no differences.

- Aggregated unavailability for DU mode: $Q_{DU} = 1.31E - 03$, consisting of:
  - FMs in rows 1–3 of Table 1, each with $Q_{FM} = 1.92E - 07$.
  - FMs in rows 4–6 of Table 1, each with $Q_{FM} = 4.37E - 04$.
  - FMs in rows 7–9 of Table 1, each with $Q_{FM} = 8.75E - 10$.
- Aggregated frequency for ST mode: $W_{ST} = 1.33E - 03$ p.h., with $W_{FM} = 50\ FIT$ for rows 17, 20 and 21 of Table 2, and $W_{FM} = 0.0$ for other rows.

---

[2] Equation 4 is commonly referred to as Esary-Proschan method and is used by FTA tools such as FaultTree+, Arbor and Item. See [1] for derivation of underlying concepts.

5   Integration with HiP-HOPS

There are three phases to the analysis process in HiP-HOPS: modeling, synthesis, and analysis [13]. In the manual modeling phase, a topological model of the system is created that details the components of the system and indicates how the components are connected together to allow the flow of data. Components can be grouped together hierarchically in sub-systems to help manage the complexity and allowing for refinement of the model as the design progresses. The components of the model are then augmented with local failure behavior that defines how each component's output can deviate from its normal expected behavior. The failure logic further documents how these output deviations can be caused by the combination of internal failure modes of the component and/or the propagation of deviations of the inputs of the component.

The second HiP-HOPS phase is the automatic synthesis of an interconnected set of fault trees that are produced by traversing the model of the system from its outputs to its inputs. It is during this phase that the failure logic defined in the modeling phase is combined by following the connections between the ports of the components and matching previously unrealized input deviations with output deviations of the same class that trigger them. This results in a model of the propagation of failure throughout the system.

The final stage is the analysis of the interconnected fault trees generated during synthesis. This begins with a qualitative pass that contracts the fault trees and removes the redundant logic resulting in the MCSs. The MCSs are then used together with the failure models of the components to run the quantitative pass and produce system unavailability and failure frequency measures.

We created a HiP-HOPS model in its user interface in the MATLAB environment. The interfacing between FMR and this model was done through an XML file exchange. The model was structured in two levels of hierarchy: system level (Fig. 2a), and component level (Fig. 2b for the final elements).

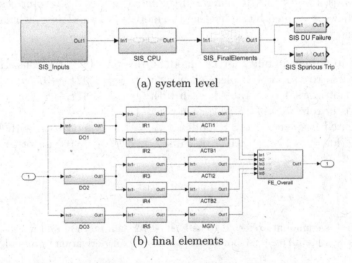

(a) system level

(b) final elements

Fig. 2. HiP-HOPS models in MATLAB

The DU and ST failures of SIS are the result of failures in SIS_Inputs, SIS_CPU or SIS_FinalElements. The component failure modes of the latter two blocks are manually implemented in MATLAB whereas the failure modes of the SIS_Inputs block are generated in FMR and automatically exported to a suitable data format in HiP-HOPS.

In Fig. 2a, the SIS_CPU block consists of two failure components: the CPU module, and the communication link between CPU and input/output modules. A DU (or ST) failure of either of these two components can result in the failure of SIS_CPU block and thus the overall failure of SIS. The SIS_FinalElement block models the failure of DO modules, interposing relays and the valves. As shown in detail in Fig. 2b, DO1 is shared between IBV1 and MBV1, and DO2 between IBV2 and MBV2. The main gas isolation valve (MGIV) is separately connected to DO3. The failure combinations for final elements are defined as follows: Out1.DU=(In1.DU AND In3.DU) OR (In2.DU AND In4.DU) and Out1.ST=(In1.ST OR In.2-ST OR In3.ST OR In4.ST OR In5.ST). The analysis in HiP-HOPS produced the MCSs for all SIS subsystems. The CPU and final elements (FE) parts are shown in Tables 3 and 4. The MCSs of inputs were the same as Tables 1 and 2.

Table 3. CPU and FE MCSs for SIF ST

No.	Min Cut Set	Frequency
1	CPU.CPUST	5.00E-09
2	Comm.CommST	1.00E-09
3	ACTB1.ACTBST	8.00E-07
4	ACTB2.ACTBST	8.00E-07
5	ACTI1.ACTIST	8.00E-07
6	ACTI2.ACTIST	8.00E-07
7	DO1.DOST	1.00E-09
8	DO2.DOST	1.00E-09
9	DO3.DOST	1.00E-09
10	IR1.IRST	4.00E-08
11	IR2.IRST	4.00E-08
12	IR3.IRST	4.00E-08
13	IR4.IRST	4.00E-08
14	IR5.IRST	4.00E-08
15	MGIV.ACTMST	1.20E-06

Table 4. CPU and FE MCSs for SIF DU

No.	Min Cut Set		Unavailability
1	CPU.CPUDU		1.90E-04
2	Comm.CommDU		1.00E-05
3	ACTB1.ACTBDU	ACTB2.ACTBDU	1.70E-04
4	ACTB1.ACTBDU	DO2.DODU	1.14E-07
5	ACTB1.ACTBDU	IR4.IRDU	6.86E-06
6	ACTB2.ACTBDU	DO1.DODU	1.14E-07
7	ACTB2.ACTBDU	IR2.IRDU	6.86E-06
8	ACTI1.ACTIDU	ACTI2.ACTIDU	1.70E-04
9	ACTI1.ACTIDU	DO2.DODU	1.14E-07
10	ACTI1.ACTIDU	IR3.IRDU	6.86E-06
11	ACTI2.ACTIDU	DO1.DODU	1.14E-07
12	ACTI2.ACTIDU	IR1.IRDU	6.86E-06
13	DO1.DODU	DO2.DODU	7.69E-11
14	DO1.DODU	IR3.IRDU	4.61E-09
15	DO1.DODU	IR4.IRDU	4.61E-09
16	DO2.DODU	IR1.IRDU	4.61E-09
17	DO2.DODU	IR2.IRDU	4.61E-09
18	IR1.IRDU	IR3.IRDU	2.77E-07
19	IR2.IRDU	IR4.IRDU	2.77E-07

The SIS inputs failure data were transferred automatically from FMR whereas the failure data for CPU and final elements were manually annotated in HiP-HOPS. We used the manufacturer's data as shown in Table 5.

Table 5. SIS component failure data

Component	Dormant (DU, SU), p.h.	Rate (DD, SD), p.h.	Fixed (PFD$_{avg}$)
SIS CPU		5.00E-9	1.90E-4
SIS Comm		1.00E-9	1.00E-5
Digital Output Module	1.00E-9	1.00E-9	
Interposing Relay	6.00E-8	4.00E-8	
Igniter/Burner Block Valve	1.50E-6	8.00E-7	
Main Gas Valve		1.20E-6	

With the same MTTR = 8 h and Risk Assessment Time and Proof Test Interval of 2 years, the overall model, including the imported FMR part, was analyzed in HiP-HOPS and the following results were obtained for the overall SIF: $Q_{DU} = 1.88E-03$ and $W_{ST} = 4.75E-06$. The results generated by HiP-HOPS matched up the ones of our reference model in FaultTree+.

6   Integration with CFT

A CFT is a Boolean model associated to system development elements such as components [9]. It has the same expressive power as classic fault trees and, likewise, it is used to model failure behavior of safety-critical systems.

In CFTs, every component is represented by a CFT element. Each element has its own in-ports and out-ports that are used to express propagation of failure modes through the tree. Similar to classic fault trees, the internal failure behavior that influences the output failure modes is modeled by Boolean gates.

The main difference between the two methods is that unlike classic fault trees, CFTs can have multiple top events (e.g. both the DU and ST modes) within the same model. Thus, the tree structure in CFT is extended towards a Directed Acyclic Graph. This eliminates the need for artificial splitting of common cause failure into multiple repeated events, and makes it possible to have more than one path to start from the same basic event or sub-tree.

A small example of a CFT was presented in [10] (see Fig. 3). The example shows an exemplary controller system *Ctrl*, including two redundant *CPU*s (i.e. two instances of the same component type) and one common power supply *Sply*, which would be a repeated event in traditional fault tree. The controller is unavailable if both CPUs are in the "failed" state. The inner fault tree of the CPU is modeled as a type. Since the CPUs are identical, they only have to be modeled once and then instantiated twice in the main model. The failure of a

CPU can be caused by some inner basic event E1, or by an external failure which is connected via the in-port. As both causes result in a CPU failure, they are joined via an OR gate. The power supply module is modeled as another type. In this example the power supply is in its "failed" state if both basic failures E1 and E2 occur. Hence, instead of a single large fault tree, the CFT model consists of small, reusable and easy-to-review components.

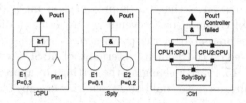

Fig. 3. Example of a simple CFT

Similar to the HiP-HOPS experiment, we implemented an automatic data link between FMR and CFT. The list of MCSs, including the model types and failure rates of basic events were exported in CSV format to the CFT tool, where a new add-on script would read the data and compose a CFT element for SIS Inputs. The rest of the modeling, i.e. for CPU and final elements, was implemented manually in the CFT tool. Figure 4 shows the CFT model for ST failure. The highlighted box represents the SIS Inputs, to which the FMs are imported from FMR. A similar model was developed for analyzing DU failure.

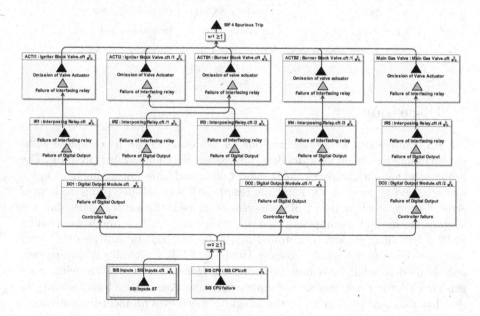

Fig. 4. CFT model for ST failure

CFT analysis produced the same list of MCSs as in HiP-HOPS and Fault-Tree+. Using the model types and failure rates of basic events shown in Table 6, the tool generated the following quantitative results:

- Average failure probability in DU mode $Q_{DU} = 1.0E - 3$
- Mean failure rate in ST mode $W_{ST} = 4.61E - 6$ p.h.

It is apparent that the CFT results differ from what we saw in the previous section. The main reason is that the approximation methods used for calculating the impact of common basic events are different in different tools. The quantitative results presented in the previous two sections used Eqs. 4 and 5, whereas CFT is based on the Siemens' internal tool ZUSIM, which uses the approach described in [15, 16]. By changing the settings of approximation method, in FaultTree+ for instance, we could observe narrower gaps between the results.

Table 6. Types and rates used for CFT modeling

Basic Event	DU	ST
SIS CPU	Probability = 1.9E-4	$\lambda = 5.0E\text{-}9$
SIS Comm	Probability = 1.0E-5	$\lambda = 1.0E\text{-}9$
Digital output module	$\lambda = 1.0E\text{-}9$	$\lambda = 1.0E\text{-}9$
Interposing relay	$\lambda = 6.0E\text{-}8$	$\lambda = 4.0E\text{-}8$
Igniter/burner block valve	$\lambda = 1.5E\text{-}6$	$\lambda = 8.0E\text{-}7$
Main gas valve		$\lambda = 1.2E\text{-}6$
Input "healthy"	Probability = 0.999	Probability = 0.999
Input "faulty"	Probability = 2.0E-6	Probability = 2.0E-6
Input "healthy & higher/lower"	Probability = 4.379E-4	Probability = 4.379E-4

7   Discussion

All SIS components are important, but no SIS analysis can be complete without including the behavior of its data-processing, decision-making program. The problem is that such analyses can be painstaking and time-consuming in complex systems, and when done by hand the results will still be susceptible to human error. Consequently, current SIS analyses often lack this critical part, and use simplifications and assumptions instead, which can lead to unreliable results. FMR solves this problem by automating the process and by studying the exact program that the SIS would execute. However, FMR's visibility is understandably limited to what influences the program. Hence, an integration with other generic FTA tools can provide a complete coverage. As such, each tool would still do what they are good at while the integration achieves an inclusive outcome.

We demonstrated through a case study how such integration can be implemented in practice. We chose HiP-HOPS and CFT as two different examples, both with proven records in other applications, and both from industries other than process. The fact is that FMR can integrate with any FTA-based method that allows standard file formats, e.g. XML and CSV, for data exchange.

The underlying question in FMR is: given a resultant deviation at the output and given the actual system program, what are the possible causing deviations at the input. This is obviously different to FTA, where we "know" the failure behavior of a system and we build a model (fault tree) to summarize our understandings. FMR is rather a failure identification method, one that can be used in failure modeling applications. Nonetheless, FMR shares a key aspect with FTA-based modeling methods such as HiP-HOPS and CFT: a component-based approach in failure analysis. Compared to conventional FTA, component-based methods provide better visibility to failure behavior of systems. Traditional fault trees become visually hard to navigate as the model size grows. Hierarchical, topographic models, such as the one in Fig. 2, offer an easier and more transparent understanding of the relationship between subsystems and components at various levels, which enhances the qualitative analysis of safety systems.

Furthermore, a safety analysis can be improved by selecting the "right" method of calculation. There are different approximation methods, referred to by different names, including Rare Event (RE), Inclusion-Exclusion (IE), Esary-Proschan (EP) and Cross-Product, depending on which the results may vary. This may in turn lead to requiring structural changes in the SIS design, if the reliability targets are not met [5]. See Table 7 as an example from FaultTree+; the results would change if we chose a different method in our case study.

Table 7. FaultTree+ calculations for different approximation methods

Calculation	Default	Esary-Proschan	Rare Event
DU unavailability	1.00E-3	1.88E-3	1.88E-3
ST frequency	4.75E-6	4.75E-6	4.76E-6

Among various approximation methods, we use the EP [1] method for FMR, as it is more conservative than the IE formula itself but less of the one of RE [17]. The same selection was set in HiP-HOPS and FaultTree+ so that we could compare the results. A different calculation method as described in [16] is used to analyze CFTs. Here, we set the selection in FaultTree+ to its default upper bound approximation so we could verify the CFT results.

Modeling of CPU and final elements (FE) in HiP-HOPS and CFT was done manually. However, the effort required for modeling these parts is not comparable to analyzing the program, which was done automatically. Our case study SIS implemented 34 SIFs. Considering an average of 30 MCSs for each SIF (our case study SIF had 45), the analyst would need to identify 1020 MCSs for SIS inputs. The number of MCSs in CPU and FE parts combined was only 34, which is almost 3% of the overall. This is because the CPU and FE parts are common between all those 34 SIFs, and thus they are modeled once; but the inputs to each SIF need a separate model on its own. Besides, the level of complexity in CPU and FE failures is considerably lower than those in a program.

8   Conclusion

We demonstrated two practical examples of integrating FMR with model-based methods HiP-HOPS and CFT. The purpose of this study was to experience comprehensive safety analyses, that included the impact of an SIS program in precise detail. In this project, FMR was used to analyze the SIS input subsystem while the random failure of logic solver and final elements were modeled in the other tools. Add-on codes were developed in each individual tool to enable automated data interfacing while the analysis methods in each tool remained unchanged. In parallel, we created a separate model in FaultTree+, to compare and verify the results of our own models with one same reference.

The main achievement of this study was showing how SIS programs can be included in safety analyses and how integrating between FMR and other FTA-based tools can help overcome modeling challenges associated with programs. Benefits of the integration include enhanced model accuracy, expanded modeling coverage, reduced modeling effort and improved analysis performance. The success of this project provided a platform for improved safety analyses in the process industry. Future research work will include expanding the interfacing features of the FMR tool, extending FMR to analyzing failure modes of system parameters, and adapting the method for modeling generic systems. In the meantime, we are in the process of publishing a formal proof for the theoretical foundations of FMR to better support its use in safety-related analyses.

References

1. Henley, E.J., Kumamoto, H.: Probabilistic Risk Assessment and Management for Engineers and Scientists, 2nd edn. IEEE Press, New York (1996)
2. IEC: IEC 61025: fault tree analysis (FTA) (2006)
3. IEC: IEC 61508: Functional safety of electrical/electronic/programmable electronic safety related systems - part 6: guidelines on the application of IEC 61508-2 and IEC 61508-3 (2010)
4. IEC: Programmable controllers - Part 3: programming languages (2013)
5. IEC: Functional safety-safety instrumented systems for the process industry sector - Part 1: framework, definitions, system, hardware and application programming requirements (2016)
6. ISA: ISA-TR84.00.02-2015, Safety integrity level (SIL) verification of safety instrumented functions (2015)
7. Jahanian, H.: Generalizing PFD formulas of IEC 61508 for KooN configurations. ISA Trans. **55**, 168–174 (2015)

8. Jahanian, H.: Failure mode reasoning. In: 2019 4th International Conference on System Reliability and Safety (ICSRS), pp. 295–303. IEEE (2019)
9. Kaiser, B., Liggesmeyer, P., Mäckel, O.: A new component concept for fault trees. In: Proceedings of the 8th Australian workshop on Safety Critical Systems and Software-Volume 33, pp. 37–46. Australian Computer Society, Inc. (2003)
10. Kaiser, B., et al.: Advances in component fault trees. In: Proceedings of ESREL (2018)
11. Papadopoulos, Y., McDermid, J., Sasse, R., Heiner, G.: Analysis and synthesis of the behaviour of complex programmable electronic systems in conditions of failure. Reliab. Eng. Syst. Saf. **71**(3), 229–247 (2001)
12. Papadopoulos, Y., et al.: A synthesis of logic and bio-inspired techniques in the design of dependable systems. Annu. Rev. Control **41**, 170–182 (2016)
13. Parker, D., Walker, M., Papadopoulos, Y.: Model-based functional safety analysis and architecture optimisation, pp. 79–92. IGI Global (2013)
14. Rausand, M.: Reliability of Safety-Critical Systems. Wiley, Hoboken (2014)
15. Stecher, K.: Fault tree analysis, taking into account causes of common mode failures. Siemens Forsch. Entwicklungsberichte (1984)
16. Stecher, K.: Evaluation of large fault-trees with repeated events using an efficient bottom-up algorithm. IEEE Trans. Reliab. **35**(1), 51–58 (1986)
17. Vesely, W.E., Goldberg, F.F., Roberts, N.H., Haasl, D.F.: Fault Tree Handbook (NUREG-0492). US Nuclear Regulatory Commission (1981)

Safety Assessment in the Automotive Domain

A Systematic Approach to Analyzing Perception Architectures in Autonomous Vehicles

Iwo Kurzidem[✉], Ahmad Saad, and Philipp Schleiss

Fraunhofer Institute for Cognitive Systems, Munich, Germany
{iwo.kurzidem,ahmad.saad,philipp.schleiss}@iks.fraunhofer.de

Abstract. Simulations are commonly used to validate the design of autonomous systems. However, as these systems are increasingly deployed into safety-critical environments with aleatoric uncertainties, and with the increase in components that employ machine learning algorithms with epistemic uncertainties, validation methods which consider uncertainties are lacking. We present an approach that evaluates signal propagation in logical system architectures, in particular environment perception-chains, focusing on effects of uncertainty to determine functional limitations. The perception based autonomous driving systems are represented by connected elements to constitute a certain functionality. The elements are based on (meta-)models to describe technical components and their behavior. The surrounding environment, in which the system is deployed, is modeled by parameters that are derived from a quasi-static scene. All parameter variations completely define input-states for the designed perception architecture. The input-states are treated as random variables inside the model of components to simulate aleatoric/epistemic uncertainty. The dissimilarity between the model-input and -output serves as measure for total uncertainty present in the system. The uncertainties are propagated through consecutive components and calculated by the same manner. The final result consists of input-states which model uncertainty effects for the specified functionality and therefore highlight shortcomings of the designed architecture.

Keywords: Uncertainty modeling · Logical system architecture · Design-time validation · ADAS safety.

1 Introduction

The usage of autonomous systems (AS) has seen an extensive advancement in various industrial fields, such as navigation, robotics and recently in automated vehicles [31]. As AS are deployed increasingly into safety-critical environments, e.g., urban settings and areas with higher-levels of automation, safety aspects with quantification of uncertainty are gaining a lot of significance [1,28].

© Springer Nature Switzerland AG 2020
M. Zeller and K. Höfig (Eds.): IMBSA 2020, LNCS 12297, pp. 149–162, 2020.
https://doi.org/10.1007/978-3-030-58920-2_10

The importance of safety during development and operation of AS has therefore triggered the creation of new guidelines and standardizations, in particular in the automotive industry.

ISO 26262 and ISO/PAS 21448 (SOTIF) are two established industry standards which address challenges of AS, especially advanced driver assistance systems (ADAS), and safety of road vehicles [12,13]. While ISO 26262 covers functional safety aspects of AS based on conventional software, SOTIF highlights uncertainties, aleatory (randomness of nature) and epistemic (lack of fundamental knowledge), due to artificial intelligence (AI) or environment perception, which are key components of many ADAS nowadays [33]. However, the mentioned standards do not provide practical methods to verify and validate safety of ADAS. With many degrees of freedom, common in real-world scenarios, the corresponding state-space expands rigorously and validation of all possible states is computationally expensive, with the given exemplary methods in ISO [3]. This makes safety assessment a time-consuming task, especially if the whole procedure needs to be repeated if part of the ADAS are changed or updated. The manual effort can be decreased by simulations, which are often the first step to validate a systems design.

Logical system behavior simulations, especially for signal propagation and alteration, can be challenging, if high amounts of varying influencing factors are present, constituting a complex system with possible interdependence [25]. Furthermore, AI based elements and sensor based perception, which are probabilistic in nature, add to the complexity. Nevertheless, determining the system behavior for all possible combinations of critical input parameters and uncertainty estimates, is pivotal for any comprehensive safety analysis. Decisive input factors for safety analyses depend on the systems function and the environment of deployment. For instance, measurement uncertainty regarding two separate objects are related to different factors, e.g., spacial proximity is decisive for RADAR detections, while high contrasts (between the two different objects) are decisive for image based systems. For AI elements, uncertainty estimates are dependent on various factors, such as the trained model and the diversity of training data [23]. To validate any system given such circumstances, the uncertainties and their propagation through a given logical architecture should to analyzed, since they limit the achievable performance and therefore reliability and ultimately safety.

The proposed approach constitutes a systematic methodology to analyze logical system architectures of ADAS with consideration of uncertainty to determine performance limits. The framework will enable a thorough analysis of perception-chain architectures to identify main influences on performance created by uncertainties. The identified influences can aid to refine the functionality, for instance, via reduction of the operational design domain (ODD). The idea emphasizes the validation of system design.

This paper is organized as follows: first we give an overview of existing methods and ideas in Sect. 2, followed by a detailed description of our proposed approach in Sect. 3. We continue with certain elements and their implementation into a stand-alone tool in Sect. 4. Finally, Sect. 5 concludes the paper and outlines the future scope.

2   Related Work

Validation of architecture design, especially Electrical/Electronics architectures, is quite common in the automotive sector and a variety of tools exists for different design phases. P. Waszecki et al. [32] give a broad overview of all available tools and which development stages they support, including details about their functionality. Most of the tools are compliant to ISO 26262 and do not explicitly consider uncertainty effects. In addition, most validations do not factor in features from the environment the systems are deployed in. However, *Simulink* [22] recently offers toolboxes to validate ADAS, but developed systems are only based on predefined algorithms and only with uncertainty effects created by noise.

Structured validation methodologies, only for functional safety aspects, to generate ISO 26262 safety artifacts can be found in [4] and [8]. Most of the established systematic safety verification methods for generic systems are based on fault tree analyses (FTA) with failure rates transformed into markov models without any consideration of uncertainty, as the examined systems do not exhibit such behavior [7]. Others consider reliability as criterion for models with decision making, but do not apply this to AI elements, sensors or other uncertainty sources, but only to failure-rates cfg. [11]. Some advances to develop an analytical modeling approach by connecting FTA with reliability has been reported by S. Kabir et al. [15], which currently enables a quantitative analysis of system architectures. If uncertainty can be adequately defined with complex basic events, which is the key part of the proposed methodology, is unclear.

Modeling of uncertainty within autonomous vehicle context has been analyzed by Y. Gal [34], but with the focus on image processing and without any consideration of the surrounding system or signal propagation through multiple components. However, some of the mentioned findings, as well as results from [16] are considered in our proposed approach and are adapted into the automobile framework. The consideration of uncertainty with safety verifications has been analyzed by S.E. Magnusson et al. [21], but the results are about fire safety and emergency exit locations, which have sparse viability for the automotive sector, as the fundamental uncertainties and scenarios are very different.

One validation method which considers uncertainty is presented by C.J. Roy et al. and incorporates the aspect of different uncertainties and its impact on the predicted system response in scientific computing [26]. The model inputs are similar to the ones of approach presented in this paper, however the framework estimates the response uncertainty mainly based on numerical approximations and extrapolations of mathematical models. Moreover, for automated driving systems, some practical technical solutions exist to reduce uncertainty, which should also be considered during validation. The use of redundant perception paths with multiple sensors coupled with data fusion is often utilized for ADAS. These practices aim to reduce uncertainty and increase performance and robustness [18]. The presented methods of C.J. Roy et al. are too abstract to include both mechanisms of redundancy and/or fusion.

Another open issue with comprehensive validation of ADAS is the missing unified ontology for scenes or situations to define the context of the designed system [24]. The description of environmental surroundings for ADAS is fundamental, as its conditions mainly determine the criticality of a scene given a specified system. For safety assessments these critical scene are of utmost importance, since they decide whether a ADAS is safe to operate or not [6]. One step towards standardizing and describing traffic scenarios is done by *PEGASUS*, a newly founded project by the German Federal Ministry for Economic Affairs and Energy. One goal of the project is to define methods to derive traffic scenarios relevant for ADAS function testing. A description of critical scenarios are also needed for the proposed approach.

3   Proposed Approach

The drawbacks and shortcomings of methods presented in Sect. 2 led to the development of the proposed approach. The proposed methodology systematically evaluates signal propagation in logical system architectures, in particular environment perception-chains, focusing on contextually relevant uncertainty to determine functional limitations. Inputs are parameters describing the state of the surrounding environment and its properties. A specified system architecture determines the propagation of these parameters. Uncertainties, within elements of the system architecture, are characterized by probability density functions (PDF) or probability mass functions (PMF). The result of the approach are inputs which produce high uncertainties after complete propagation and therefore represent shortcomings of the system.

The framework of the approach is shown in Fig. 1. The methodology is split into a design phase (top) and an analysis phase (bottom). On the right-hand side column of Fig. 1 implementations are referenced, which will be encountered throughout this paper.

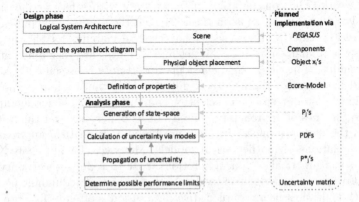

Fig. 1. Framework of the proposed approach.

During the design phase the systems architecture, including all relevant components, is being created. For this, connected components are used, cf. Fig. 4.

Components are based on specific models and meta-models to represent certain technical devices, such as sensors or AI based elements, like object classifiers based on a convolutional neural network (CNN). All unspecified elements will have a generic model which can be modified to resemble the corresponding component. The underlying model in each component allows to modify characteristics essential for the element, properties like field of view (FoV) for sensors, network calibration for CNNs to represent confidence, or simply defining the capabilities for generic components. The relations between different components, especially their in- and outputs, are simply represented by weighted connections. The designed architecture may represent a complete functionality, such as an autonomous emergency brake (AEB), or only a subsystem. As ADAS consist of distributed components (RADAR, CNN, etc.), the sequential combination of elements is a valid representation [2]. Additionally, developed architectures can be modified easily and compared to another, e.g. AEB systems, which are typically RADAR based, in comparison to camera and LIDAR based systems [17].

The logical architecture serves as setup to investigate a concrete scene. Besides physical objects, such as other road-users, pedestrians and general landmarks, environmental factors or influences, including weather and light conditions are part of scenes. Physical objects have corresponding properties such as color, size and position for pedestrians or other road users. The necessary parameters will be derived from available standard specifications, e.g. upcoming ISO 23150 [14], to achieve completeness.

Throughout this paper the following notation will be used: j is the index of a *specific scene* which can be understood as snapshot at some fixed point in time, x represent a parameter, such as the current weather condition, n denotes the total number of parameters in *one* scene, with index i *one specific parameter* can be selected and all notations associated with an asterisk ($*$) describe the *output of a computation*. Additionally, for the convenience of the readers, the abbreviation PDF will be used primarily throughout this paper, although in most cases PDF and PMF apply equally.

Properties and conditions are treated as parameters $x_i : S_i$ and are assumed to be independent from one another. Each parameter has a finite value set of possible states $S_i \rightarrow \{1, ..., k\}$, e.g the weather condition is expressed by $x = weather : \{1 = sunny, 2 = cloudy, 3 = foggy, 4 = rainy, 5 = snowy\}$. All parameters together create a point P in n-dimensional euclidean space

$$P_j(x_1^j, ..., x_n^j). \tag{1}$$

With $j = j_0$ a specific realization of P_j is noted by P_{j0}. The analysis, for the designed architecture, identifies possible combinations of parameters which have a negative impact on the performance of the represented system.

The analysis phase contains different consecutive steps. First the complete state-space of the scene is created by a systematical iterative creation of all P_j's via permutations ($j \in \{1... \prod_{i=1}^{n} S_i\}$), thus *all* possible parameter combinations are uncovered to ensure completeness. The complete state-space for the environment is of dimension n. The systematic iterative calculation of all possible P_j's prevents the oversight of critical parameter-combinations during the subsequent validation process. The creation of the state-space is deterministic.

Following the creation of the environment state-space is the calculation of uncertainty by different components of the architecture. Typical logical architectures for ADAS contain different types of uncertainties, which influence each other, as the output of one component serves as input to another. E.g. sensor signals have aleatory uncertainty, which are input to classifiers, represented by CNNs, which themselves have epistemic uncertainties.

To express aleatory uncertainties the models for sensors treat the single parameters $x_1^j, ..., x_n^j$ of input P_j as random variables $X_i : \Omega_i$, cfg. Fig. 2(a). Currently $\Omega_i \equiv S_i$ for simplicity. The exact probability density distributions of the random variables depend on the nature of the uncertainty. The PDFs are acquired by different means, e.g. empirical measurement data for sensors. The PDFs and their creation are further discussed in Sect. 5.

Not all elements contain PDFs. Fusion can be implemented via a simple logic gate, such as triple modular redundancy for fusion of three inputs, or by comparing both PDFs and their distribution, for two sources, and evaluating which x_i is more accurate or plausible [20].

The input value of some x_i determines the used PDF of some X_i, as shown in Fig. 2(b), independently of j. Thus elements contain multiple PDFs. Furthermore, the user specified characteristics (FoV etc.) are considered during simulation and immensely influence certain PDFs, cfg. Fig. 6(a). The model output $P_{j0}^*(x_1^{j0*}, ..., x_n^{j0*})$ has the same dimension as the input. However, the exact values $x_1^{j0*}, ..., x_n^{j0*}$ are influenced by the computations mentioned above. For an easier traceability the resulting value of X_i is being mapped to x_i^{j*}.

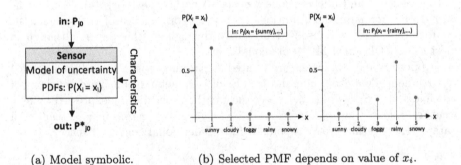

(a) Model symbolic.   (b) Selected PMF depends on value of x_i.

Fig. 2. Sensor models simulating aleatory uncertainty via PDFs.

The degree of uncertainty is determined by dissimilarity between input P_{j0} and model output P_{j0}^*. The assessment of dissimilarity is achieved via calculation of the euclidean distance D between P_j and P_j^* by [29]:

$$D(P_j, \; P_j^*) \; = \; \sqrt{\sum_{i=1}^{n}(x_i^j \; - \; x_i^{j*})^2}. \tag{2}$$

No scaling is necessary as we are already in n-dimensional euclidean space. Higher values of $D(P_j, \; P_j^*)$ correspond to higher uncertainty. The model output P_{j0}^* is probabilistic, so multiple simulations for a given P_{j0} are necessary to gain statistical confidence in the calculated uncertainty. For the architecture validation the worst case scenarios are relevant, as a consequence the P_{j0}^* which creates the highest $D(P_{j0}, \; P_{j0}^*)$ is propagated through following components, given a fixed $j = j_0$. The amount of iterations for sufficient confidence is currently being investigated.

Equation 2 can be interpreted as the cumulative uncertainty over all properties. However, for a detailed analysis a comparison between to identical properties is required as this allows for a qualitative assessment. For a single property $i = i_0$, given a certain realization $j = j_0$, the value of dissimilarity d

$$d(x_{i0}^{j0}, \; x_{i0}^{j0*}) \; = \; \frac{\mid x_{i0}^{j0} \; - \; x_{i0}^{j0*} \mid}{\mid S_{i0} \mid} \tag{3}$$

serves as measure of uncertainty for this property. Denominator $\mid S_i \mid$ denotes the cardinality of set S_i, while the numerator $\mid x_i^j \; - \; x_i^{j*} \mid$ gives the absolute value between two points. This implicitly requires that estranged elements are sorted accordingly in the PDFs. Equation 3 does not apply for certain enumerated PMFs if any x_i holds the value of zero, as this means the property is not determined and stands for maximum uncertainty, $x_i^j \vee x_i^{j*} = 0 \; \Rightarrow \; d = 1$. For all other cases results of Eq. 3 can be interpreted as magnitude of uncertainty.

The single d's are grouped into a matrix of measurement object attribute uncertainty M_A, which is used to calculate members of measurement object existence uncertainty M_E [19]. Additionally, measurement noise is quantified by M_N [5]. Complete measurement sensor data uncertainty is represented by

$$\overline{\mathbf{U}}_S \; = \; (M_E, \; M_A, \; M_N), \tag{4}$$

with $s \in \{RADAR \; (R), LIDAR \; (L), Camera \; (C)\}$. The matrix of attributes M_A has size $objects \times obj.attributes$ and contains the uncertainty about the properties of physical objects. M_E is a column vector $objects \times 1$ and holds the object existence probability. The existence probability of an object is calculated via its respective attributes uncertainty d from M_A. The noise M_N is a scalar value. As not all properties are measurable by each sensor, the exact sizes of the matrices M_A and potentially M_E, differ between the sensors. Figure 3 shows how different factors affect various uncertainties of $\overline{\mathbf{U}}_S$. Dashed lines represent potential influences.

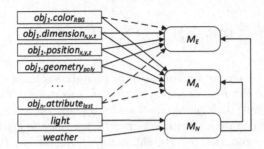

Fig. 3. Factors influencing different uncertainties.

The propagation of uncertainty depends on the elements and their connections to one another in the sketched architecture. As most ADAS are represented by sequential combination of components, the output of one model is input to the next $P_j^*[previous] * \alpha_r \rightarrow P_j[next]$. α_r represents the connection weight between to specific components. The aforementioned calculations are repeated for every component of the architecture.

Every single P_j of the input-state requires a separate simulation of the whole architecture. To prevent astronomically unlikely events to be analyzed, simulation is better suited rather then a simple analytical worst-case approach.

The validation of the designed system is grounded on the calculated uncertainties for every P_j. The final values of uncertainties serve as a quantifier for performance. The nominal performance must be defined in such a way it can be evaluated with data from $\overline{U}$ or directly from a final P_j^*, if the designed architecture allows this. Currently, the final evaluation is based on comparisons via user-defined thresholds.

4   System Description

The approach described in Sect. 3 is currently being implemented into a tool. The current implementation covers parts of the design phase, in particular the creation of the system block diagram and the definition of corresponding sensor characteristics, cfg. Fig. 1.

To showcase the approach an example logical system architecture for an AEB system is shown in Fig. 4. The simple illustrative example consists of two sensors, namely a LIDAR and Camera, as well as a CNN for object interpretation from images. The processed data from both sensors is fused and transferred to the functionality of AEB. Finally, the AEB may trigger a brake command, which is not part of the analysis procedure but completes the architecture overview.

As mentioned in Sect. 3, a building block represents a visualization of a model, cfg. Fig. 2(a). The input for the Camera and LIDAR are the P_j's derived from a designed scene. The output of P_j^* of Camera and LIDAR are input to CNN and Fusion Unit respectively. The connection weights α_r between elements are equal, so currently $\alpha_r = 1, \forall\, r \in \mathbb{N}$.

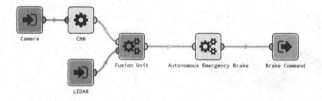

Fig. 4. A simplified example system architecture.

The characteristics for the sensors are taken into account during simulation. Figure 5 shows the model for the currently implemented sensors as an Ecore model in the eclipse modeling framework (EMF). The selected characteristics are typical vendor specific properties. Some of the properties are included for future extensions of the approach, such as *scanRate*. Each type of sensor has a different model (different PDFs), however the PDFs are adjusted for specified entries like *fovVertical*, *maxRange* and *minRange*. For sensors based on electromagnetic wave reflections off objects, some characteristics are the same, such as *fovVertical*. A few entries simply exist for implementation reasons and can be ignored. The characteristics can be customized during the design phase and taken from technical vendor specifications of the sensor. In Fig. 6(a) a visualization of a joint probability distribution for LIDAR detections is shown. The joined PDF already takes into account the specified FoV characteristics. In this case the joined PDF represents the probability of detection during rainy conditions.

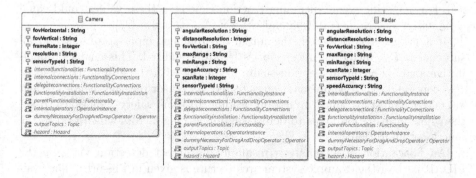

Fig. 5. Subset of the sensor meta-model.

Sensor data fusion creates a 3D-model of the surrounding environment and decreases uncertainties from single sensors. Currently the fusion acts as a filter, only passing through the more plausible value (smaller deviation from the mean), thus effectively decreasing uncertainty. The output of fusion unit is also of type P_j^*. For each component the corresponding uncertainty matrices of $\overline{U}$ are calculated, after the sample P_j^* with the highest uncertainty found using Eq. 2.

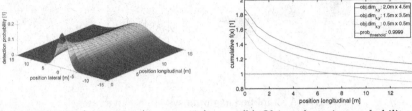

(a) Joined PDF $p(obj.x, obj.y|x_i = rain)$.   (b) Object detection probability.

Fig. 6. LIDAR detection PDF and analysis result. (Color figure online)

To objectively assess critical parameter-combinations, which create high uncertainty, the exact functionality needs to be specified in a computer understandable way, such as a condition with expression statements. For instance, the specified functionality of AEB does not require high confidence in color measurement, but rather if objects are definitely detected given a certain distance from the automated vehicle (existence uncertainty which lead to false negatives). So M_E and object position from M_A are deemed necessary and important. Note that this a somewhat simplified viewpoint of AEB system functionality. The expression statements are defined via thresholds, see Algorithm 1.

The algorithm checks two conditions, first if any object falls short of the specified existence probability and then if such an object is inside the specified range. If both conditions are true, the P_{j0} which led to this is considered critical. For a specific scene, including reaction time etc., these values could equal $obj.exist\_prob_{threshold} = 0.9999$ and $obj.pos_{threshold} = 8\,\mathrm{m}$ [27].

If a violation is detected, the initial environment input-state P_{j0} and all subsequent P_{j0}^*, including uncertainties $\overline{\mathbf{U}}$, are visualized. This enables a qualitative analysis of the perception-chain, beginning with the ground truth scene P_{j0}, continuing with what has been detected via sensor measurements P_{j0}^* and all subsequent steps, until eventually leading to some safety violation. To see the whole propagation helps to detect key influencing factors which lead to the functional limitation.

An illustration of an analysis result for an object detection via *only* the LIDAR path of the example system architecture is given in Fig. 6(b). The evaluation is based on Algorithm 1 with the aforementioned thresholds. As LIDAR sensors are not able to detect colors, this information is disregarded during the analysis, the same applies to the position uncertainty as we assume that it is negligible for objects *inside* the FoV. The geometry is fixed as cuboid. The uncertainty for LIDAR detections is mainly influenced by the weather and occlusion effects, however occlusion is not relevant for this case.

For $x_i : \{rainy\}$ the joined PDF for detection probability is assuming shape of Fig. 6(a). The identified critical parameters of the input-state are the dimensions of the object and its position relative to the sensor. In Fig. 6(b) plots of three different object size detections and their longitudinal position as distance from

---

Func. AEB_performance(M_E, M_A, $obj.exist\_prob_{threshold}$, $obj.pos_{threshold}$)
Input: Vector of object existence probability M_E, matrix of object attribute
     uncertainty M_A and threshold values $obj.exist\_prob_{threshold}$ and
     $obj.pos_{threshold}$
Output: Boolean $isViolatingNominalPerformance$

foreach $obj \in M_E$ **do**
    if $obj.exist\_prob < obj.exist\_prob_{threshold}$ **then**   // check existence
     | $isViolatingNominalPerformance$ = true;
    end
    if $isViolatingNominalPerformance$ **then**   // uncertain existence
       $obj.pos$ = getObjectAttributePosition(M_A, obj);
       if $obj.pos < obj.pos_{threshold}$ **then**   // check range
       | break;
       else
       | $isViolatingNominalPerformance$ = false;
       end
    end
end
return $isViolatingNominalPerformance$

Algorithm 1: *Simplified AEB functionality evaluation.*

---

the measurement sensor are shown. The three different object sizes are due to measurement uncertainty of the ground truth object of size 1.5 m × 3.5 m. The red line corresponds to $obj.exist\_prob_{threshold}$ = 0.9999. In this case the analysis reveals that for objects of size 0.5 m × 0.5 m, or smaller, the specified performance cannot be achieved. The detection of objects of dimension 0.5 m × 0.5 m is, in the worst case, only up to 7 m. The input-state of object dimension 0.5 m × 0.5 m and rain is therefore considered critical, as the uncertainty of existence violates the specified performance. An AEB architecture only based on LIDAR sensors is therefore not recommended.

The results enables further development steps, such as to characterize and safeguard identified sources of uncertainty in ADAS architectures, e.g. via ODD reduction.

5   Conclusion and Future Work

In this paper we describe a systematic approach to analyze perception based architectures with consideration of contextual uncertainty effects. The approach involves the design of the logical measurement system architecture and environmental scene, which enables the analysis of both in conjunction afterwards. Certain logical system components fabricate uncertainty effects, these are modeled via PDFs or calculated analytically if feasible. The dissimilarity between the model-input and -output serves as measure for total uncertainty present in the system. The uncertainties are propagated through consecutive components and are calculated by the same principle. Eventually, the resulting uncertainty is evaluated against the specified functionality of the system, generally including some safety aspect. The final result consists of input-states which produce high uncertainty effects and jeopardize a safe functionality, thus representing shortcomings of the designed architecture.

The novel contribution of this work is the combined evaluation of aleatoric *and* epistemic uncertainty via underlying models, compared to present approaches described in Sect. 2. Furthermore, the signal propagation through mixed sources of uncertainty, as well as techniques to reduce uncertainty are an integral part of the approach.

The probabilistic nature of the approach, via random variables inside models, adds itself uncertainty to the produced results. The level of abstraction from models, simplifications and assumptions (such as independence of properties) need to be evaluated [30]. Violations currently reduce the validity of this approach.

All models are currently based on some kind of statistical classification from measurement of *one* component. This implies that the model is also *only valid* for this one component, e.g. measurement data from *one* specific sensor. If and what kind of generalizations are possible within these PDFs is currently unclear. Potential mistakes during the creation of the PDFs are detrimental for this approach. The uncertainty of CNNs is currently extensively researched, see [9, 10,16], and its results will be incorporated into the approach. If the modeling of epistemic uncertainty via PDFs is a meaningful estimation for AI uncertainty is still under investigation.

The next steps for the tool include the implementation of underlying mechanics for elements based on AI. Additional components for localization, for instance GPS and a-priori perception sensors, shall also be included. Currently, only quasi-static scenes, as only parameters are varied, are examined.

The computational feasibility is currently mainly affected by the creation of the state-space

$$n * \sum_{i=1}^{n} |S_i|!, \tag{5}$$

as the calculation of all permutations has currently the highest complexity. From Eq. 5 follows, that the cardinality of S_i is decisive for the run-time. Thus the set for properties should be limited, however without jeopardizing completeness. To possibly decrease the computation time, while also allowing moderate cardinality of sets, a reduction can be accomplished by omitting properties which are unimportant for certain components, such as lighting conditions for LIDAR. A reduction via clustering could potentially be possible, however it needs to be accomplished so that Eqs. 2 and 3 are still computable.

For future iterations the investigations of scenarios, meaning the development with time t, shall be part of the analysis.

Acknowledgments. This work was funded by the Bavarian Ministry for Economic Affairs, Regional Development and Energy as part of a project to support the thematic development of the Institute for Cognitive Systems.

References

1. Alexander, R., Herbert, N., Kelly, T.: Structuring safety cases for autonomous systems (2008)
2. Bach, J., Otten, S., Sax, E.: A taxonomy and systematic approach for automotive system architectures–from functional chains to functional networks. In: International Conference on Vehicle Technology and Intelligent Transport Systems, vol. 2, pp. 90–101. SCITEPRESS (2017)
3. Bagschik, G., Reschka, A., Stolte, T., Maurer, M.: Identification of potential hazardous events for an unmanned protective vehicle. In: 2016 IEEE Intelligent Vehicles Symposium (IV), pp. 691–697. IEEE (2016)
4. Beckers, K., Côté, I., Frese, T., Hatebur, D., Heisel, M.: A structured validation and verification method for automotive systems considering the OEM/supplier interface. In: Koornneef, F., van Gulijk, C. (eds.) SAFECOMP 2015. LNCS, vol. 9337, pp. 90–108. Springer, Cham (2015). https://doi.org/10.1007/978-3-319-24255-2_8
5. Belhedi, A., Bartoli, A., Bourgeois, S., Hamrouni, K., Sayd, P., Gay-Bellile, V.: Noise modelling and uncertainty propagation for TOF sensors. In: Fusiello, A., Murino, V., Cucchiara, R. (eds.) ECCV 2012. LNCS, vol. 7585, pp. 476–485. Springer, Heidelberg (2012). https://doi.org/10.1007/978-3-642-33885-4_48
6. Chen, W., Kloul, L.: Stochastic modelling of autonomous vehicles driving scenarios using PEPA. In: Papadopoulos, Y., Aslansefat, K., Katsaros, P., Bozzano, M. (eds.) IMBSA 2019. LNCS, vol. 11842, pp. 317–331. Springer, Cham (2019). https://doi.org/10.1007/978-3-030-32872-6_21
7. Goble, W., Cheddie, H.: Safety Instrumented Systems Verification: Practical Probabilistic Calculations. ISA-The Instrumentation, Systems, and Automation Society, USA (2005)
8. Grönninger, H., Hartmann, J., Krahn, H., Kriebel, S., Rothhart, L., Rumpe, B.: View-centric modeling of automotive logical architectures. Technical report, TU Braunschweig (2014)
9. Henne, M., Schwaiger, A., Roscher, K., Weiss, G.: Benchmarking uncertainty estimation methods for deep learning with safety-related metrics. In: SafeAI@ AAAI, pp. 83–90 (2020)
10. Henne, M., Schwaiger, A., Weiss, G.: Managing uncertainty of AI-based perception for autonomous systems. In: AISafety@ IJCAI Proceedings, pp. 57–60 (2019)
11. Hillenbrand, M.: Funktionale Sicherheit Nach ISO 26262 in Der Konzeptphase Der Entwicklung von Elektrik/Elektronik Architekturen von Fahrzeugen. Ph.D. thesis, KIT Scientific Publishing 4 (2012)
12. International Organization for Standardization: Road vehicles—functional safety (ISO 26262). ISO (2011)
13. International Organization for Standardization: Safety of the intended functionality - SOTIF (ISO/PAS 21448). ISO (2019)
14. International Organization for Standardization: Road vehicles—data communication between sensors and data fusion unit for automated driving functions—logical interface. ISO (2020)
15. Kabir, S., Aslansefat, K., Sorokos, I., Papadopoulos, Y., Gheraibia, Y.: A conceptual framework to incorporate complex basic events in HiP-HOPS. In: Papadopoulos, Y., Aslansefat, K., Katsaros, P., Bozzano, M. (eds.) IMBSA 2019. LNCS, vol. 11842, pp. 109–124. Springer, Cham (2019). https://doi.org/10.1007/978-3-030-32872-6_8

16. Kendall, A., Cipolla, R.: Modelling uncertainty in deep learning for camera relocalization. In: 2016 IEEE International Conference on Robotics and Automation (ICRA), pp. 4762–4769. IEEE (2016)
17. Khastgir, S., Sivencrona, H., Dhadyalla, G., Billing, P., Birrell, S., Jennings, P.: Introducing ASIL inspired dynamic tactical safety decision framework for automated vehicles. In: 2017 IEEE 20th International Conference on Intelligent Transportation Systems (ITSC), pp. 1–6. IEEE (2017)
18. Kocić, J., Jovičić, N., Drndarević, V.: Sensors and sensor fusion in autonomous vehicles. In: 2018 26th Telecommunications Forum (TELFOR), pp. 420–425. IEEE (2018)
19. Kuka, C.: Processing the uncertainty: quality-aware data stream processing for dynamic context models. In: 2012 IEEE International Conference on Pervasive Computing and Communications Workshops, pp. 560–561. IEEE (2012)
20. Luo, R., Lin, M.H., Scherp, R.: Dynamic multi-sensor data fusion system for intelligent robots. Technical report 4/4. IEEE (1988)
21. Magnusson, S., Frantzich, H., Harada, K.: Fire safety design based on calculations: uncertainty analysis and safety verification. Technical report 27/4. Elsevier (1996)
22. MathWorks: Sensor fusion and tracking for autonomous systems. The MathWorks, Inc. (2019)
23. Mikołajczyk, A., Grochowski, M.: Data augmentation for improving deep learning in image classification problem. In: 2018 International Interdisciplinary PhD Workshop (IIPhDW), pp. 117–122. IEEE (2018)
24. Pollard, E., Morignot, P., Nashashibi, F.: An ontology-based model to determine the automation level of an automated vehicle for co-driving. In: Proceedings of the 16th International Conference on Information Fusion, pp. 596–603. IEEE (2013)
25. Rakotonirainy, A.: Design of context-aware systems for vehicle using complex systems paradigms. In: Proceedings Workshop on Safety and Context in Conjunction with CONTEXT 2005, pp. 43–51. QUTePrints, Paris (2005)
26. Roy, C.J., Oberkampf, W.L.: A comprehensive framework for verification, validation, and uncertainty quantification in scientific computing. Technical report 200/25-28. Elsevier (2011)
27. Russo, J., Sproesser, T., Drouhin, F., Basset, M.: Risk level assessment for rear-end collision with Bayesian network. Technical report 50/1. Elsevier (2017)
28. Sanfeliu, A., Hagita, N., Saffiotti, A.: Network robot systems. Technical report 56/10. Elsevier (2008)
29. Scheidt, C., Caers, J.: Representing spatial uncertainty using distances and kernels. Technical report 41/4. Springer (2009)
30. Struck, C.: Uncertainty propagation and sensitivity analysis techniques in building performance simulation to support conceptual building and system design. Ph.D. thesis, University of Technology Eindhoven, Department of the Built Environment (2012)
31. Tzafestas, S.G.: Advances in Intelligent Autonomous Systems. Springer, Dordrecht (2012). https://doi.org/10.1007/978-94-011-4790-3
32. Waszecki, P., Lukasiewycz, M., Masrur, A., Chakraborty, S.: How to engineer toolchains for automotive E/E architectures? Technical report 10/4. ACM, New York (2013)
33. Wood, M., et al.: Safety first for automated driving (2019)
34. Yarin, G.: Uncertainty in deep learning. Ph.D. thesis, University of Cambridge (2016)

Identification and Quantification of Hazardous Scenarios for Automated Driving

Birte Kramer[1(✉)], Christian Neurohr[1(✉)], Matthias Büker[2], Eckard Böde[1], Martin Fränzle[1], and Werner Damm[1]

[1] OFFIS, Oldenburg, Germany
{kramer,neurohr,boede,fraenzle,damm}@offis.de
[2] BTC Embedded Systems, Oldenburg, Germany
matthias.bueker@btc-es.de

Abstract. We present an integrated method for safety assessment of automated driving systems which covers the aspects of functional safety and safety of the intended functionality (SOTIF), including identification and quantification of hazardous scenarios. The proposed method uses and combines established exploration and analytical tools for hazard analysis and risk assessment in the automotive domain, while adding important enhancements to enable their applicability to the uncharted territory of safety analyses for automated driving. The method is tailored to support existing safety processes mandated by the standards ISO 26262 and ISO/PAS 21448 and complements them where necessary. It has been developed in close cooperation with major German automotive manufacturers and suppliers within the PEGASUS project (https://www.pegasusprojekt.de/en). Practical evaluation has been carried out by applying the method to the PEGASUS Highway-Chauffeur, a conceptual automated driving function considered as a common reference system within the project.

Keywords: Automated driving · Hazard analysis · Risk assessment · SOTIF · Scenario identification · Environmental triggers

1 Introduction

In order to bring automated driving systems (ADS) [17] to the market, there are several challenges that need to be overcome. One of them is the verification

This study was partially supported and financed by AUDI AG, BMW Group, Continental Teves AG & Co. oHG, Daimler AG, Robert Bosch GmbH, TÜV SÜD GmbH and Volkswagen AG within the context of PEGASUS, a project funded by the German Federal Ministry for Economic Affairs and Energy (BMWi). (**P**roject for the **E**stablishment of **G**enerally **A**ccepted quality criteria, tools and methods as well as **S**cenarios and **S**ituations for the release of highly-automated driving functions).

© Springer Nature Switzerland AG 2020
M. Zeller and K. Höfig (Eds.): IMBSA 2020, LNCS 12297, pp. 163–178, 2020.
https://doi.org/10.1007/978-3-030-58920-2_11

and validation of such systems. It has been well-established [11] that a mileage-based approach is infeasible. This is mainly due to the impossibility of driving the vast distance that is required to obtain a statistically valid argument in support of a positive safety statement. The most promising alternative for verification and validation of automated driving is a scenario-based approach where testing is guided by a manageable set of logical scenarios [13] that have been identified as crucial. Recent research projects, such as PEGASUS[1] and ENABLE-S3[2], explored and pushed this scenario-based approach to testing. A central challenge for this is the systematic identification and quantification of scenarios that are likely to exhibit hazardous behavior of the ADS. While analyzing already existing real-world data (such as accident databases, real world driving, etc.) reveals which scenarios are hazardous for human drivers, the set of hazardous scenarios for automated driving can only be partially obtained from this data prior to the large-scale deployment of ADS. Therefore, a complementary, knowledge-based approach is needed in order to identify and quantify such hazards early on in the development process. This cannot be replaced by massive testing. In Sect. 2 we revisit the challenges for automated driving and explain why existing methods for Hazard Analysis and Risk Assessment (HARA) used in the automotive domain, as suggested by the ISO 26262 [9] and the ISO/PAS 21448 [10], cannot adequately identify hazardous scenarios for automated vehicles. Moreover, we briefly introduce the Highway-Chauffeur, a conceptual ADS with the operational design domain 'German Highway', that serves as running example in PEGASUS and throughout this paper. In Sect. 3 we propose a method for the identification of hazardous scenarios for automated driving that combines established methods for HARA with a focus on detecting hazard-triggering environmental conditions. Moreover, we propose a method for estimating the probability of such a scenario in real-world traffic and show how the results can be used for risk assessment, leading to an integrated iterative risk mitigation process. An in-depth review and application of the method have been conducted within the PEGASUS project. More detailed information on the method as well as its application and evaluation targeting the PEGASUS highway-chauffeur have been made public in a German language technical report [5].

2   Problem Characterization and Challenges

Hazardous Scenarios. The ISO 26262 [9] defines a **hazard** as a potential source of harm. In PEGASUS [14], different sources of hazards for automated driving were distinguished, namely hazards arising from (1) the impact of the environment on the ADS, (2) the impact of the ADS on the environment and (3) the interaction between human driver and ADS. Although the methods presented in this paper were developed with a focus on (1), it may be applied to class (2) as well. As Class (3) has a different focus (e.g. HMI concept) it needs different methods to consider the specific problems.

---

[1] www.pegasusprojekt.de/en.
[2] www.enable-s3.eu.

According to [19], a **scene** describes a snapshot of the environment, while a scenario describes the temporal development between several scenes in a sequence of scenes. Thus, a **hazardous scenario** can be characterized by adding contextual information to an identified hazard by means of environmental triggers. A comprehensive catalog of such scenarios then enables a test-driven verification approach for automated driving.

Challenges for Automated Driving. Advanced Driving Assistance Systems currently on the market only perform individual sub-tasks of vehicle control, while the residual tasks remain the responsibility of the driver. With the driver acting as a redundant control system, a fail-safe safety concept is sufficient. Safety mechanisms, as addressed in [10], are therefore primarily concerned with avoiding false-positive reactions. With SAE Level $\geq$ 3 [17], ADS (temporarily) relieve the driver of the driving task. Consequently, the driver is no longer available as a fallback at all times and missing (re-)actions of the ADS's (false negative reactions) play a decisive role for operational safety and thus, requiring a fail-operational (or even fail-silent) safety concept. While hazardous scenarios for human drivers can be reconstructed relatively well from existing data (e.g. accident data bases), the question arises whether the corresponding triggers are the same for ADS. Reflections from metallic objects (e.g. crash barriers) could lead to erroneous recognition of objects by a radar sensor, an unknown accident cause for humans. Extensive databases of observed accidents for automated driving are lacking, so possible hazardous scenarios are not known a priori, rendering safety assessment of automated vehicles particularly challenging. In addition, the criticality of automated driving may be highly discontinuous along the parameter ranges of environmental models: algorithms make discrete decisions, the thresholds of which are only partially known, especially machine learning methods. For example, only a few differences in images that are hardly visible to the human eye can lead to a false object classification [2]. It is therefore dangerous to solely rely on a data-driven approach (i.e. a combination of existing driving data and variation methods) when identifying hazardous scenarios. Although this problem could, in principle, be countered with a complete characterization of all scenarios in the Operational Design Domain (ODD), it is impossible to explicitly describe all relevant scenes and scenarios. Thus, it is inherently difficult to appropriately specify the ADS's behaviour. The intended functionality can therefore neither assumed to be safe nor fully specified (SOTIF). This problem is addressed in [10], but only for advanced driver assistance systems. In order to address the aforementioned issues, it is essential to adapt existing methods for HARA according to the challenges presented by analyzing the safety of ADS. An integrative HARA, which facilitates an iterative feedback loop into the development process, should be performed early in the development of the ADS so that the results can be incorporated appropriately. With this goal in mind, the proposed method for identification and quantification of hazardous scenarios has been developed.

Existing techniques for Hazard Analysis and Risk Assessment. In the proposed method, we use, combine and extend established techniques for hazard analysis and risk assessment. Thus, we briefly summarize them here.

Hazard and Operability Study (HAZOP) was developed and successfully applied in the chemical industry in the 1970s. Starting in the 1990s HAZOP was used in other areas and finally also adapted for the automotive industry. HAZOP is a structured, keyword-based brainstorming approach that investigates significant deviations from the specified behavior in order to identify possible hazards. Optimally, a HAZOP should be performed by a diverse group of specialists from different areas of expertise, who study the system under consideration from various points of view. Selected keywords are applied to process variables and components of the system to investigate deviations from the ideal state. In the process, possible causes, their consequences and potential countermeasures are identified, without making any claims of exhaustiveness. For more details on classical HAZOP we refer to [6]. In this paper we use two different versions of HAZOP (see step (2.1) and (2.2) of Sect. 3) that were specifically adapted for the application to ADS.

Fault Tree Analysis (FTA) is a widely used method to identify fault chains and was originally developed by the U.S. Air Force. The Fault Tree Handbook [20] provides an excellent overview of the method. FTA follows a top-down approach, i.e. starting from a certain event (called Top Level Event), causes for this event are systematically identified down to basic events. These causes are logically entangled using boolean algebra. With quantitative fault trees, minimal sets of triggering events, so-called minimal cut sets, are identified after the fault tree has been created and a probability of occurrence of the Top Level Event is calculated from probabilities of the basic events. Classical quantitative fault trees assume that each Top Level Event is caused by faults of some other component inside the system. This assumption is no longer tenable for automated driving, since every environmental conditions could potentially trigger or propagate faults. Another problem of fault trees are unknown dependencies between events. Therefore, the FTA is often complemented by a Common Cause Analysis [7].

System-Theoretic Process Analysis (STPA) is a relatively new hazard analysis technique that uses STAMP (System-Theoretic Accident Model and Processes, [12]). In this accident model, hazards arise from untreated environmental influences, untreated or uncontrolled defects of components, unsafe interactions between components or from insufficiently coordinated control actions between control loops. In STAMP, safety is understood as an emergent property, which occurs when system components interact in a larger context. This is in contrast to the safety process of ISO 26262 (and other methods such as FTA or FMEA), where only defects and malfunctions of components are considered. Based on this accident model, STPA identifies unsafe control actions and derives safety constrains. The next step is to identify the causal factors for the occurrence of the previously identified unsafe control actions. The causes identified here within the control loop help to refine the previously defined safety constraints into safety requirements.

Related Work. As the presented method aims at identifying and quantifying hazardous scenarios for scenario based testing while deriving safety requirements for the further development, there is related work for serveral parts of the method. For example, in [3] an ontology is proposed to automatically generate scenes for the development of automated vehicles. However, this does not generate a classification of hazardous/relevant scenarios. [1] uses STPA to identify unsafe interactions of ADS in the absence of system malfunctions. Thus, this may be used to generate scenarios. However, this is not done there and they do not use methods to quantify scenarios/malfunctions. [18] uses STPA to identify hazards that arise from expectations that other road users have of the ADS (because driving styles of automated vehicles may differ from human driving styles) which corresponds to class (2) of the before-mentioned sources of hazards. [21] uses a scenario based STPA and compares it with more traditional HARA methods. However, they are also only focused on identifying hazards in specific scenarios and do not present an approach on how to generate and quantify them.

The PEGASUS Highway Chauffeur. [15] is an example of a ADS, thus not requiring the driver to monitor the system but needing to be able to take back the driving task within a defined time margin. The ODD and basic functionality of the Highway Chauffeur were defined to include highways in Germany, a speed range of $[0, 130]\frac{km}{h}$, lane changes, following in stop & go traffic and emergency braking and collision avoidance. It excludes construction sites, driving onto/exiting the highway and extreme weather conditions.

Contribution. We outline an integrated safety process for ADS that addresses functional safety as well as safety of the intended functionality (SOTIF). Our method is composed of an identification part (Hazard Analysis) and a quantification part (Risk Assessment) for hazardous scenarios. Identification builds on a combination of established methods used for Hazard Analysis, which we adapted to uncover the safety-relevant weaknesses and blind spots of ADS. In the second part, we propose quantification of hazards via probability estimation of the hazard's context. In contrast to the process of ISO 26262, the subsequent risk assessment abandons the factor of 'controllability', which is practically nonexistent (or strongly diminished, at least) for automated driving. Moreover, we integrate risk mitigation into the safety process. Lastly, we indicate how regulatory requirements on hazard exposure, can be used to systematically derive requirements on error rates. The method introduces the iterative feedback loops between concept and development phase that are required for establishing a fail-operational safety concept for ADS, while remaining compatible with the ISO 26262 and ISO/PAS 21448. Moreover, the method identifies and quantifies hazardous scenarios for scenario based testing. These can be incorporated into logical scenarios [13]. This enables specific selection of potentially critical scenarios in the testing process and serves to support the argument for a sufficiently complete test space coverage.

3   Method for Identification of Hazardous Scenarios

In the following we describe an iterative method for the identification and quantification of hazardous scenarios for highly automated driving. The method, as seen in Fig. 1, is divided into two parts. The identification part, described in this section, consists of steps (1)–(5). For more examples of the steps see [5].

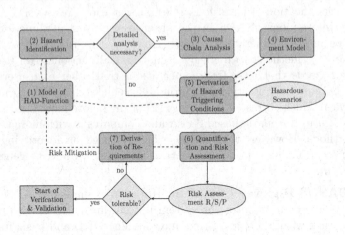

Fig. 1. Overview of the method to identify and quantify hazardous scenarios

Step (1): Modeling of the ADS. specifies the functional architecture and the intended functionality of the ADS. In particular, this needs to include the flow of information between the components of the system (i.e. inputs and outputs of each component). This model serves as the starting point for the method (see Fig. 1) and is iteratively refined in the process as indicated by the dotted lines leading back to step (1). For the Highway Chauffeur this information flow can be seen in Fig. 2 where each arrow represents that information is given to the next component.

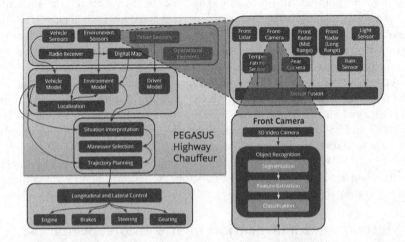

Fig. 2. High-level functional architecture for the PEGASUS highway chauffeur.

Step (2): Hazard Identification aims at identifying hazards related to the ADS, corresponding to causes in the ADS and possible triggers in the environment. The focus lies on hazards that are <u>not</u> caused by random hardware faults, but rather by performance limitations or functional insufficiencies of the ADS in its perception, in the modeling and interpretation of its environment and in the planning of maneuvers and trajectories. In particular, this includes hazards which result from the absence of SOTIF. The hazard identification is split into two substeps (2.1) and (2.2).

Step (2.1): Scenario-based Identification of Hazards on Vehicle-Level. We start by identifying generic hazards on vehicle-level using a keyword-based, HAZOP-inspired brainstorming approach. We start from a set of basic scenarios and a set of basic maneuvers that are chosen according to the ODD of the ADS. For each combination of basic scenario and basic maneuver, we systematically determine the observable effects of this behavior, potential hazards and additional environmental conditions triggering these hazards. The results of this step are denoted in a modified HAZOP table (see Table 1), which consists of 9 columns. In the 1st column (cln) we denote a unique **ID** for later reference. The **basic scenario** and **basic maneuver** under consideration are entered in the 2nd and 3rd cln respectively. While the set of basic scenarios is highly dependent on the ODD, the basic maneuvers (BM) form a subset of the set of all maneuvers that an (automated) vehicle can perform [16], i.e. BM(ODD) $\subseteq$ {start, follow, approach (includes braking), pass, traverse crossover, lane change, turn left/right, turn back, park, safe stop}. In the 4th cln **Correct (if context)** we denote the context in which this vehicle behavior would be considered correct. Now we apply a set of **Keywords**, denoted in the 5th cln, to the respective maneuver under consideration to determine possible **Incorrect Vehicle Behavior** (IVB), denoted in the 6th cln. We propose the following list of keywords

Table 1. Table (two exemplary rows) for Identification of Hazards on Vehicle-Level.

ID	Basic scenario	Basic maneuver	Correct if (context)	Keyword	Incorrect vehicle behaviour	Observable effect(s) in scenario	Additional scenario conditions (necessaroy for Top Level Event)	Potential top level event
1	Slower turn into path challenger	Decelerate/ braking	Front distance < safety distance	no	Necessary breaking maneuver not initiated	Ego continues with constant speed	Challenger with significantly lower speed or critical Time-To-Collision	Front/side collision with challenger
2				less	Braking maneuver not strong enough	Ego does not decelerate to prvent collision	Challenger with significantly lower speed or critical Time-To-Collision	Front/side collision with challenger

- **no, less, more, too early, too late** (classical HAZOP keywords)
- **non-existent, too large, too small, too many, too few, not relevant, physically not possible** (specific keywords for driving assistance systems according to the Sense-Plan-Act paradigm [4])
- **provided in inappropriate context, stopped too soon, provided too long** (STPA-inspired keywords)
- **outdated, misapprehended, inappropriate, falsified, too slow, too fast** (keywords found to be relevant during application of the method)
- **wrong** (generic, only to be applied if no other keyword is applicable)

Based on the IVB, the 7th cln is filled with **Observable Effect(s) in Scenario**. These effects are then used to derive potential hazards at vehicle level (top level events) in the 9th cln **Potential Top Level Event**. If **Additional Scenario Conditions** are **Necessary for Top Level Event** to happen, this is denoted in the 8th cln. The results of step (2.1) are essentially independent of the concrete implementation and can be used for the development of other ADS within the same ODD.

Step (2.2): Identification of Functional Insufficiencies with Hazardous Effects. Now we systematically apply the keywords from step (2.1) to the triple (Input, Computation, Output) for each functional unit (FU) of the system in order to examine deviations that may lead to hazards. In particular, we analyze the effects of these deviations locally, system-wide and on vehcile-level. Again, the results are documented in a table consisting of 11 columns (Table 2).

Table 2. Table for Identification of Local Failures/Functional Insufficiencies.

Functional Unit	Function			Key-word	Local Failure / Functional Insufficiency	Basic Scenario	System Effect(s) in Scenario	Incorrect Vehicle Behavior	ID(s) of IVB	Possible System Cause(s)	Environmental Condition	Relevant for human driver?
	Input	Compu-tation	Output									
Sensors > Front camera > object recognition	camera image	segmen-tation	seg-mented camera image	no	segmented camera image not generated	slower turn into path challenger	challenger not detected by front camera > maneuver planning without information about the challenger	necessary braking maneuver not initiated	1	HW-failure, degradation or design fault	none	no statement
					no segments in camera imaged recognized	s/a	s/a	s/a	s/a	no night vision, lacking sensibility at dark	darkness	likely (human vision also impaired by darkness)

Using the model of the ADS from step (1), we denote in the 1st cln the considered **Functional Unit** followed by the triple (Input, Computation, Output) in the 2nd cln. Then we check whether this triple, in combination with a **Keyword** (3rd cln) exhibits incorrect behavior that leads to a **Local Failure/Functional Insufficiency** (4th cln). Afterwards, the worst-potential consequences of these are investigated (bottom-up, inductive). This is done separately for each **Basic Scenario** (5th cln). Based on this we derive negative **System Effect(s) in** this **Scenario** (6th cln) leading to **Incorrect Vehicle Behavior** (IVB) on vehicle level (7th cln). If the respective IVB was already identified in step (2.1), we denote the corresponding **ID** in the 8th cln. Otherwise, go back to step (2.1) and create a new row in the table for this IVB. Additionally, local causal chains are already identified here. If they exist, we denote **Possible System Cause(s)** (9th cln) as well as **Environmental Trigger(s)** (10th cln). Finally, in the 11th cln, we rate a human driver's ability to cope with the environmental condition. If a human driver is also likely to struggle in this situation, it can be argued that no 'new' cause of risk was identified here. For this, we propose an estimation using an ordinal scale (e.g. no statement, very unlikely, unlikely, likely very likely). Optimally, this estimation is supported by measured real-word data obtained from accident databases (e.g. GIDAS[3]), Field Operational Tests, Naturalistic Driving Studies, simulator studies or tests on proving grounds.

Step (3): Causal Chain Analysis analyzes environmental conditions that were identified as 'triggering' in step (2.2) thoroughly. While in step (2.2) we merely considered single causes and conditions, the goal here is to identify all combinations of triggering environmental conditions. The necessity (or expendability) of a Causal Chain Analysis must not be based on the above estimates for humans alone, but on expert judgment. It is performed via an extended fault tree analysis focused on identifying design- and specification faults (i.e. systemic faults) that may, in conjunction, expose hazards. These faults are inherent in the system, but usually only lead to actual hazards under additional conditions. These can be other faults in the system, but also environmental conditions.

In order to be able to identify and model them, we extend the classical fault tree analysis [20] by using inhibit-gates to specify environmental conditions (rather than classical events inside the system) as being necessary for the propagation of a fault. Using such an **environment fault tree (EFT)**, environmental conditions can be modeled as basic events that trigger higher-level faults. A hazard H (identified in step (2.1)) constitutes the Top Level Event and therefore the root of the EFT. Additionally, we assume as context the corresponding basic scenario Z. Starting from the Top Level Event H, we create a new node in the tree and connect it to the root (using AND/OR-Gates), for every deviation D from the correct behavior of an internal signal S. The hypothesized causes for these deviations are then subdivided into (random) hardware faults, (systemic) design faults in hardware or software, (systemic) specification faults, i.e. fault in some (sub-)specification, either due to incorrect assumptions (SOTIF) or lacking structural approach. Orthogonal to these classes of faults are so-called propagated faults, i.e. the input of a component is already errorenous; these can be either random or systemic faults. In order to uncover systemic faults, it is particularly useful to compare its functionality (and potential faults) to conventional vehicle operation by human drivers. Additionally, we model every combination of environmental conditions that propagate systemic faults to the underlying FU using inhibit-gates. This process is iterated until we either arrive at the level of

---

[3] German In-Depth Accident Study - www.gidas.org.

perception or the corresponding FU has no further output and thus, there cannot be any more propagated faults. This way of constructing EFTs focuses on identifying systemic faults that arise newly in the context of automated driving and are not already covered by accident databases for conventional vehicles. The first levels of a generic EFT are illustrated in Fig. 3.

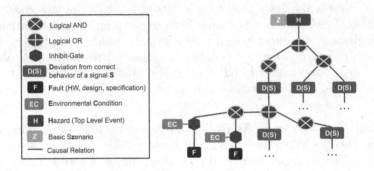

Fig. 3. Generic structure of an environment fault tree (EFT).

The input on the level of perception (i.e. sensory data) is the ADS's environment. For each type of sensor we can use its characteristics to identify environmental conditions that might cause the faults at the leafs of the EFT, e.g. rain drops, glare or reflections confusing the camera, metal reflections irritating the radar or objects with bad light reflection compromising the lidar.

Step (4): Environment Model builds a model of the environment that is first used for expressing the environmental conditions from Step (3) and later on for the translation into the output scenario specification language. This intermediate step ensures independence from the limitations of a specific scenario modeling language. The environment model has to be built with regard to the ADS and its ODD. Iterative refinements of this model may become necessary later in the process (as indicated by the dashed arrow from (5) back to (4) in Fig. 1). In the context of PEGASUS, we built an exemplary environment model for the ODD 'German Highway' which is based on the functional description of the Highway-Chauffeur [15] and the PEGASUS-ontology as described in [3].

Step (5): Derivation of Hazard Triggering Scenario Properties formalizes the previously identified environmental conditions for individual faults such that these are unambiguous and formulated in a language suitable for the description of scenarios. From this we derive properties of scenarios that potentially trigger the corresponding hazard. First, each of the EFTs from step (3) is reduced to those nodes that represent environmental conditions while maintaining the logical structure of the tree. The next step consists of a Common Cause Analysis [7] and expressing the environmental conditions in the reduced tree using the environment model from step (4). Here, it may be necessary to introduce some extra nodes (using AND-/OR gates) in the tree in case the non-formal descriptions of the environmental conditions contain implicit con-/disjunctions. If the environment model is not or only insufficiently able to represent some EC, we have to go back to step (4), as indicated by the dashed back arrow in Fig. 1, and extend our environment model accordingly. As of now, the identified environmental conditions are still described statically, although the events may have to occur chronologically in order to actually trigger the hazard. Therefore, the formalized environmental conditions are divided into discrete time steps $(\ldots, t_{-1}, t_0, t_1, \ldots)$ corresponding to scenes $S(t_i)$ such that the relative ordering $S(t_{i-1}) < S(t_i)$ describes a possible evolution of situations in time likely to trigger a hazardous event, resulting in a hazardous scenario $Sc = \{S(t_i)\}_i$. Here, $S(t_0)$ is the starting scene of the scenario, while $\{S(t_i)\}_{i<0}$ describe previous scenes and $\{S(t_i)\}_{i>0}$ describe possible evolutions of $S(t_0)$, as illustrated in Fig. 4.

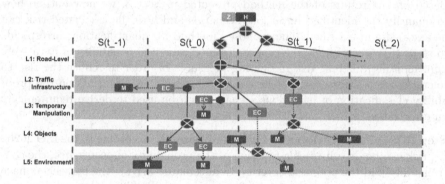

Fig. 4. Introducing chronological ordering of the events.

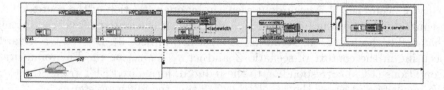

Fig. 5. A hazardous scenario specified as Traffic Sequence Chart.

For each EC, the pertinent time to trigger the hazard (according to the logical structure) must be determined. Here, the environmental conditions may extend over multiple time steps. In a final step, the identified hazardous scenarios should be specified using a sufficiently powerful language for specification of traffic scenarios which allows formal expression of environmental conditions on an adequate level of abstraction, such as Traffic Sequence Charts (TSCs) [8]. Hazardous scenarios, that are output of the presented method, are more abstract than logical scenarios, i.e. scenarios described as parameter ranges, but more concrete than functional scenarios, i.e. scenarios described using natural language (cf. [13]). Figure 5 depicts a hazardous scenario that was identified during the application of the method to the PEGASUS Highway-Chauffeur, specified as a TSC. In this scenario, the weather is foggy (impacting the Lidar) while the ego-vehicle (gray car) enters a tunnel (bad lighting conditions impacting the cameras). Subsequently, the green car, driving much slower than the ego, challenges the ego to react by turning into its path from the left (therefore, not being in the field of view of ego's front radar). The final snapshot of the TSC points at the potential hazard.

4   Method for Quantification of Hazardous Scenarios

Based on the results of the method presented in Sect. 3, we now outline how to quantify the identified hazardous scenarios and how the associated risk can be assessed and classified. The proposed method for quantification corresponds to steps (6)–(7) in Fig. 1. We propose to integrates the possibility of iteratively implementing different risk mitigating measures in order to reduce the risk to tolerable levels. Moreover, we sketc.h how imposing requirements on the probability classification of hazardous scenarios can be used to derive requirements on error rates.

Step (6): Quantification and Risk Assessment. According to the ISO 26262 [9], risk can be described as a function of the probability of occurrence, the controllability and the potential severity. In automated driving the passengers have very limited control over the driving task and controllability only applies to persons outside the ADS. Thus, it is highly questionable whether controllability should be a parameter for risk assessment of ADS. However, assessing the risk associated to a hazard by estimating its probability of occurence and its severity remains a valid strategy. We propose obtaining an upper bound on the probability of occurence of a hazardous scenario by quantification of the context, i.e. estimating the exposure of a ADS to the triggering environmental conditions that define the hazardous scenario (as identified in Sect. 3). Let H be a hazard occuring in the context of scenario Z and let $c_1, \ldots, c_m$ be the Environmental Conditions (ECs) corresponding to the reduced, formalized EFT from Step (5). We quantify and assess the risk $R(H \cap Z)$ using the following steps:

(1) Quantify the ECs $c_1, \ldots, c_m$ as **probability of occurence** per hour of driving (exposure), i.e. $e_1 = P(c_1), \ldots e_m = P(c_m) \in [0, 1]$. Optimally, this happens on the basis of data that is representative for the ADS's ODD. If that is not possible, choose upper bounds $e_1 \geq P(c_1), \ldots e_m \geq P(c_m) \in [0, 1]$ on the basis of exposure catalogues and/or expert judgement.

(2) For each EC c_i determine the **error rate** $\mu_i \in (0, 1]$, i.e. the probability that the error propagates in the fault tree under the assumptions that c_i occurs.

If to some EC an error rate cannot be associated or it is simply unknown at this point, pessimistically set $\mu_i = 1$.

(3) Every Minimal Cut Set (i.e. conjunction of triggering ECs) of the reduced, formalized environment fault tree corresponds to a sub-scenario $Z_j (j = 1 \ldots n)$ of Z. The probability of the hazard occuring in a subscenario is estimated as $P(H|Z_j) \leq \prod_{i=1,\ldots,m \,:\, U_i \in Z_j} \mu_i e_i$.

(4) Under the assumption that $Z_1, \ldots, Z_n$ exhaustively cover the scenario Z, we obtain an upper bound B for the probability of occurence of hazard H in scenario Z via $P(H \cap Z) = P(Z)P(H|Z) \leq P(Z)\sum_{j=1}^{n} P(H|Z_j) \leq P(Z)\sum_{j=1}^{n} \prod_{i=1,\ldots,m \,:\, U_i \in Z_j} \mu_i e_i =: B$.

If B is too large (especially if $B > 1$) it is not a useful bound and the process should be reiterated under use of more accurate values for e_i and μ_i. If $B \leq 1$ is reasonably small, it can be sorted into an a probability class, i.e. $B \in P_k$ for some k where $\bigcup_k P_k = (0, 1]$, according to its order of magnitude, e.g. $E_1 = (0, 10^{-7}]/h$, $E_2 = (10^{-7}, 10^{-5}]/h$, $E_3 = (10^{-5}, 10^{-3}]/h$, $E_4 = (10^{-3}, 1]/h$.

(5) Estimate the potential severity $S(H \cap Z)$ of hazard H in scenario Z and sort it into S_0, S_1, S_3, S_4 according to the classification in [9, Table B.1].

(6) Finish the risk assessment by determing whether risk mitigating measures (RMMs) are necessary, using an appropriate table featuring the dimensions 'probability' and 'severity', see e.g. Fig. 5. In contrast to the automotive safety integrity level (ASIL) assigned to a hazardous event in the ISO 26262 process, this risk assessment indicates whether RMMs have to be implemented or not (nM=no measures); and if RMMs are necessary, how impactful do they need to be ($M_1 < M_2 < M_3$) in order to reduce $R = R(H \cap Z)$ to a tolerable level (Fig. 6).

R	E_1	E_2	E_3	E_4
S_0	nM	nM	nM	nM
S_1	nM	nM	nM	M_1
S_2	nM	nM	M_1	M_2
S_3	nM	M_1	M_2	M_3

Fig. 6. Table for Risk Assessment.

Step (7): Derivation of Requirements checks whether regulatory guidelines and requirements have been complied with. The existence of such requirements/guidelines is a prerequisite for step (7), because as long as there are no guidelines for automated driving, no requirements for error rates or exposures can be derived. Reducing the risk $R(H \cap Z)$ can be realized by either (i) using tighter bounds for the exposures e_i, (ii) using more exact values for the error rates μ_i, (iii) implementing and verifying risk mitigating measures (RMMs). While changes of type (i) or (ii) require reiteration of step (6) using the updated values, the identification part of the method, i.e. steps (1)–(5), does not have to be repeated. The method indicates this possibility by the dotted arrow from step (7) back to step (6) in Fig. 1. However, this is no longer true for RMMs: they do lead to (far-reaching) changes in the ADS and can trigger a complete reiteration of the method, indicated by the dotted arrow from step (7) back to step (1).

Classes of Risk Mitigating Measures (RMMs). Each RMM can be effective by reducing exposure (E-effective) or severity (S-effective). We distinguish four classes of RMMs: (1) **Functional Safety Measures** according to ISO 26262, such as implementing redundancies, monitors, fault-resistent or reconfigurable systems, can be E-effective (reduction of error rates) or S-effective, (2) **Restriction of the ODD** to exclude hazardous scenarios is E-effective, (3) **Behavioral Safety Measures**, such as a more defensive driving profile for the ADS, can be E-effective (e.g. proactive driving) or S-effective (e.g. keeping larger safety distances, driving more slowly), (4) **External Measures**, such as better traffic infrastructure for ADS or changes in law that aid automated driving. External measures passively mitigate risks (S-effective or E-effective) in the long-run. After implementing a RMM, depending on its class, its effectiveness has to be verified appropriately. Beware that implementing RMMs may lead to crucial changes in the ADS's functional architecture, its ODD, its behavior or its environment and may therefore invalidate the results of steps (1)–(5).

Derivation of Requirements on Error Rates. Under the assumption that there exists a regulatory requirement on the E-classification of a hazardous scenario, stated as $P(H \cap Z) \in E_k$ for some k, it is possible to derive **requirements on the error rates** μ_i such that in the next iteration of step (6) evaluating $P(H \cap Z)$ will fall into probability class. More precisely, the requirement on the E-classification of $P(H \cap Z)$ induces an inequality for every sub-scenario $Z_j (j = 1, \ldots, n)$ that can be reformulated as requirements on the error rates. Even if not all of these n equalities can be satisfied, formulating these requirements gives us an idea about the required error rates. Let H be a hazard occuring in the context of scenario Z, let $e_1, \ldots, e_m$ be upper bounds for exposure and $\mu_1, \ldots, \mu_m$ the associated error rates from the previous iteration of step (6). We derive conditions on the error rates which ensure $P(H \cap Z) \in E_k$ using:

(1) Translate the requirement into a worst-case probability $p_{\max} \in (0, 1]$ such that $P(H \cap Z) \leq P(Z) \sum_{j=1}^{n} P(H|Z_j) \leq p_{\max}$. Here, $p_{\max}$ should be chosen as the upper bound of the interval E_k.

(2) From each sub-scenario $Z_j (j = 1, \ldots, n)$, derive the requirement $\prod_{i=1,\ldots,m : U_i \in Z_j} \mu_i e_i = P(H|Z_j) \leq p_{\max}/(n \cdot P(Z))$. These can be aggregated into n requirements on the product of error rates $\prod_{i=1,\ldots,m : U_i \in Z_j} \mu_i \leq p_{\max}/(n \cdot P(Z) \cdot \prod_{U_i \in Z_j} e_i)$ for $j = 1, \ldots, n$.

In total, we obtain n requirements on products of error rates. In case, the exact number of sub-scenarios n and/or the probability $P(Z)$ are unknown, upper bounds for these values should be approximated.

5   Conclusion

The approach presented in this paper is a first step towards an integrated safety assessment for automated driving systems. On the one hand, it identifies relevant scenarios for scenario based testing while on the other hand deriving requirements for the further development of the ADS. Application to the PEGA-SUS Highway-Chauffeur demonstrated usability of the method in practice, more examples can be found in [5]. A full assessment on how well it performs to identify potential hazards in comparison to e.g. STPA or existing standards will need to be evaluated thoroughly and can (as usual with safety analysis methods) only be determined later (e.g. through comparisons of hazard rates in real traffic).

For automation at SAE levels 4/5 and more complex environments (e.g. urban areas), as addressed in the PEGASUS follow-up projects 'VVMethoden' and 'SET Level 4to5', we aim to extend our method towards analyzing structural criticalities in traffic and thus combining the expert based analysis with a data driven approach. Concerning the specification of hazardous scenarios, we plan on extending Traffic Sequence Charts in order to capture more accurately the critical phenomena and associated causal relations that trigger hazardous behavior.

References

1. Abdulkhaleq, A., Baumeister, M., Böhmert, H., Wagner, S.: Missing no Interaction - using STPA for identifying hazardous interactions of automated driving systems. Int. J. Saf. Sci. **02**, 115–124 (2018)
2. Akhtar, N., Mian, A.: Threat of adversarial attacks on deep learning in computer vision: a survey. IEEE Access **6**, 14410–14430 (2018)
3. Bagschik, G., Menzel, T., Maurer, M.: Ontology based scene creation for the development of automated vehicles. In: IEEE Intelligent Vehicles Symposium (IV), pp. 1813–1820 (2018)
4. Bagschik, G., Reschka, A., Stolte, T., Maurer, M.: Identification of potential hazardous events for an Unmanned Protective Vehicle. In: IEEE Intelligent Vehicles Symposium (IV), pp. 691–697 (2016)
5. Böde, E., et al.: Identifikation und Quantifizierung von Automationsrisiken für hochautomatisierte Fahrfunktionen. Tech. report, OFFIS e.V. (2019)
6. International Electrotechnical Commission, International Electrotechnical Technical Commission, et al.: Hazard and operability studies (HAZOP Studies)-Application guide. BS IEC 61882 (2001)
7. S.I.S. Committee, et al.: Guidelines and Methods for Conducting the Safety Assessment Process on Civil Airborne System and Equipment. SAE International (1996). https://doi.org/10.4271/ARP4761
8. Damm, W., Möhlmann, E., Peikenkamp, T., Rakow, A.: A formal semantics for traffic sequence charts. In: Lohstroh, M., Derler, P., Sirjani, M. (eds.) Principles of Modeling. LNCS, vol. 10760, pp. 182–205. Springer, Cham (2018). https://doi.org/10.1007/978-3-319-95246-8_11
9. ISO: ISO 26262:2018: Road vehicles - Functional safety (2018)
10. ISO: ISO/PAS 21448: Road vehicles - Safety of the intended functionality (2019)
11. Kalra, N., Paddock, S.M.: Driving to safety: how many miles of driving would it take to demonstrate autonomous vehicle reliability? Transp. Res. Part A: Pol. Pract. **94**, 182–193 (2016)
12. Leveson, N.G.: STAMP: an accident model based on systems theory. In: Systems Thinking Applied to Safety, Engineering a Safer World (2012)

13. Menzel, T., Bagschik, G., Maurer, M.: Scenarios for development, test and validation of automated vehicles. In: IEEE Intelligent Vehicles Symposium (IV), pp. 1821–1827. IEEE (2018)
14. PEGASUS: Critical Scenarios for and by the HAD (2017). www.pegasusprojekt. de/files/tmpl/PDF-Symposium/06_Critical-Scenarios-for-and-by-the-HAD.pdf
15. PEGASUS: The Highway Chauffeur (2019). www.pegasusprojekt.de/files/tmpl/ Pegasus-Abschlussveranstaltung/04_The_Highway_Chauffeur.pdf
16. Reschka, A.: Fertigkeiten-und Fähigkeitengraphen als Grundlage des sicheren Betriebs von automatisierten Fahrzeugen im öffentlichen Straßenverkehr in städtischer Umgebung. Ph.D. thesis, TU Braunschweig (2017)
17. SAE, T.: Definitions for Terms Related to On-Road Motor Vehicle Automated Driving Systems. J3016, SAE International Standard (2014)
18. Steck, J.: Methodological Approach to Identify Automation Risks of Highly Automated Vehicles Using STPA. Technische Universität München, Masterarbeit (2018)
19. Ulbrich, S., Menzel, T., Reschka, A., Schuldt, F., Maurer, M.: Defining and substantiating the terms scene, situation, and scenario for automated driving. In: 2015 IEEE 18th International Conference on Intelligent Transportation Systems, pp. 982–988. IEEE (2015)
20. Vesely, W.E., Goldberg, F.F., Roberts, N.H., Haasl, D.F.: Fault tree handbook. Tech. report Nuclear Regulatory Commission Washington DC (1981)
21. Yan, F., Tang, T., Yan, H.: Scenario based STPA analysis in Automated Urban Guided Transport system. In: 2016 IEEE International Conference on Intelligent Rail Transportation (ICIRT), pp. 425–431 (2016)

An Integrated Approach to Support the Process-Based Certification of Variant-Intensive Systems

Lucas Bressan[1]([⊠]), André L. de Oliveira[1], Fernanda Campos[1],
Yiannis Papadopoulos[2], and David Parker[2]

[1] Universidade Federal de Juiz de Fora (UFJF), Juiz de Fora, MG, Brazil
{lucasbressan,andre.oliveira,fernanda.campos}@ice.ufjf.br
[2] University of Hull, Hull, UK
{y.i.papadopoulos,d.j.parker}@hull.ac.uk

Abstract. Component-based approaches and software product lines have been adopted by industry to manage the diversity of configurations on safety-critical software. Safety certification demands compliance with standards. ISO 26262 standard uses the concept of Automotive Safety Integrity Level (ASIL) to allocate safety requirements to components of a system under design. Compliance with standards is demonstrated through achieving those ASILs which can be very expensive when requirements are high. While achieving safety certification of variant-intensive components without being unnecessarily stringent or expensive is desirable for economy, it poses challenges to safety engineering. In this paper, we propose an approach to manage the diversity of safety goals and supporting safety certification of software components. Our approach is built upon the integration among ASIL decomposition, software process modeling, and variability management techniques. The approach supports cost-effective safety certification and the efficient tailoring of process models to components according to their ASILs. We evaluated our approach in the automotive domain. The approach is feasible in supporting the management of the diversity of safety goals, and cost-effective safety certification of software components.

Keywords: Safety certification · Safety critical software · Software development process · Model-based engineering

1 Introduction

Safety-critical systems are systems in which failures may lead to catastrophic consequences to the environment and/or to people involved with their operation. This critical nature demands addressing dependability properties, e.g., safety, reliability. Safety standards provide guidance to analyze and demonstrate safety properties at different levels of abstraction. The ISO 26262 [10] automotive standard prescribes a set of safety goals to be achieved, activities to be performed, and artefacts to be produced, depending on the criticality of an item, stated through an Automotive Safety Integrity Level (ASIL). The

© Springer Nature Switzerland AG 2020
M. Zeller and K. Höfig (Eds.): IMBSA 2020, LNCS 12297, pp. 179–193, 2020.
https://doi.org/10.1007/978-3-030-58920-2_12

development lifecycles of automotive system components (items) may change according to their assigned ASILs. Safety goals and ASILs are assigned to a function via systematic evaluation of severity, probability of occurrence and controllability of a hazardous event. Highly critical functions demand addressing more expensive safety goals and development lifecycle processes in comparison with functions that pose lower risks to the overall safety. Assigning stringent ASILs to classify the risk of failures on less critical system functions may incur in unnecessary certification costs [15, 16]. To counter this, prescriptive safety standards [10, 23] establish rules for decomposing ASILs assigned to top-level failure conditions (hazards) through contributing component faults.

Recent extensions in the scope of ISO 26262 have included support for functional safety on all road vehicles, with the introduction of requirements on trucks, buses, trailers, semi-trailers, motorcycles and their supporting processes. Such extensions introduce more variability in the development of automotive systems. Component-based approaches and Software Product Lines (SPL) have been adopted in the automotive [24] and aerospace [7] industry for their benefits of reduction of the time to market and development effort, and increased product quality [21]. SPL approaches have been extended to consider safety engineering and certification issues [15, 24]. A SPL is a variant-intensive architecture with common and variable functions shared among different systems from an application domain. Common and variable functions can be combined to derive different configurations. In variant-intensive automotive systems, variation in the design choices and usage context may impact hazard analysis, assignment of top-level safety goals (ASILs) and their decomposition through components [7, 15, 16].

Existing Model-Based Safety Assessment (MBSA) techniques provide automated support for ASIL decomposition in standalone [1, 19, 20] and variant-intensive system architectures [16]. ASIL decomposition results provide information to support the management of the diversity of safety goals and cost-effective safety-certification of system and software components in compliance with safety standards. Lifecycle models defined in cross-domain standards can be specified with the support of OMG Software & Systems Process Engineering Metamodel (SPEM) version 2.0 [17] compliant modeling tools, e.g., EPF Composer[1]. The integration of process modeling and variability management techniques [8] within AMASS[2] Platform enables variant management on EPF software process models. However, achieving safety certification and deriving EPF process models for variant-intensive software components without being unnecessarily stringent is challenging. Moreover, the manual configuration of EPF process models for each software intensive component in complex and large-scale system architectures can be burden. In addition, changes in the system design may impact on the ASIL allocation at the system level and decomposition at the component level, leading to modifications on the safety goals, and consequently the reconfiguration/generation of EPF process models for each individual component.

This paper proposes an approach, enhancing Oliveira et al. [16] work, supporting the management of the diversity of safety goals and cost-effective safety certification of variant-intensive components. It integrates MBSA and ASIL decomposition techniques, EPF Composer and BVR tools within the AMASS Platform. We evaluated our approach

---

[1] https://www.eclipse.org/epf/.
[2] https://www.amass-ecsel.eu/content/about.

in an automotive braking system. This paper is organized as follows: Sect. 2 presents the background information needed for the reader understanding our approach. Section 3 presents our approach to support process-based certification of variant-intensive software components and its evaluation in the automotive domain. In Sect. 4, we discuss the related work. Finally, Sect. 5 presents the conclusions and future work.

2 Background

2.1 ISO 26262

ISO 26262 is a safety standard that postulates requirements for functional safety on electrical and electronic systems embedded into small and medium sized (up to 3.5 tons) general purpose road vehicles [10]. It is important for the development of software intensive systems.

ASILs are initially assigned to classify the risks that hazards pose to the overall safety, during the ISO 26262 Part 3 – Concept phase [10], after 3–7 Hazard Analysis and Risk Assessment. A hazard is a *"potential source of harm caused by malfunctioning behavior of the item"*. ASILs are assigned based on the *severity* of the harm, the *probability* of exposure to operational situations, and *controllability* of each hazardous event at the 3–8: Functional safety concept. A safety goal is then derived for each hazard, according to its ASIL. Safety goals are top-level safety requirements, from which functional safety requirements are derived, thus, characterizing the Functional Safety Concept. The definition of the functional safety concept requires an analysis of how component faults contribute to hazards. Therefore, ASILs initially assigned to classify the risk posed by hazardous events are further decomposed throughout architectural component faults according to rules described in ISO 26262 Part 9. The benefits of ASIL decomposition are obtained when architectural elements are sufficiently independent. In the case where only two independent components failing together leads to the occurrence of a hazard, the responsibility of addressing an stringent ASIL D assigned to a hazard, is shared between the components (ASIL B + ASIL B). ASIL decomposition allows addressing a higher ASIL assigned to a hazard without being unnecessarily expensive.

ASIL allocation and decomposition are qualitative concepts that address systematic issues (i.e.: design and architecture) rather than random faults (i.e.: hardware reliability). If applied correctly, it allows engineers allocating lower ASILs to components and reusing third party pre-certified parts, while still meeting the safety goals derived from the ASILs assigned to hazardous events [10]. ASIL D is assigned to the most critical hazards/items that demand rigorous assessment process. On the other hand, ASIL QM is usually assigned to hazards/items that pose no safety risks, i.e., not required to satisfy or demonstrate any specific safety goals. ISO 26262 prescribes a set of safety goals, activities, guidance, and work products that should be produced at each phase per ASIL. ASIL D demands more risk reduction measures, e.g., lower failure rates and extensive software verification, compared to ASIL A.

2.2 HiP-HOPS and ASIL Decomposition

HiP-HOPS [19] is a method and tool for model-based safety analysis. HiP-HOPS supports ISO 26262 safety-lifecycle, fault tree analysis and FMEA, via semi-formal languages for specification, composition, and analysis of the system failure behavior based on a set of dependability information about the system components. Once the system models have been annotated with hazards and local failure logic, HiP-HOPS synthesizes fault trees for each hazard, and then combines them to create an FMEA for the system that can record the effect of combinations of component faults.

HiP-HOPS design optimization extension [1] implements ISO 26262 ASIL decomposition rules [10]. HiP-HOPS tool uses the information within fault trees and FMEA results and rationalizes the allocation of ASILs to hazards and their decomposition through system components, by showing how combinations of component failures lead to hazards. The HiP-HOPS design optimization capability was further extended to support ASIL decomposition through components of a variant-intensive system design [16]. This extension supports co-analysis of files containing HiP-HOPS ASIL decomposition results for each system variant, to obtain the ASILs that should be assigned to components to ensure their safe use across a set of variants relevant for the stakeholders. This is achieved by allocating the most stringent ASIL assigned to a failure mode of a component in a given system variant as the required ASIL to ensure the safely use of that component across all variants.

ASIL decomposition results are inputs for deriving ISO 26262 lifecycle process models for individual variant-intensive components without being unnecessarily stringent or expensive. A component process model comprises a set of activities, guidance and artefacts to be produced at each lifecycle phase to comply with the targeted ASIL requirements. Thus, the process of verifying the design of an ASIL C component should comprise design inspection and walkthroughs, control and data flow analyses, and simulation of the dynamic parts of the design to comply with ASIL C safety goals. The verification of the design of an ASIL D component, however, should address other safety goals demanding more costly guidance, e.g., formal verification. Component ISO 26262 life-cycle models can be specified with the support of SPEM 2.0 process modeling tools, e.g., EPF Composer, and their variability can be managed with the support of variant management tools like BVR.

2.3 EPF Composer and BVR

The EPF Composer is a tool built upon the Unified Method Architecture (UMA), which supports the specification and deployment of OMG SPEM 2.0 [17] compliant software process models [6]. UMA incorporates SPEM 2.0 and defines a library for method plugins and configurations. An EPF method plugin is divided into two categories: method content and processes. The method content describes the required steps and skills to achieve specific development goals comprising: content packages, standard custom categories [12]. Therefore, tasks, roles, work products and guidance are specified in a content package, and disciplines, domains, work product kinds, role sets and tools are standard categories. EPF Composer stores all method library content in a repository of XMI files. XMI is an OMG specification for storage and interchanging metadata in

XML format. The method content elements are semi-ordered, thus, providing the means to create a process lifecycle. EPF capability patterns are building blocks used for holding process knowledge for a given area of interest, and complete lifecycles are modeled as delivery processes. A method configuration is a subset within a method library. EPF Composer supports the generation of a method configuration as a HTML web page that can be deployed in a web server for distributed collaboration between team members.

BVR [8] is a language and toolset, built upon CVL [9], which supports standard variability modeling in Eclipse Modeling Framework (EMF) models. Since BVR defines variability orthogonally for Meta-Object Facility (MOF) [18] compliant models, e.g., EPF method plugins, communication with other tools is required to map elements of a target configuration to variability abstractions. BVR supports the generation of configurations from a base model via VSpec, Realization and Resolution editors. The *VSpec* editor supports the specification of feature models [3]. A feature is a characteristic of the system visible to the end user. In the *VSpec* model, the mandatory features are connected to the parent feature via solid lines, and dashed lines represent optionality. The VSpec also supports the specification of constraints between features using implication, alternative, and negation operators. The Resolution editor allows engineers resolving variability in a base model to obtain configuration models representing the desired product variants.

The BVR Realization editor supports engineers on mapping variability abstractions (features) to elements of a base model based on placements and replacements within fragment substitution elements. A fragment substitution removes base model elements within placements and substitutes them with replacement elements based on feature selection. BVR [8] provides an intuitive and visual representation where placement and replacement elements are highlighted in red and blue colors respectively. Fragment substitutions are executed based the variability definitions in the abstract (VSpec) and realization layers for deriving configuration models from a base model. The integration of EPF Composer and BVR within the AMASS platform allows mapping EPF method plugin elements to VSpec features in the BVR realization editor, and it supports variability resolution in method plugins.

3   The Proposed Approach

The purpose of our approach is supporting the management of the diversity of safety goals in variant-intensive platform system architectures and safety certification without being unnecessarily stringent or expensive. In this section, we present the structure (Sect. 3.1) and the steps (Sect. 3.2) of our approach. We evaluated our approach in an automotive braking system platform.

3.1   Approach Structure

Our approach provides a conceptual framework to manage the diversity of safety goals, supporting the design and safety-certification of variant-intensive platform components based on optimal and cost-effective ASIL allocation results, and automated (re)configuration of standard-compliant component process models. It relies on the integration of model-based safety analysis and ASIL decomposition, software process modeling, and variability management techniques. In this work, we considered HiP-HOPS

ASIL decomposition extension for variant-intensive systems and product lines [16], EPF Composer for safety standard process modeling, and BVR for variability management on safety goals and EPF process models. This work enhances AMASS Platform with the support for configuring component process models according to product line ASIL decomposition results provided by HiP-HOPS. In addition to the support for safety certification, our approach intends reduce the burden on configuring process models for components of large-scale and variant-intensive safety-critical software platforms.

Figure 1 shows an overview of our framework, comprising modules and their relationships in a SysML block diagram. The design of variant-intensive systems can be performed with the support of EAST-ADL [4] or MATLAB/Simulink and pure::variants integration. Preliminary ASIL decomposition for a given product variant is obtained through integration of HiP-HOPS [19] with Simulink or EAST-ADL based tools (e.g., EPM). Cross variant component lifecycle models are generated according to component ASILs provided by product line HiP-HOPS ASIL decomposition extension. The generated process models provide standard-compliant guidance for specification and verification of the design of architectural subsystems and components. Our approach requires the following input artefacts: ASIL decomposition results for a variant-intensive system design (provided by HiP-HOPS), the specification of a superset (150%) process model for the targeted standard, e.g., produced using EPF Composer, the variability specification (VSpec) and realization models for the targeted standard Process Line using BVR tool.

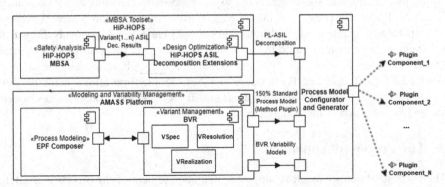

Fig. 1. Tool framework modules and their relationships.

The concept of 150% model relates to the superset approach where different 100% configuration models are obtained, via selection and resolution of variation points from a 150% model containing both base and variable elements [2]. In our case, the 150% model is an EPF/SPEM 2.0 standard Process Line. ASIL decomposition results for a variant-intensive system design are obtained from the analysis of ASIL decomposition results from multiple system configurations (variants) relevant for the stake-holders. Although the specification of 150% process model and its variability model seems to be a burden, these artefacts can be further reused across different projects and companies.

The ASIL decomposition results, 150% process model for the targeted safety standard, and the BVR variability model are input artefacts to our Process Model Configurator and Generator algorithm[3]. For each system component, our algorithm invokes the BVR API to generate a new resolution model based on the assigned ASIL and it executes the BVR resolution method. We provide the following input parameters to this method: the *VSpec*, *VResolution*, and *VRealization* models for generating an EPF method plugin that only contains the required activities, tasks and guidance to address the ASIL assigned to the component. This is done for each component of the hierarchical platform architecture. If a component contains subcomponents, the same procedure is executed to generate process models for each subcomponent. The algorithm uses a recursive call for configuring and generating process models for architectural subcomponents. This algorithm was implemented in Java and will be further deployed as an Eclipse plugin.

The generated component process models provide development guidance and the basic *claims* for structuring an argument of conformance of component's development processes with safety goals established by the standard for the targeted ASIL. The produced lifecycle artifacts to address the safety goals provide the *evidence* that substantiate *claims* of conformance with safety standards. Component *claims* provided by development lifecycle models and the produced *evidence* can be used for structuring *modular safety arguments* arguing the conformance of component development processes with safety standards, supporting the certification of platform components. Although there are similarities of our approach with what was done in EAST-ADL [4], the issue of variability is addressed more extensively here and it allows ASIL decomposition across a product line which was not done in EAST-ADL.

3.2   Variant Management and EPF Model Configuration/Generation Process

In this section, we describe the steps of our approach considering the ISO 26262 standard and an automotive variant-intensive wheel braking system.

Automotive Hybrid Braking System
The Hybrid Braking System[4] (HBS) [5] comprises one electrical motor per wheel. Figure 2 shows the HBS architecture in a block diagram. The term hybrid means the braking occurs through the combined action of electrical In-Wheel Motors (IWMs), and frictional Electromechanical Brakes (EMBs). During braking, IWMs transform the vehicle kinetic energy into electricity, which charges the power train battery, increasing the vehicle's range. The HBS architecture comprises 4 variant wheel-brake modules (subsystems), 30 components with 69 connections. Each wheel brake module comprises a Wheel Node Controller (WNC) for calculating the amount of braking torque to be produced by each wheel braking actuator, and it sends commands to EMB and IWM power converters that control EMB and IWM braking actuators. While braking, the electric power flows from the Auxiliary Battery to the EMB via EMB Power Converter; and IWM acts as a power generator providing energy for the Powertrain Battery via IWM Power Converter.

The wheel brake module is the HBS variation point. We can combine the four HBS wheel-brake modules into different ways to derive different system configurations. The

---

[3] https://github.com/bressan3/HBS-HipHops-Results/tree/master/pseudocode.

[4] https://github.com/bressan3/HBS-PL.

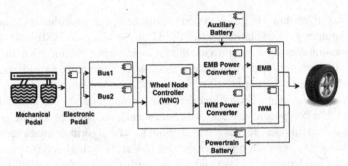

Fig. 2. Hybrid braking system architecture [5].

three HBS configurations for generating cost-effective EPF software process models are: four wheel braking (4WB), front wheel braking (FWB), and rearwheel braking (RWB). The front-wheel brake modules and their connections to other components (Fig. 2) represent the realization of FWB configuration. Different hazards with different ASILs can rise from the interaction between components in each configuration, impacting on ASIL decomposition. FWB and RWB raise two ASIL D hazards each with different causes. 4WB configuration raises two ASIL C and four ASIL D hazards [16].

The Process: Figure 3 illustrates the approach steps, in an activity diagram, to support variability management on safety goals, configuration and generation of cost-effective EPF process models for variant-intensive software components. The starting points of the process are performing ASIL decomposition for a variant-intensive system design and the specification of 150% EPF process models. These steps can be performed in parallel. After that, we should manage variability on the process model(s) specified with the support of EPF Composer. In our approach, we use BVR for variability specification (i.e., specification of ASIL features) and variability realization (i.e., linking ASIL features to their respective process activities and guidance). Finally, the ASIL decomposition results, along with the EPF process model(s), BVR VSpec and realization models are inputs to the process configurator. Finally, we derive process models for individual variant-intensive components according to their ASILs. We describe the inputs, purpose, and outputs of each step, considering the braking system and ISO 26262 *Part 6-7.4.8.1: System design and verification methods*, as follows.

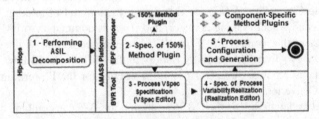

Fig. 3. Steps for configuration and generation of process variants.

1 - Performing ASIL Decomposition in variant-intensive system design: Inputs: a set of ASIL decomposition results for configurations of a variant-intensive system design relevant for the stakeholders, obtained via execution of HiP-HOPS from configuration's fault trees and FMEA. **Purpose**: analyzing ASIL decomposition results from different system configurations to identify the ASILs that should be assigned to ensure the safe use of components across configurations. In our approach, we perform this activity with the support of HiP-HOPS ASIL decomposition extension for variant-intensive system design [16]. We send a set of configuration-specific ASIL decomposition results (XML files) to the HiP-HOPS extensions performing the analysis. **Outputs**: the required ASILs to ensure the safe use of the components across system configurations. Three variants were examined from the HBS and the allocated requirements (i.e., ASILs) to 30 components from which the variants are composed. The possible space allocations that satisfy the safety requirements in each HBS variant design is large, ranging from 1 to 850. The vast majority of those allocations would incur unnecessary costs, i.e., leading to component development at unnecessarily higher ASILs. From the analysis of the results provided by HiP-HOPS, one could see many allocations where costs were higher among those representing good solutions. For example, one allocation solution for a given HBS variant prescribes a stringent ASIL D to the BrakeUnit4.IWM component. Doing the allocation of ASILs manually could incur significantly higher waste of resources. Table 1 shows the best ASIL allocation solutions for HBS components per variant (see columns "4WB", "FWB" and "RWB") provided by HiP-HOPS. We further sent these allocations to the HiP-HOPS extension [16] for analyzing the ASILs assigned to 30 HBS components in each configuration to identify the allocations that ensure the safe use of components across configurations (column "MAX ASIL").

2 - Specification of 150 % EPF Process Models: Inputs: the targeted safety standard(s), e.g., automotive ISO 26262, to be modeled using EPF Composer. **Purpose**: specifying the superset (150%) standard process model(s) based on the standard(s) documentation. This steps aims to obtain a superset model(s) with the required processes, phases, activities, tasks, roles, work products and guidance per ASIL. We recommend engineers to follow the Snowball approach [14] rules for analyzing standard(s) and specifying EPF process models. The Snowball rules describe mappings between safety standard concepts and EPF/SPEM 2.0 abstractions. The ISO 26262 *Life-Cycle, Section*, and *ASIL recommendation* concepts correspond to SPEM *processes, activities*, and *guidance* respectively. In the EPF Composer, a process is a *Delivery Process*, activity is a *Capability Pattern*, and guidance is a *Content Package: Guidance*. Each content package contains optional,

Table 1. ASIL decomposition results for HBS variant-intensive system components.

Component	MAX ASIL	4WB	FWB	RWB
Auxiliary Battery	D (4)	D(4)	D (4)	D (4)
BrakeUnit1.WheelNodeController	B (2)	A (1)	B (2)	–
BrakeUnit1.EMB Power Converter	B (2)	A (1)	B (2)	–
BrakeUnit4.IWM	B (2)	QM (0)		B (2)

recommended, and highly recommended *Tasks, Roles, Work Products*, and *Guidance* to perform an *Activity* in compliance with all ASILs. **Outputs**: 150% EPF model(s), i.e., ISO 26262 Standard Process Line. We have followed the Snowball approach for specifying the EPF method plugin for the ISO 26262 *Part 6-7.4.8.1: Verification of system design* guidance (illustrated in Fig. 6a). Guidance can be *highly recommended, recommended* or *optional* according to the targeted ASIL. We specified a method library with one content package with all the *verification of system design* guidance.

3 - Specification of the Process(es) BVR VSpec Model: Inputs: the specification of superset (150%) standard(s) process models as an EPF method library with the required processes, phases, activities, roles, work products, and guidance per ASIL. **Purpose**: specify the VSpec model, using BVR, for the targeted standard(s) based on the standard guidance and the taxonomy of safety integrity levels. For example, ISO 26262 defines five ASILs: QM, A, B, C, and D and a set of phases, activities, tasks, and recommended guidance to be followed per ASIL. Firstly, we create a *VSpec* model with an ASIL mutually exclusive feature group with the specification of each ASIL as a feature. We should also specify standard processes, phases, activities, tasks and/or guidance as features. For each task, we should create a feature group containing guidance features that represent the optional guidance to comply with each ASIL. Finally, we should specify constraints, using Basic Constraint Language (BCL) from BVR, to establish relationships between a given ASIL and its corresponding guidance feature. **Outputs**: the VSpec model for the EPF standard process model(s) with constraints highlighting the relationships between ASILs and their corresponding processes, phases, activities, tasks, work products and guidance. Figure 4 shows an excerpt of the VSpec model for the ISO 26262 Part 6-4.7.4.8.1: *Verification of system design*. We created an ASIL feature group with A, B, C, and D mutually-exclusive selection features. We also created features to represent: ISO 26262 Part 6 (process), clauses (tasks) and guidance that may present variability, e.g., Prototype generation and Formal verification features were specified as optional (Fig. 3). We specified constraints to link ASIL features to guidance features, e.g., (C or D) implies (not G_1d).

4 - Specification of Process(es) BVR Variability Realization Model: Inputs: the specification of superset (150%) standard(s) EPF process models and the VSpec model. **Purpose**: specifying mappings linking features in the VSpec model with their realization into EPF method plugin elements, e.g., content packages. For each ASIL/guidance related feature in the VSpec model, e.g., "G_1d", we specify placement and replacement

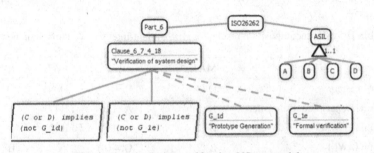

Fig. 4. System design verification VSpec model.

(elements highlighted in blue in Fig. 5b) fragments, and create a fragment substitution by following the steps described in Sect. 2.3. After that, we link the created fragment substitution to a VSpec feature. **Outputs**: the variability realization model with mappings linking VSpec features to their realization into the EPF method plugin elements as illustrated in Fig. 5b. The variability realization model comprises two fragment substitutions that represent the realization of "G_1d" and "G_1e" VSpec features in the EPF process model. When G_1d feature is selected in the resolution model, we generate an EPF method plugin excluding the Prototype Generation guideline (highlighted in red in Fig. 5a) from the method plugin. If ASIL C or D is selected, then "G_1d" and "G_1e" features are chosen.

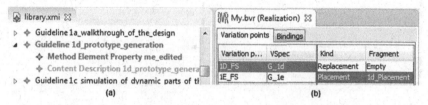

Fig. 5. BVR variability realization model. (Color figure online)

5 - Process Configuration and Generation for Variant-Intensive Components:
Inputs: ASIL decomposition results for a variant-intensive system design, 150% EPF method plugin, BVR VSpec and realization models. **Purpose**: generating EPF method plugins according to the ASILs assigned to each variant-intensive system component. We do this by providing the four aforementioned inputs to the Process Configurator and Generator program, which analyzes the ASIL decomposition results, and for each component: it selects the proper ASIL feature in the BVR resolution model, and invokes BVR resolution passing the following parameters: VSpec, resolution, realization, and the 150% EPF method plugin. These steps are performed to generate cost-effective EPF method plugins for all system components. **Outputs**: a set of EPF method plugins, one per component. We generated EPF method plugins to 30 HBS components, e.g., ASIL D Auxiliary Battery and ASIL B IWM. Only ASIL D processes contain stringent system design verification guidance. Therefore, we achieved a cost-effective configuration and generation of EPF method plugins for the HBS variant-intensive software components according to their ASILs. Figure 6 shows the base and derived component-specific method plugin models. It is important to highlight that any change in the system design and ASIL decomposition results directly impact on the structure of component's EPF process models. Our approach supports the management of the diversity on safety goals that can emerge from changes in the platform design, via automatic regeneration of EPF process models for components.

The generated EPF process models provide the *claims* for arguing conformance of development processes of individual components with the allocated ASILs. The resultant software development, verification, validation and testing artifacts from process activities, provide the evidence that substantiate *claims* of compliance with safety goals defined for the targeted component ASIL requirements. Process conformance arguments for a given component can be automatically generated, with the support for model-based techniques, from component EPF process model and the respective development artifacts.

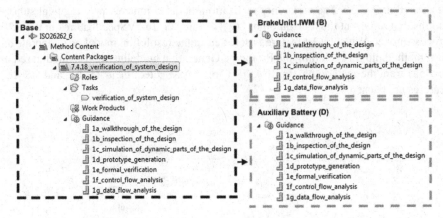

Fig. 6. Base method plugin and the generated component-specific process models.

Considering an excerpt of the EPF process model for BrakeUnit1.IWM component (Fig. 6) to address ASIL B safety goals, we can build a safety argument with a *claim* arguing the *"minimum torque is not violated while braking (ASIL B)"*. This *claim* is further supported by *sub-claims* arguing the verification of system design (ISO 26262 Part 4 Sec. 7.4.1.8) was performed following the recommended guidance to address ASIL B. These *sub-claims* argue that the following techniques were applied to verify the BrakeUnit1.IWM design: *walkthrough, inspection, model simulation, control and data flow analyses*. Finally, *design walkthrough* and *inspection, control and flow analyses reports* together with *simulation results* provide the *evidence* that substantiate the *sub-claims*. The derived safety argument for each component can be organized into modules.

Component *argument modules* can be further used to support safety certification of the whole configurable platform defined in the HBS design, instead of a specific configuration. A configurable platform allows engineers deriving different variants by combining alternative components. Thus, platform *safety argument modules* provide valid assurance *claims*, supported by *evidence* that demonstrate that the *components* are acceptably safe to operate across a set of targeted *configurations*.

4   Related Work

Existing work on this topic comprises modeling techniques [11, 13, 14] and tools [12], and ASIL allocation and decomposition [16]. Krammer et al. [13] proposed a method content approach based on the EPF Composer to define and formalize software development processes, improving process management and tailoring activities. Their approach supports the tailoring of ISO 26262 lifecycle processes according to ASILs assigned to items, thus, improving reusability and extensibility of method definitions. Our 150%

variability modeling approach on EPF process models also considers the impact of ASILs on process activities, tasks, and guidance with the advantage of using only one method content, avoiding the specification of redundant guidance in different method contents as present in the Krammer et al. [13] approach. Krammer et al. also provides mappings between EPF Composer and SPEM elements and ISO 26262 concepts, which are the basis for the "Snowball" [14] approach for extracting SPEM 2.0 process models from standards. Luo et al. [14] propose the "Snowball" approach to support the extraction of the conceptual and process models from safety standards to enable the usage of these models for demonstrating compliance and reusing assurance artefacts. This is a rule-based approach that contributes to reduce the manual work and it provides traceability between conceptual and process models, and the standard. The Snowball approach was applied in the automotive domain for specifying ISO 26262 Part 3 process models using EPF Composer. The approach can also be used to specify process models of standards from other domains, e.g., aerospace DO-178C [22], and industry IEC 61508. The work of Luo et al. is not focused on the generation of cost-effective process models for components as presented in this paper.

Javed and Gallina [12] propose the integration between the EPF Composer and BVR Tool to support variant management and resolution on EPF method libraries, establishing the concept of Safety-oriented Process Lines (SoPL). In [11], Javed et al. integrated BVR, CHESS Toolset and EPF Composer to support co-engineering and integration of SoPLs and SPLs. The approach supports the specification of traceability links between variability in the software architecture and process elements, and automatic generation of component variants and their respective process models. Although Javed and Gallina consider the association between ASILs and process activities, work products, and guidance in the BVR realization model, the generation of process models for multiple components with different ASILs demands the manual configuration of resolution models, which can be burden in the case of a complex system design. Our approach automates the configuration EPF models based on ASIL assignment. Oliveira et al. [16] propose an extension to the HiP-HOPS design optimization to support ASIL decomposition throughout components of variant-intensive system architectures. Our approach enhances Oliveira et al. [16] work with the support for variability management on safety-oriented process lines and automated configuration of EPF method plugins for components accordingly to their ASILs.

5   Concluding Remarks and Future Work

In this paper, we presented an approach to support variability management on safety goals and semi-automatic configuration and generation of software process models for certification of variant-intensive components. The approach comprises a conceptual framework, tooling integration and a systematic process. In this work, we integrated HiP-HOPS ASIL decomposition extensions [16] for variant-intensive system design, EPF Composer, and BVR tools, to support variability management on safety goals, configuration and automatic generation of cost-effective EPF process models for software components according to ASIL assignment. The process provides a set of steps to support engineers on generating cost-effective EPF process models for individual components based on ASIL decomposition results. This work contributed to reducing the costs and effort for certifying individual components within a system family. The approach automated tailoring of development processes, and enabled component safety certification in compliance with the assigned ASILs, without being unnecessarily expensive. Our approach also enabled the reuse and customization of process models across multiple projects. The generated process models provide the basis for arguing the conformance of component development processes with ASIL requirements. A limitation in our approach is the need for manually creating a 150% EPF process model for the whole standard and a BVR model. As future work, we intend to evaluate our approach in other domains, e.g., aerospace. We also intend to enable support for automatic generation of process-based conformance arguments for individual components from EPF process models. Furthermore, we intend to improve and implement the process configurator algorithm as an Eclipse plugin.

References

1. Azevedo, L.S., Parker, D., Walker, M. Papadopoulos, Y.: Automatic decomposition of safety integrity levels: optimization by tabu search. In: Proceedings of the 2nd Workshop on Critical Automotive applications : Robustness & Safety (CARS), Safecomp (2013)
2. Beuche, D., Schulze, M., Duvigneau, M.: When 150% is too much: supporting product centric viewpoints in an industrial product line. In: 20th International Systems and Software Product Line Conference on (SPLC), pp. 262–269. ACM, Beijing (2016)
3. Capilla, R., Bosch, J., Kang, K.C.: Systems and Software Variability Management: Concepts, Tools and Experiences. Springer, Heidelberg (2013). https://doi.org/10.1007/978-3-642-365 83-6
4. Chen, D.J., Mahmud, N., Walker, M., Feng, L., Lonn, H., Papadopoulos, Y.: Systems modeling with EAST-ADL for fault tree analysis through HiP-HOPS. In: IFAC Proceeding Volumes (IFAC-PapersOnline), vol. 4, pp. 91–96 (2013)
5. De Castro, R., Araújo, R.E., Freitas, D.: Hybrid ABS with electric motor and friction brakes. In: 22nd International Symposium on Dynamics of Vehicles on Roads and Tracks, Manchester, UK, pp. 1–7 (2011)
6. Eclipse. EPF Composer Manual. https://www.eclipse.org/epf/general/EPF_Installation_Tut orial_User_Manual.pdf. Accessed 28 Feb 2020
7. Habli, I., et al.: Challenges of establishing a software product line for an aerospace engine monitoring system. In: 11th International Software Product Line Conference (SPLC), pp. 193–202. ACM, Japan (2007)
8. Haugen, Ø., Øgård, O.: BVR – better variability results. In: Amyot, D., Fonseca i Casas, P., Mussbacher, G. (eds.) SAM 2014. LNCS, vol. 8769, pp. 1–15. Springer, Cham (2014). https://doi.org/10.1007/978-3-319-11743-0_1
9. Haugen, Ø., Møller-Pedersen, B., Oldevik, J., Olsen, G.K., Svendsen, A.: Adding standardized variability to domain specific languages. In: 12th International Conference on Software Product Lines, Limerick, Ireland, pp. 139–148. IEEE (2008)
10. ISO. ISO 26262: Road vehicles - Functional safet (2018)
11. Javed, M.A., Gallina, B., Carlsson, A.: Towards variant management and change impact analysis in safety-oriented process-product lines. In: Proceedings of the 34th ACM/SIGAPP Symposium on Applied Computing, pp. 2372–2375. ACM (2019)
12. Javed, M.A., Gallina, B.: Safety-oriented process line engineering via seamless integration between EPF composer and BVR tool. In: 22nd International Systems and Software Product Line Conference - Volume B, Gothenburg, Sweden, pp. 1–6. ACM (2018)

13. Krammer, M., Armengaud, E., Bourrouilh, Q.: Method library framework for safety standard compliant process tailoring. In: 37th EUROMICRO Conference on Software Engineering and Advanced Applications, Oulu, pp. 302–305. IEEE (2011)
14. Luo, Y., van den Brand, M., Engelen, L., Favaro, J., Klabbers, M., Sartori, G.: Extracting models from ISO 26262 for reusable safety assurance. In: Favaro, J., Morisio, M. (eds.) ICSR 2013. LNCS, vol. 7925, pp. 192–207. Springer, Heidelberg (2013). https://doi.org/10.1007/978-3-642-38977-1_13
15. de Oliveira, A.L., Braga, R.T.V., Masiero, P.C., Papadopoulos, Y., Habli, I., Kelly, T.: Variability management in safety-critical software product line engineering. In: Capilla, R., Gallina, B., Cetina, C. (eds.) ICSR 2018. LNCS, vol. 10826, pp. 3–22. Springer, Cham (2018). https://doi.org/10.1007/978-3-319-90421-4_1
16. Oliveira, A.L., et al.: Automatic allocation of safety requirements to components of a software product line. In: 9th IFAC Symposium on Fault Detection, Supervision and Safety for Technical Processes, Paris, France, Elsevier, vol. 48, no. 41, pp. 1309–1314 (2015)
17. OMG. Software & Systems Process Engineering Metamodel Specification (SPEM) Ver 2.0, http://www.omg.org/spec/SPEM/2.0/. Accessed 25 Feb 2020
18. OMG: Meta-Object Facility. https://www.omg.org/mof/. Accessed 01 Mar 2020
19. Papadopoulos, Y., et al.: Engineering failure analysis and design optimization with HiP-HOPS. J. Eng. Fail. Anal. 18(2), 590–608 (2011)
20. Parker, D., Walker, M., Azevedo, L.S., Papadopoulos, Y., Araújo, R.E.: Automatic decomposition and allocation of safety integrity levels using a penalty-based genetic algorithm. In: Ali, M., Bosse, T., Hindriks, K.V., Hoogendoorn, M., Jonker, C.M., Treur, J. (eds.) IEA/AIE 2013. LNCS (LNAI), vol. 7906, pp. 449–459. Springer, Heidelberg (2013). https://doi.org/10.1007/978-3-642-38577-3_46
21. Pohl, K., Böckle, G., van der Linden, F.J.: Software Product Line Engineering: Foundations, Principles, and Techniques. Springer, Heidelberg (2005). https://doi.org/10.1007/3-540-28901-1
22. RTCA: DO-178C Software Considerations in Airborne Systems and Equipment Certification. Radio Technical Commission for Aeronautics (2011)
23. S.A.E. ARP 4754A: Guidelines for development of Civil Aircraft and Systems (2010)
24. Schulze, M., Mauersberger, J., Beuche, D.: Functional safety and variability: can it be brought together? In: 17th International SPLC, pp. 236–243. ACM, New York (2013)

Artificial Intelligence (AI) and Safety Assurance

SafeML: Safety Monitoring of Machine Learning Classifiers Through Statistical Difference Measures

Koorosh Aslansefat[1]([✉]) [iD], Ioannis Sorokos[2] [iD], Declan Whiting[1,3] [iD],
Ramin Tavakoli Kolagari[4] [iD], and Yiannis Papadopoulos[1] [iD]

[1] University of Hull, Kingston upon Hull HU6 7RX, UK
{k.aslansefat-2018,d.whiting-2018,y.i.papadopoulos}@hull.ac.uk
[2] Fraunhofer Institute for Experimental Software Engineering (IESE),
Fraunhofer-Platz 1, 67663 Kaiserslautern, Germany
ioannis.sorokos@iese.fraunhofer.de
[3] APD Communications, Kingston upon Hull HU1 1RR, UK
[4] Nuremberg Tech, Keßlerplatz 12, 90489 Nürnberg, Germany
ramin.tavakolikolagari@th-nuernberg.de

Abstract. Ensuring safety and explainability of machine learning (ML) is a topic of increasing relevance as data-driven applications venture into safety-critical application domains, traditionally committed to high safety standards that are not satisfied with an exclusive testing approach of otherwise inaccessible black-box systems. Especially the interaction between safety and security is a central challenge, as security violations can lead to compromised safety. The contribution of this paper to addressing both safety and security within a single concept of protection applicable during the operation of ML systems is active monitoring of the behavior and the operational context of the data-driven system based on distance measures of the Empirical Cumulative Distribution Function (ECDF). We investigate abstract datasets (XOR, Spiral, Circle) and current security-specific datasets for intrusion detection (CICIDS2017) of simulated network traffic, using distributional shift detection measures including the Kolmogorov-Smirnov, Kuiper, Anderson-Darling, Wasserstein and mixed Wasserstein-Anderson-Darling measures. Our preliminary findings indicate that there is a meaningful correlation between ML decisions and the ECDF-based distances measures of the input features. Thus, they can provide a confidence level that can be used for a) analyzing the applicability of the ML system in a given field (safety/security) and b) analyzing if the field data was maliciously manipulated. (Our preliminary code and results are available at https://github.com/ISorokos/SafeML.)

Keywords: Safety · SafeML · Machine Learning · Deep Learning · Artificial Intelligence · Statistical difference · Domain adaptation

© Springer Nature Switzerland AG 2020
M. Zeller and K. Höfig (Eds.): IMBSA 2020, LNCS 12297, pp. 197–211, 2020.
https://doi.org/10.1007/978-3-030-58920-2_13

1   Introduction

Machine Learning (ML) is expanding rapidly in numerous applications. In parallel with this rapid growth, the expansion of ML towards dependability-critical applications raises societal concern regarding the reliability and safety assurance of ML. For instance, ML in medicine by [28], in autonomous systems e.g. self-driving cars by [6,9], in military [25], and in economic applications by [7]. In addition, different organizations and governmental institutes are trying to establish new rules, regulations and standards for ML, such as in [1,15,20].

While ML is a powerful tool for enabling data-driven applications, its unfettered use can pose risks to financial stability, privacy, the environment and in some domains even life. Poor application of ML is typically characterized by poor design, misspecification of the objective functions, implementation errors, choosing the wrong learning process, or using poor or non-comprehensive datasets for training. Thus, safety for ML can be defined as a set of actions to prevent any harm to humanity by ML failures or misuse. However, there are many perspectives and directions to be defined for ML safety. In fact, [2] have addressed different research problems of certifying ML systems operating in the field. They have categorized safety issues into five categories: a) safe exploration, b) robustness to distributional shift, c) avoiding negative side effects, d) avoiding "reward hacking" and "wire heading", e) scalable oversight. We find this categorization to facilitate the framing of ML safety. In the work presented here, we will be focusing on addressing distributional shift, however using a non-standard interpretation. Distributional shift is usually interpreted as the gradual deviation of the initial state of learning of an ML component and its ongoing state as it performs online learning. As will be shown later, distributional shift will instead be used by our approach to evaluate the distance between the training and observed data of an ML component.

Statistical distance measures can be considered as a common method to measure distributional shift. Furthermore, in modern ML algorithms like Generative Adversarial Nets (GANs), statistical distance or divergence measures are applied as a loss function, such as the Jensen-Shannon divergence [12], the Wasserstein distance [13], and the Cramer distance [5]. For dimension reduction, the t-SNE (t-distributed stochastic neighbour embedding) algorithm uses the Kullback-Leibler divergence as a loss function [27].

This paper studies the applicability of safety-security monitoring based on statistical distance measures on the robustness of ML systems in the field.

The basis of this work is a modified version of the statistical distance concept to allow the comparison of the dataset during the ML training procedure and the observed dataset during the use of the ML classifier in the field. The calculation of the distance is carried out in a novel controller-in-the-loop procedure to estimate the accuracy of the classifier in different scenarios. By exploiting the accuracy estimation, applications can actively identify situations where the ML component may be operating far beyond its trained cases, thereby risking low accuracy, and adjust accordingly. The main advantage of this approach is its flexibility in potentially handling a large range of ML techniques, as it is not dependent on the ML approach. Instead, the approach focuses on the quality of the training data and its deviation from the field data. In a comprehensive case study we have analyzed the possibilities and limitations of the proposed approach.

Our analysis of the research literature did not reveal any reference to existing publications dealing with the safety, security and accuracy of ML-based classification using statistical measures of difference. Nevertheless, there are publications that provide a basis for comparison with the current study. A Resampling Uncertainty Estimation (RUE)-based algorithm has been proposed by [23] to ensure the point-wise reliability of the regression when the test or field dataset is different from the training dataset. The algorithm has created prediction ensembles through the modified gradient and Hessian functions for ML-based regression problems. An uncertainty wrapper for black-box models based on statistical measures has been proposed by [17]. Hobbhahn M. et al. [14] have proposed a method to evaluate the uncertainty of Bayesian Deep Networks classifiers using Dirichlet distributions. The results were promising but to a limited class of classifiers (Bayesian Network-based classifiers). A new Key Performance Index (KPI), the Expected Odds Ratio (EOR) has been introduced in [10]. This KPI was designed to estimate empirical uncertainty in deep neural networks based on entropy theories. However, this KPI has not yet been applied to other types of machine learning algorithms. A comprehensive study on dataset shift has been provided by [21] and the dataset issues such as projection and projectability, simple and prior probability shift are discussed there. However, the mentioned study does not address the use of statistical distance and error bound to evaluate the dataset shift, in contrast to the work presented here.

In Sect. 2, the problem definition is provided. The proposed method is addressed in Sect. 3. Numerical results are demonstrated in Sect. 4 with a brief discussion. The capabilities and limitations of the proposed method are summarised in Sect. 5 and the paper terminates with a conclusion in Sect. 6.

2   Problem Definition

Classification ML algorithms are typically employed to categorize input samples into predetermined categories. For instance, abnormality detection can be performed by detecting whether a given sample falls within known ranges i.e. categories. A simple example of a classifier for 1-dimensional input can be a line or threshold. Consider a hypothetical measurement t (e.g. time, temperature etc.) and a classifier D based on it, as shown in Fig. 1-(a) and defined as (1). Note that Fig. 1 shows the true classes of the input.

$$D(t) = \begin{cases} Class1, & \text{if } 0 < n \leq 100 \\ Class2, & \text{if } 100 < n \leq 200 \end{cases} \tag{1}$$

The classifier $D(t)$ can predict two classes which represent, in this example, the normal and abnormal state of a system. From measurement input 0 to 100,

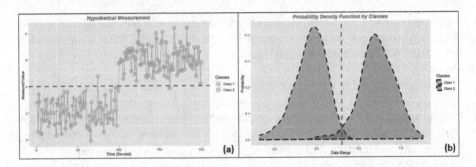

Fig. 1. (a) A hypothetical measurement (i.e. from 0 to 100 is Class 1 and from 101 to 200 is Class 2) (b) The estimated probability density function for both Class 1 and Class 2 with a classifier threshold equal to four

the sample is considered to fall under class 1 and from above 100 to 200 under class 2. The Probability Density Functions (PDFs) of the (true) classes can be estimated as shown in Fig. 1-(b). In this figure, the threshold of the classifier has been represented with a red vertical dash-line and value of four. The area with an overlap in this figure can cause false detection to occur, as the classifier misclassifies the input belonging to the opposite class. These type of misclassifications are also known as false positive/type I errors (e.g. when misclassifying input as being class 1) and false-negative/type II errors (e.g. when misclassifying input as not being class 1). Considering Fig. 1-(b) of probability density functions, we notice that in the area where the two probability density functions merge, misclassifications and thus errors can occur. The probability of the error or misclassification can be calculated with (2) [26]. Note that the error probability is also related to the threshold value (x considered as the threshold value), (for more details see [4]).

$$P\left(error\right) = \int_{-\infty}^{+\infty} P\left(error|x\right) P\left(x\right) dx \qquad (2)$$

In listing (2), the $P\left(error|x\right)$ can be calculated as the minimum of both PDFs as (3). The minimization is subject to variation of threshold value from $-\infty$ to $+\infty$.

$$P\left(error|x\right) = min\left[P\left(Class\ 1|x\right),\ P\left(Class\ 2|x\right)\right] \qquad (3)$$

By dividing the space into two regions as R_1 and R_2, the probability of error can be written in two parts.

$$P\left(error\right) = P\left(x \in R_1, Class\ 1\right) + P\left(x \in R_2, Class\ 2\right)$$

$$= \int_{R_1} P\left(x|Class\ 1\right) P\left(Class\ 1\right) dx + \int_{R_2} P\left(x|Class\ 2\right) P\left(Class\ 2\right) dx \qquad (4)$$

To ease the minimization problem, consider the following inequality rule [11].

$$min\left[a, b\right] \le a^\lambda b^{1-\lambda}\ where\ a, b\ \ge 0\ and\ 0 \le \alpha \le 1 \qquad (5)$$

Equation (3) can be rewritten as (6). Note that in (5) the "$\leq$" can be considered as "$=$", when we consider the worst-case scenario or upper bound error.

$$P(error|x) = min[P(Class\ 1|x),\ P(Class\ 2|x)] =$$
$$min\left[\frac{P(x|Class\ 1)\ P(Class\ 1)}{P(x)},\ \frac{P(x|Class\ 2)\ P(Class\ 2)}{P(x)}\right] \quad (6)$$

Using the inequality rule and Eq. (6), the conditional probability of error can be derived as (7).

$$P(error|x) \leq \left(\frac{P(x|Class\ 1)\ P(Class\ 1)}{P(x)}\right)^{\lambda} \left(\frac{P(x|Class\ 2)\ P(Class\ 2)}{P(x)}\right)^{1-\lambda} \quad (7)$$

The Eq. (8) can be obtained using Eqs. (2) and (7).

$$P(error) \leq (P(Class\ 1))^{\lambda} (P(Class\ 2))^{1-\lambda}$$
$$\int_{-\infty}^{+\infty} (P(x|Class\ 1))^{\lambda} (P(x|Class\ 2))^{1-\lambda} dx \quad (8)$$

In safety assurance, it is important to consider the worst-case scenario which can lead us to (9), known as the "Chernoff upper bound of error" [11].

$$P(error) = P(Class\ 1)^{\lambda} P(Class\ 2)^{1-\lambda}$$
$$\int_{-\infty}^{+\infty} P(x|Class\ 1)^{\lambda} P(x|Class\ 2)^{1-\lambda} dx \quad (9)$$

If the probability distributions of the features obey normal or exponential distribution families, the integral part of (9) can be solved through (10) [11].

$$\int_{-\infty}^{+\infty} P(x|Class\ 1)^{\lambda} P(x|Class\ 2)^{1-\lambda} dx = e^{-\theta(\lambda)} \quad (10)$$

The $\theta(\lambda)$ can be calculated using (11) where μ and Σ are the mean vector and variance matrix of each class respectively.

$$\theta(\lambda) = \frac{\lambda(1-\lambda)}{2} [\mu_2 - \mu_1]^T [\lambda\Sigma_1 + (1-\lambda)\Sigma_2]^{-1} [\mu_2 - \mu_1]$$
$$+ 0.5\ log\frac{|\lambda\Sigma_1 + (1-\lambda)\Sigma_2|}{|\Sigma_1|^{\lambda} |\Sigma_2|^{(1-\lambda)}} \quad (11)$$

Considering $\alpha = 0.5$ the Eq. (11) effectively becomes the Bhattacharyya distance. It can be proven that this value is the optimal value when $\Sigma_1 = \Sigma_2$ [11,18]. In this study, for simplicity, the Bhattacharyya distance will be used to demonstrate the approach. It should be noted that there may be cases where the estimated error bound is lower than the real value. However, this is acceptable as an overestimation of the classifier error would not introduce safety concerns (although it may impact performance). As the $P(error)$ and $P(correct)$ are complementary, the probability of having a correct classification can be calculated using (12).

$$P\left(correct\right) = 1 - \sqrt{P\left(Class\ 1\right)P\left(Class\ 2\right)}\ e^{-\theta(\lambda)} \tag{12}$$

The Chernoff upper bound of error is usually used as a measure of separability of two classes of data, but in the above context, Eq. (12) measures the similarity between two classes. In other words, in an ideal situation, by comparing the $P\left(error\right)$ of a class, with itself, the response should be equal to one while $P\left(correct\right)$ should be zero. The intuitive explanation is to determine whether the distribution of the data during training is statistically the same as the distribution observed in the field (or not).

Assuming $P\left(Class\ 1\right) = P\left(Class\ 2\right)$, the integral part of $P\left(error\right)$ can be converted to the cumulative distribution function as (13).

$$
\begin{aligned}
P\left(error\right) &= \left(\int_{-\infty}^{T} P_{Class\ 1}\left(x\right)dx + \int_{T}^{\infty} P_{Class\ 2}\left(x\right)dx\right) \\
&= \left(\int_{-\infty}^{T} P_{Class\ 1}\left(x\right)dx + \int_{T}^{+\infty} P_{Class\ 2}\left(x\right)dx\right) \\
&= \left(F_{Class\ 1}\left(T\right) + \left(1 - F_{Class\ 2}\left(T\right)\right)\right) \\
&= 1 - \left(F_{Class\ 2}\left(T\right) - F_{Class\ 1}\left(T\right)\right)
\end{aligned}
\tag{13}
$$

Equation (13) shows that the probability of error (and also accuracy) and statistical difference between two Cumulative Distribution Functions (CDF) of two classes are related. Using this fact and considering that the Empirical CDFs of each class is available, ECDF-based statistical measures such as the Kolmogorov-Smirnov distance (Eq. 14) and similar distance measures can be used [8,22].

$$P(error) \approx \sup_{x}\left(F_{Class\ 2}\left(x\right) - F_{Class\ 1}\left(x\right)\right) \tag{14}$$

It should be mentioned that such ECDF-based distances are not bounded between zero and one and, in some cases, need a coefficient to be adjusted as a measure for accuracy estimation. More discussion regarding the ECDF-based statistical distances can found at [3].

3   SafeML Method

To begin with, we should note that while this study focuses on ML classifiers, the proposed approach does not prohibit application on ML components for regression tasks either. Figure 2 illustrates how we envision the approach to be applied practically. In this flowchart, there are two main sections; the training phase and the application phase. A) The 'training' phase is an offline procedure in which a trusted dataset is used to train the ML algorithm. Once training is complete, the classifier's performance is measured with user-defined KPIs. Meanwhile, the

PDF and statistical parameters of each class are also computed and stored for future comparison in the second phase. B) The 'application' phase is an online procedure in which real-time and unlabelled data is provided to the system. For example, consider an autonomous vehicle's machine vision system. Such a system has been trained to detect obstacles (among other tasks), so that the vehicle can avoid collisions with them. A critical issue to note in the application phase is that the incoming data is unlabeled. So, it cannot be assured that the classifier will perform as accurately as it had in during the training phase. As input samples are collected, the PDF and statistical parameters of each class can be estimated. The system requires enough samples to reliably determine the statistical difference, so a buffer of samples may have to be accumulated before proceeding. Using the modified Chernoff error bound in 12, the statistical difference of each class between the training phase and the application phase is compared. If the statistical difference is very low, the classifier results and accuracy can be trusted. In the example mentioned above, the autonomous vehicle would continue its operation in this case. Instead, if the statistical difference is greater than the threshold, the classifier results and accuracy are no longer considered valid (as the difference between the training and observed data is too great). In this case, the system should use an alternative approach or notify a human operator. In the above example, the system could ask the driver to take over control of the vehicle.

4   Case Studies

In this section, the proposed method described in Sect. 3 is applied on typical synthetic benchmarks for ML classification. The proposed method has been implemented in three different programming languages including R, Python and MATLAB. Three well-known ML classification benchmarks have been selected: a) the XOR dataset, b) the Spiral dataset and c) the Circle dataset. Each dataset has two features (i.e. input variables) and two classes. Figure 3 illustrates the scatter plots of the selected benchmarks. More examples and benchmarks are available at SafeML Github Repository.

4.1   Methodology for Evaluation Against Benchmark Datasets

To start the ML-based classification, 80% of each dataset was used for training and testing and 20% of the dataset has been used for validation, with 10-fold cross-validation. Both linear and nonlinear classifiers have been selected for classification. The Linear Discriminant Analysis (LDA) and the Classification And Regression Tree (CART) are used as linear methods. Moreover, the Random Forest (RF), K-Nearest Neighbours (KNN) and Support Vector Machine (SVM) are applied as nonlinear methods. As KPIs, the accuracy and Kappa measure are used to measure the performance of each classifier. Finally, as Empirical Cumulative Distribution Function (ECDF)-based statistical

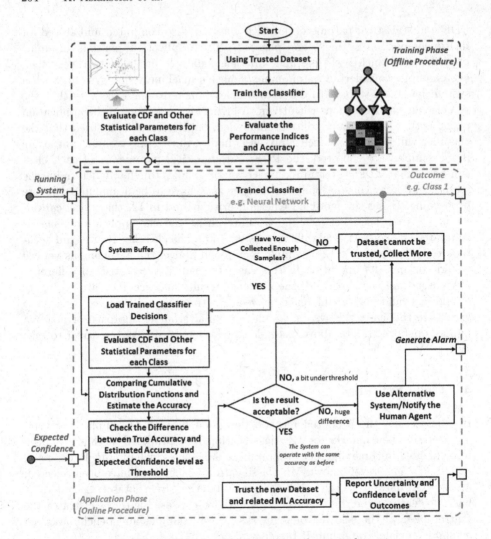

Fig. 2. Flowchart of the proposed approach

distance measures, the Kolmogorov-Smirnov Distance (KSD), Kuiper Distance, Anderson-Darling Distance (ADD), Wasserstein Distance (WD), and a combination of ADD and Wasserstein-Anderson-Darling Distance (WAD) have been selected for evaluation.

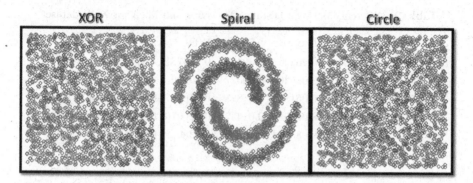

Fig. 3. Scatter plot of XOR, spiral and circle benchmarks

XOR Dataset: The XOR dataset has two features and two classes in which features have the same mean and variance characteristics. Table 1 compares the estimated accuracy, based on the ECDF measures, with the Minimum True Accuracy (MTA) and the Average True Accuracy (ATA) over 10 folds. For instance, the second column of this table provides the estimated accuracy based on the KSD measure. As a matter of safety, MTA is more important because it represents the worst-case scenarios, where the lowest accuracy may be experienced and impact safety. We observe that the KSD measure reports low accuracy for the LDA classifier (.77). Instead, the ADD and WAD measures significantly overestimate the accuracy of the LDA.

Table 1. Comparison of estimated accuracies vs minimum true accuracy for XOR dataset

Method	KSD	Kuiper	ADD	WD	WAD	BD	MTA	ATA
LDA	0.772217	0.770600	0.902818	0.755064	0.985666	0.154506	0.50833	0.59121
CART	0.928179	0.921982	0.987722	0.92545	0.995211	0.497243	0.98744	0.99415
KNN	0.93057	0.913063	0.993151	0.958768	0.997076	0.497102	0.97489	0.98666
SVM	0.931045	0.917586	0.993489	0.95819	0.997064	0.496731	0.97916	0.98791
RF	0.92962	0.910749	0.992742	0.957821	0.997018	0.496856	0.99583	0.99833

Based on Table 1, Table 2 represents the (absolute) difference between accuracy estimations of each measure and the MTA of each classifier. The ADD, WD and WAD measures have the best accuracy estimations overall. In particular, when a LDA classifier is used, the WD measure provides an estimated accuracy with comparatively less error.

Table 2. Difference between Distance Measures and MTA for XOR dataset

Method	KSD	Kuiper	ADD	WD	WAD	BD
LDA	0.263883	0.262267	0.394484	0.246731	0.477333	0.353828
CART	0.059269	0.065466	0.000274	0.06199	0.007763	0.490205
KNN	0.044320	0.061833	0.018256	0.016127	0.02218	0.477793
SVM	0.048122	0.061580	0.014322	0.020976	0.017897	0.482310
RF	0.066207	0.085084	0.003092	0.038012	0.001184	0.499102

Spiral Dataset: Similar to the XOR dataset, the proposed method can be applied for the spiral dataset. Table 3 presents difference between ECDF-based distance measures and minimum true accuracy for this dataset. For brevity, for this dataset and the next one, only the difference table is provided. Based on this table, the KSD and Kuiper distance measures have better estimation for accuracy of the classifiers for the spiral dataset.

Table 3. Difference between Distance Measures and MTA for Spiral dataset

Method	KSD	Kuiper	ADD	WD	WAD	BD
LDA	0.099447	0.088252	0.269975	0.248396	0.528852	0.043445
CART	0.056131	0.031092	0.149191	0.09477	0.158529	0.355675
KNN	0.047526	0.075598	0.001468	0.014756	0.002734	0.496559
SVM	0.047526	0.075598	0.001468	0.014756	0.002734	0.496608
RF	0.024471	0.050261	0.018778	0.003885	0.019643	0.479893

Circle Dataset: The circle dataset has similar statistical characteristics with the spiral dataset. Table 4 provides the difference between ECDF-based distance measures and MTA for this dataset. As can be seen, the worst accuracy estimation is related to the accuracy estimation of the LDA classifier. For the LDA, the Kuiper distance estimates with less error, with the KSD and WD being in second and third place respectively.

4.2 Security Dataset

This case-study applies the proposed method towards the CICIDS2017 dataset, which was originally produced by [24] at the Canadian Institute for Cyber Security (CICS). The purpose of the dataset is to act as an aide to the development and research of anomaly-based intrusion detection techniques for use in Intrusion Detection Systems (IDSs) and Intrusion Prevention Systems (IPSs) [19]. The labelled dataset includes both benign (Monday) and malicious (Tuesday, Wednesday, Thursday, Friday) network activity. The benign network traffic is

Table 4. Difference between distance measures and MTA for Circle dataset

Method	KSD	Kuiper	ADD	WD	WAD	BD
LDA	0.329391	0.250345	0.412382	0.347450	0.49826	0.236670
CART	0.114312	0.019111	0.168596	0.099549	0.24322	0.455675
KNN	0.004833	0.037554	0.027649	0.010871	0.02775	0.498459
SVM	0.016133	0.043604	0.019147	0.001695	0.01935	0.498808
RF	0.004663	0.034529	0.027776	0.012814	0.02782	0.468893

simulated by abstraction of typical user activity using a number of common protocols such as HTTP, HTTPS, FTP and SHH. Benign and malicious network activity is included as packet payloads in packet capture format (PCAPS).

Wednesday Attack: This attack occurred on Wednesday, July 5, 2017, and different types of attacks on the availability of the victim's system have been recorded, such as DoS/DDoS, DoS slowloris (9:47–10:10 a.m.), DoS Slowhttptest (10:14–10:35 a.m.), DoS Hulk (10:43–11 a.m.), and DoS GoldenEye (11:10–11:23 a.m.). Regarding the cross-validation, a hold-out approach has been used, in which 70% of data has been randomly extracted for testing and training and the rest has been used for accuracy estimation. Additionally, traditional classifiers including 'Naive Bayes', 'Discriminant Analysis', 'Classification Tree', and 'Nearest Neighbor' have been used.

Figure 4 has been generated over 100 iterations. For each iteration, 70% of the data has been randomly extracted for testing and training and the rest has been used for accuracy estimation. Figure 4 shows the box plot of the statistical distance measurements vs. the evaluated accuracy over 100 iterations. By observing the average values (red lines) of each box plot, the relationship between each measure and the average change in accuracy can be understood. In addition, this plot shows which method has less variation. For instance, the Kuiper distance and WD have the best performance while Chernoff has the poorest performance.

Thursday Attack: This attack occurred on Thursday, July 6, 2017, and various attacks, such as the Web Attack – Brute Force (9:20–10 a.m.), Web Attack – XSS (10:15–10:35 a.m.), and Web Attack – Sql Injection (10:40–10:42 a.m.) have been recorded.

Similar to the previous example, accuracy vs. distances have been generated over 100 times and the box plot of Fig. 5 can be seen. In this figure, the Kolmogorov-Smirnov, Kuiper and Wassertein distance measures have a better performance, however, their decision variance is a bit high.

The rest of results for Security Intrusion Detection in the CICIDS2017 dataset are available in the SafeML Github Repository. Using Pearson's correlation between the class labels of Wednesday's dataset and the statistical ECDF-based distances KSD, KD, ADD, WD, and WAD had 0.6279, 0.5935, 0.6478, 0.7364, and 0.7326 respectively. We note that the WD and WAD distance measures are more strongly correlated with the class labels. P-values for

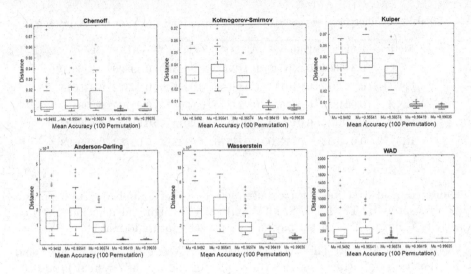

Fig. 4. Box plot of statistical distance measures vs. accuracy over 100 iterations

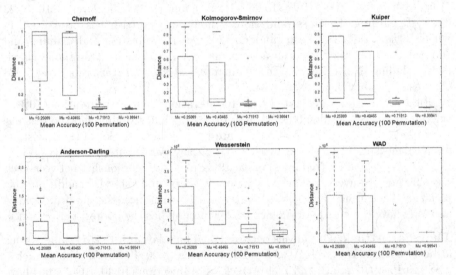

Fig. 5. Box plot of statistical distance measures vs. accuracy over 100 iterations for Thursday Security Intrusion Detection in CICIDS2017 dataset

the above correlations were evaluated to be zero, thereby validating the correlation hypotheses above.

5   Discussion

Overall, our preliminary investigation indicates that statistical distance measures offer the potential for providing a suitable indicator for ML performance, specifically for accuracy estimation. In particular, we further denote the following capabilities and limitations for the proposed approach.

5.1 Capabilities of SafeML

- By modifying the existing statistical distance and error bound measures, the proposed method enables estimation of the accuracy bound of the trained ML algorithm in the field with no label on the incoming data.
- A novel human-in-loop monitoring procedure is proposed to certify the ML algorithm during operation. The procedure has three levels of operation: I) nominal operation allowed with assured ML-accuracy based on the distance estimation, II) buffering data samples to generate estimation, and III) low estimated accuracy estimated, leading to external intervention by automated/human controller being needed.
- The proposed approach is easy to implement, and can support a variety of distributions (i.e. exponential and normal distribution families).
- The outcome of the proposed approach can be used as an input for runtime safety analysis in adaptive systems [16]

5.2 Limitations of the Proposed Method

- The proposed algorithm is currently only tackling the safety evaluation problem of the machine-learning-based classification. However, we believe it can be easily expanded for clustering, dimension reduction or any problem that can be evaluated through statistical difference.
- Some of the machine learning algorithms can be robust to a certain distributional shift or variation in the dataset distribution. This may limit the effectiveness of the discussed distance measures. That being said, the proposed measures can then be used as additional confirmation of the robustness, contributing to certification arguments.

6   Conclusion

The expansion of ML applications to safety-critical domains is a major research question. We investigate the problem of context applicability of an ML classifier, specifically the distributional shift between its training and observed data. We have identified and evaluated sets of statistical distance measures that can provide estimated upper error bounds in classification tasks based on the training and observed data distance. Further, we have proposed how this approach can be used as part of safety and security-critical systems to provide active monitoring and thus improve their robustness. The overall most effective distance measure for XOR, Spiral and Circle datasets was identified to be the Kolmogorov-Smirnov and for security dataset was identified as Wasserstein Distance. The proposed human-in-the-loop procedure uses this statistical distance measure to monitor the estimated accuracy of the ML component and notify its AI or human controller when the deviation exceeds specific boundaries. The study is still in its early stages, but we believe the results to offer a promising starting point. The strengths and weaknesses of the proposed approach are discussed in the previous section. As a future research, we aim to use SafeML for explainable artificial intelligence purposes.

Acknowledgements. This work was supported by the DEIS H2020 Project under Grant 732242. We would like to thank EDF Energy R&D UK Centre, AURA Innovation Centre and the University of Hull for their support.

References

1. Alexander, R., et al.: Safety assurance objectives for autonomous systems (2020)
2. Amodei, D., Olah, C., Steinhardt, J., Christiano, P., Schulman, J., Mané, D.: Concrete problems in AI safety. arXiv preprint arXiv:1606.06565 (2016)
3. Aslansefat, K.: How to make your classifier safe (2020). https:// towardsdatascience.com/how-to-make-your-classifier-safe-46d55f39f1ad
4. Aslansefat, K., Gogani, M.B., Kabir, S., Shoorehdeli, M.A., Yari, M.: Performance evaluation and design for variable threshold alarm systems through semi-Markov process. ISA Trans. **97**, 282–295 (2020)
5. Bellemare, M.G., et al.: The Cramer distance as a solution to biased Wasserstein gradients. arXiv preprint arXiv:1705.10743 (2017)
6. Burton, S., Habli, I., Lawton, T., McDermid, J., Morgan, P., Porter, Z.: Mind the gaps: assuring the safety of autonomous systems from an engineering, ethical, and legal perspective. Artif. Intell. **279**, 103201 (2020)
7. Davenport, T.H., Brynjolfsson, E., McAfee, A., Wilson, H.J.: Artificial Intelligence: The Insights You Need from Harvard Business Review. Harvard Business Press, Boston (2019)
8. Deza, M.M., Deza, E.: Distances in probability theory. Encyclopedia of Distances, pp. 257–272. Springer, Heidelberg (2014). https://doi.org/10.1007/978-3-662-44342-2_14
9. Du-Harpur, X., Watt, F., Luscombe, N., Lynch, M.: What is AI? Applications of artificial intelligence to dermatology. Br. J. Dermatol. 1–8 (2020). https://doi.org/10.1111/bjd.18880
10. Finlay, C., Oberman, A.M.: Empirical confidence estimates for classification by deep neural networks. arXiv preprint arXiv:1903.09215 (2019)
11. Fukunaga, K.: Introduction to Statistical Pattern Recognition. Elsevier, Amsterdam (2013)
12. Goodfellow, I., et al.: Generative adversarial nets. In: Advances in Neural Information Processing systems, pp. 2672–2680 (2014)
13. Gulrajani, I., Ahmed, F., Arjovsky, M., Dumoulin, V., Courville, A.C.: Improved training of Wasserstein GANs. In: Advances in Neural Information Processing Systems, pp. 5767–5777 (2017)
14. Hobbhahn, M., Kristiadi, A., Hennig, P.: Fast predictive uncertainty for classification with Bayesian deep networks. arXiv preprint arXiv:2003.01227 (2020)
15. ISO: Iso/iec jtc 1/sc 42: Artificial intelligence (2017). https://www.iso.org/committee/6794475.html. Accessed 10 May 2020

16. Kabir, S., et al.: A runtime safety analysis concept for open adaptive systems. In: Papadopoulos, Y., Aslansefat, K., Katsaros, P., Bozzano, M. (eds.) IMBSA 2019. LNCS, vol. 11842, pp. 332–346. Springer, Cham (2019). https://doi.org/10.1007/978-3-030-32872-6_22

17. Kläs, M., Sembach, L.: Uncertainty wrappers for data-driven models. In: Romanovsky, A., Troubitsyna, E., Gashi, I., Schoitsch, E., Bitsch, F. (eds.) SAFE-COMP 2019. LNCS, vol. 11699, pp. 358–364. Springer, Cham (2019). https://doi.org/10.1007/978-3-030-26250-1_29

18. Nielsen, F.: The chord gap divergence and a generalization of the Bhattacharyya distance. In: 2018 IEEE International Conference on Acoustics, Speech and Signal Processing (ICASSP), pp. 2276–2280. IEEE (2018)

19. Panigrahi, R., Borah, S.: A detailed analysis of cicids2017 dataset for designing intrusion detection systems. Int. J. Eng. Technol. **7**(3.24), 479–482 (2018)

20. U.C. on Standards in Public Life: Artificial intelligence and public standards (2020). https://www.gov.uk/government/publications/artificial-intelligence-and-public-standards-report. Accessed 10 May 2020

21. Quionero-Candela, J., Sugiyama, M., Schwaighofer, A., Lawrence, N.D.: Dataset Shift in Machine Learning. The MIT Press (2009)

22. Raschke, M.: Empirical behaviour of tests for the beta distribution and their application in environmental research. Stochast. Environ. Res. Risk Assess. **25**(1), 79–89 (2011)

23. Schulam, P., Saria, S.: Can you trust this prediction? auditing pointwise reliability after learning. arXiv preprint arXiv:1901.00403 (2019)

24. Sharafaldin, I., Lashkari, A.H., Ghorbani, A.A.: Toward generating a new intrusion detection dataset and intrusion traffic characterization. In: International Conference on Information Systems Security and Privacy (ICISSP), pp. 108–116 (2018). https://doi.org/10.5220/0006639801080116

25. Sharkey, A.: Autonomous weapons systems, killer robots and human dignity. Ethics Inf. Technol. **21**(2), 75–87 (2018). https://doi.org/10.1007/s10676-018-9494-0

26. Theodoridis, S., Koutroumbas, K.: Pattern Recognition. Elsevier, New York (2009)

27. Van Der Maaten, L.: Accelerating t-SNE using tree-based algorithms. J. Mach. Learn. Res. **15**(1), 3221–3245 (2014)

28. Wiens, J., et al.: Do no harm: a roadmap for responsible machine learning for health care. Nat. Med. **25**(9), 1337–1340 (2019)

Model-Based Error Detection for Industrial Automation Systems Using LSTM Networks

Sheng Ding[1]([✉]), Andrey Morozov[2], Silvia Vock[3], Michael Weyrich[2], and Klaus Janschek[1]

[1] Institute of Automation, Technische Universität Dresden, Dresden, Germany
{sheng.ding,klaus.janschek}@tu-dresden.de
[2] Institute of Industrial Automation and Software Engineering,
University of Stuttgart, Stuttgart, Germany
{andrey.morozov,michael.weyrich}@ias.uni-stuttgart.de
[3] Bundesanstalt für Arbeitsschutz und Arbeitsmedizin, Dresden, Germany
Vock.Silvia@baua.bund.de

Abstract. The increasing complexity of modern automation systems leads to inevitable faults. At the same time, structural variability and untrivial interaction of the sophisticated components makes it harder and harder to apply traditional fault detection methods. Consequently, the popularity of Deep Learning (DL) fault detection methods grows. Model-based system design tools such as Simulink allow the development of executable system models. Besides the design flexibility, these models can provide the training data for DL-based error detectors.

This paper describes the application of an LSTM-based error detector for a system of two industrial robotic manipulators. A detailed Simulink model provides the training data for an LSTM predictor. Error detection is achieved via intelligent processing of the residual between the original signal and the LSTM prediction using two methods. The first method is based on the non-parametric dynamic thresholding. The second method exploits the Gaussian distribution of the residual. The paper presents the results of extensive model-based fault injection experiments that allow the comparison of these methods and the evaluation of the error detection performance for varying error magnitude.

Keywords: Error detection · Simulink · Deep learning · LSTM · Time-series data · Industrial robots

1 Introduction

Modern automation systems contain numerous heterogeneous components connected over a network. On the one hand, the increasing complexity leads to inevitable faults that may result in severe system failures. The sensors are subject to noise, drift, offset, and stuck-at faults. The networks are prone to delays,

M. Zeller and K. Höfig (Eds.): IMBSA 2020, LNCS 12297, pp. 212–226, 2020.
https://doi.org/10.1007/978-3-030-58920-2_14

jitters, and package drops. Controllers suffer from computing hardware faults such as bit flips. On the other hand, the complexity, together with structural variability and untrivial interaction of the sophisticated components, makes it harder and harder to apply traditional fault detection and isolation methods effectively. Because of these two factors, the popularity of Artificial Intelligence and Deep Learning (DL) fault detection methods based on the anomaly detection principle grows.

Model-based system design, in general, is a common approach for developing complex networked automation systems. Moreover, the tools such as Simulink allow the development of executable system models. Besides the design flexibility and early system analysis, these models are perfect sources of big data for training and tuning of DL-based error detectors.

Contribution: This paper describes the case study application of an LSTM-based error detector for a system of two industrial robotic manipulators. A detailed Simulink model of the target automation system was built in order to obtain the training data for an LSTM predictor. Error detection is achieved via intelligent processing of the residual between the original signal and the LSTM prediction using two methods. The first method is based on the non-parametric dynamic thresholding. The second method exploits the Gaussian distribution of the residual. The paper presents the results of extensive model-based fault injection experiments that allow the comparison of these methods. The evaluation of the error detection performance for varying error magnitude is the main contribution of this paper.

2   State of the Art

2.1   Classical and Deep Learning Based Error Detection

An extensive survey of various anomaly detection methods is given in [4] including deep learning based methods. Deep learning approaches outperform the traditional methods as the scale of data increases. The primary reason is their ability to learn hierarchical distinctive features and high-level representations from data. This automatic feature learning capability eliminates the need for professional manual engineering by domain experts, therefore helps to solve the problem end-to-end taking raw input data. Recent survey of deep learning based anomaly detection methods is presented in [3].

2.2   Deep Learning Based Time-Series Data Error Detection Approaches

In this paper we focus on deep learning based error detection in time-series data. This can be achieved using three different groups of methods.

- *Classification methods* directly exploit DL-based classifiers to distinguish between normal and erroneous system states. This is a supervised technique that can achieve good performance, but requires sufficient and balanced labeled normal and erroneous instances.

- *Reconstruction methods* are based on LSTM encoder-decoder frameworks that reconstruct the normal time-series data [15,18]. These methods are based on the assumption that such a model would perform badly to reconstruct the erroneous time-series that have not been encountered during training. It requires an encoder-decoder architecture that has a high computational complexity and does not show on-line error mitigation capability.
- *Prediction methods* are commonly used under the assumption that the normal time-series is predictable to some extent and when erroneous instances are hard to obtain. The classifier, usually an LSTM [11], plays the role of a predictor [16]. Given current and past values it predicts next one in the time-series. An error is considered to be detected if the residual of the actual and predicted values is higher than a certain threshold.

Unlike the classification and reconstruction, the prediction methods can localize and even mitigate temporary errors, by replacing the actual erroneous values with the predicted ones. Therefore the prediction method is used in this work.

Many recent papers [1,2,5,12,21,22,24] propose to train an LSTM or an LSTM encoder-decoder for anomaly detection. This helps to differentiate between normal and anomalous behavior in time-series data assuming a high prevalence of normal instances over abnormal data instances. In our previous paper [7], we trained an LSTM network as a single step predictor to detect errors such as bit flips, sensor spikes, and offsets. We also trained an LSTM encoder-decoder as a multi-step prediction model to detect long-duration errors, e.g., network delays. Moreover, we mitigate errors by temporarily replacing the detected errors with the predicted values.

2.3 Anomaly Scoring and Threshold Setting

Most of the existing works about anomaly detection using the prediction methods are only focused on the prediction rather than on the detection. However, it is equally important to set the threshold intelligently. Certain works address this problem [25]. We categorize them into parametric and non-parametric.

Parametric techniques assume that the distribution of underlying data is known. An adaptive threshold approach was introduced in [6] to overcome the common issues of the fixed thresholds: high false alarm rate or a low anomaly detection rate. Sensor signals are data streams, and the time series's data distribution may shift over time because of concept drift. Therefore it is challenging to distinguish between the natural changes in distribution and anomalies. The zero hypothesis is defined as there exists no concept drift in the current sliding window, and there is no need for threshold update. The threshold is updated when significant changes in the mean of the anomaly score are detected by Z-test. Similarly, the work presented in [20] considers the identification of the anomaly as rejecting the null hypothesis by applying p-value scoring. In [16], a Gaussian Distribution method is presented. The error vectors are used to estimate the parameters μ and σ using Maximum Likelihood Estimation. The authors approach this problem by fitting the prediction errors into a multivariate normal distribution. A parametric double window scoring method is introduced in [1]. It maintains two windows, a history long term window and a recent short term window to identify the change of the distribution between long trend and short term. This method is potentially able to address the concept drift problem [25]. There are three main limitations of parametric methods. First, anomalies do not always follow the assumed statistical distribution. In data-driven methods, the parametric assumption can be violated, and residuals are not random. Second, the hypothesis test is not always dependable because it asserts the unavailability of other alternative hypotheses, which is often theoretical but not realistic [12]. Third, the monitored data are often heterogeneous, noisy, and high-dimensional. This fact is ignored by parametric methods and leads to a great number of false alerts.

Non-parametric methods do not assume the availability of data distribution. Generally, they are usually computationally light weighted and more preferable than the parametric methods. They typically use some distance measure between a new test instance and the statistical model and apply a threshold on this distance to determine whether the observation is an anomaly. In [23], the authors exploit distance-based methods by assigning anomaly score to new data based on the distance to other groups. These methods are supervised, which bring additional restrain on the real application. Moreover, finding a threshold is a big challenge for the distance-based method. One of the approaches to reduce the false alarm, particularly for the long-duration errors, is discussed in [21]. Another unsupervised thresholding method for residual evaluation is presented [12]. This method is followed by an anomaly pruning procedure that basically removes some non-prominent anomalies if a new, more obvious anomaly is detected.

In this paper, we have chosen two representative methods for comparison, one parametric and one non-parametric. As for parametric, we choose the Gaussian Distribution method [16]. As for non-parametric, we choose the dynamic threshold along with the anomaly pruning techniques, which is introduced in [12].

2.4 Anomaly Detection for Industrial Automation System

Finally, several works about anomaly detection in industrial automation systems exist. The authors of [13,14] have applied the LSTM autoencoder to detect anomalies within large amounts of machine and process data. They have also compared it to the k-means clustering method and state that the LSTM autoencoder is more accurate in case of slinking anomalies. In another representative work [19], the authors apply the LSTM method to an industrial robot manipulator and compare it to other traditional methods. They also emphasize the advantage of the LSTM method. The LSTM is only considered as a classifier. The error localization abilities are ignored.

3 Simulink Model of Two Industrial Robotic Manipulators

Simulink is widely used in the modeling and simulation of control systems and digital signal processing. One of the advantages of the method presented in this paper is its model-based application. So, we apply it to a comprehensive Simulink model of two industrial robotic manipulators.

Our reference system is based on the ROBOTIS OpenManipulator project [17]. It is an open-source Simulink model of a robotic manipulator available in the GitHub [10]. We have extended it into a system of two robotic manipulators that share a tool. The top layer of the Simulink model is shown in Fig. 1. The robots emulate a mutual work using a shared tool represented as a gray cylinder. The first robot takes the tool from the tool holder A, highlighted in blue, moves it through several random waypoints located between the robots, and puts it to the tool holder B. Then the second robot takes the tool, moves it through other random waypoints, and puts back to the tool holder A.

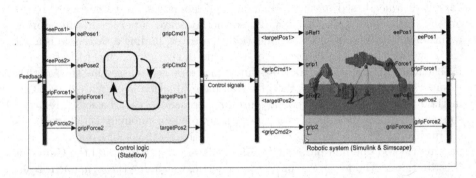

Fig. 1. The top layer of the Simulink model of two robotic manipulators. (Color figure online)

The Simulink model consists of two major parts. The high-level control logic is implemented in the Stateflow block shown on the left side of Fig. 1. It receives the feedback measurements from sensors and identifies whether the robot has reached a waypoint, is the gripper holding the tool, or has the other robot completed its task. The low-level computation is implemented with Simulink blocks inside the Robotic System sub-model shown on the right side of Fig. 1. Figure 2 shows the blocks of this sub model. Forward and inverse kinematics are modeled with Simulink blocks from the Robot System Toolbox. The robots are masked with the robot icon.

The detailed model of a robot is shown in Fig. 3. The physical parts of the robot are implemented in Simscape Multibody. Each robot consists of five links and two grippers. The relations between the links are modeled via the joint blocks. The robot receives four command signals to the joints position and two

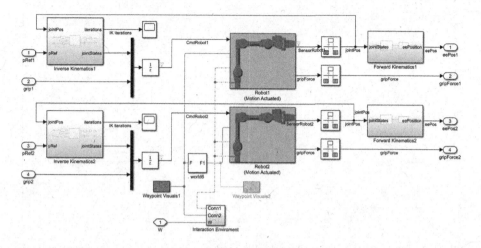

Fig. 2. The sub-model of the robotic system block from Fig. 1.

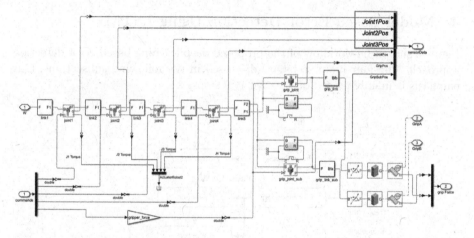

Fig. 3. The physical model of a robot, the sub-model of the robot blocks from Fig. 2. (Color figure online)

command signals to the gripper. The real position signal, along with the contact force of the grippers, is measured through sensors.

The Simulink model, as instrumented with special fault injection blocks [9]. The type, probability, and duration of a fault can be specified with different kinds of fault injection parameters.

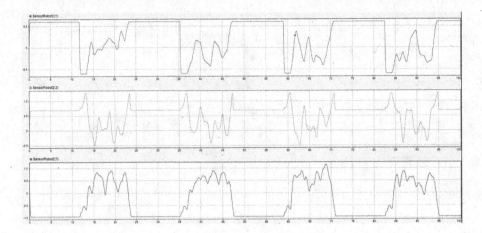

Fig. 4. Positions of the three joints, highlighted in red in Fig. 3. (Color figure online)

4   Model-Based Error Detection Using LSTM

Figure 5 shows the workflow of the proposed deep learning based error detection approach. The four main steps are discussed in the following subsections. Our emphasis is mainly placed on the last two steps.

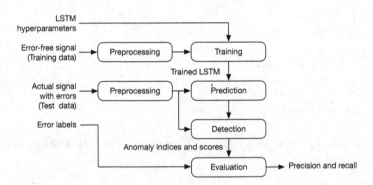

Fig. 5. The workflow of the proposed error detection approach.

4.1   Preprocessing

The data needs to be pre-processed because the values could come from different sources. This step is pretty much standard for machine learning. First, the collected sensor data should be re-sampled to have a consistent sampling rate. Second, the data should be standardized to have zero-mean and unit-variance. Third, the data need to be reshaped, i.e., transformed into the format required by the prediction model. Specifically for the LSTM model, the data set should be transformed into a three-dimensional array with three axes: (i) the number of data samples, (ii) the number of lookback time steps, and (iii) the number of features.

We get our "Fault-free signal" data (see Fig. 5) by monitoring and logging the normal behavior of robot signals for 2500 s. From the 12 original signals, we choose three channels. We get our "Actual signal with faults" data (see Fig. 5) by monitoring and logging the robot signals with fault injections. We were injecting offset faults with varying magnitude from 0.1 to 1.0 with step 0.1. We inject the faults 100 times for each magnitude value in order to achieve acceptable statistical confidence.

The Fig. 6 illustrate how we get the training, validation, and test data. The fault-free data is divided into two sets, a training set S_N, and a validation set V_N. The normal training data set S_N is used for the LSTM training. The normal validation data set V_N is used for early stopping to prevent the model from overfitting. The erroneous data is also divided into two sets, a validation set V_A, and a test set T_A. The abnormal test set T_A is used for evaluation of the performance of the trained prediction model and the corresponding anomaly detection method. The validation set V_A is used specifically for the threshold decision in the Gaussian distribution method and will be further mentioned in Sect. 4.3.

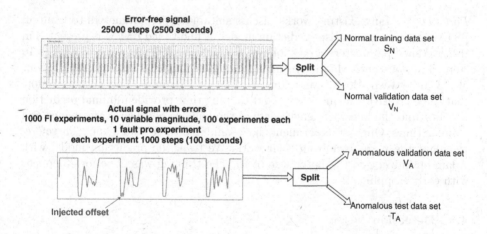

Fig. 6. The splitting of the training, validation, and test data.

4.2   Training and Prediction

We use a standard Long Short-Term Memory (LSTM) network as a predictor. LSTM networks [11] is a special kind of recurrent neural network that overcomes the vanishing gradients problem by replacing an ordinary neuron with a complex architecture called the LSTM Cell unit. The LSTM neural network structure is shown in Fig. 7. The input at each time step is processed by the LSTM cell.

The zones marked with yellow, purple, blue, and green are the network parts of the forget gate, input gate, output gate, and candidate input value, respectively. These gates allow gradients to flow back in time up to arbitrary lengths, enabling the learning of diverse temporal dependencies. For sequential and temporal data, LSTM has become the deep learning model of choice because of its ability to learn long-range patterns. LSTM-based algorithms for anomaly detection have been investigated and reported to produce significant performance gains over conventional methods [8].

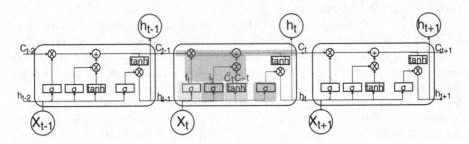

Fig. 7. The structure of a Long Short-Term Memory (LSTM) network. (Color figure online)

Parameters: Many existing works discuss suitable hyperparameters to train an LSTM network as a precise prediction model. A fine-tuned LSTM is presented in [12]. Detailed parameters are as follows. Lookback is 250 steps. Lookahead is 10 steps. Two consecutive hidden recurrent layers are fully connected with a dropout of 0.3 in-between. Both layers consist of 80 LSTM units. The authors report that the increase of the model size and training time provide minimal prediction benefits, and the lookback length defines the balance between performance and training times. Our test experiments have validated these statements. Therefore, we adopt the parameter from their work. We train the prediction model with Adam optimizer and the batch size of 70. The training was done for 35 epochs with early stopping.

4.3   Detection

As it was mentioned, the error detection can be achieved using either a parametric or non-parametric method. In this paper, we compared two methods, one from each category.

The parametric method, which we used, is the Gaussian method [16]. It is based on the assumption that the residual between predicted and actual signal is normally distributed. Basically, we fit the prediction error into a multivariate normal distribution, see Fig. 8. First, we use Gaussian distribution to model the prediction errors on the normal training set S_N. We use Maximum Likelihood Estimation (MLE) to estimate the mean and variance of the distribution. Second, the trained prediction model is applied on the V_A. The calculated distribution parameters are used to compute the log probability density of the errors from the V_A. Third, we set the threshold on the log Probability density values that can distinguish the errors with the minimal number of false alarms.

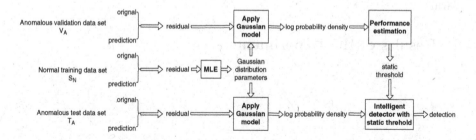

Fig. 8. The error detection using the Gaussian method.

As for non-parametric, we choose the dynamic thresholding method that is described in [12]. The method is sketched in Fig. 9 most of the implementation details are omitted and can be found in [12]. First, we compute the residual between the original and predicted values of the anomalous test data set. After that, we use Exponentially-Weighted Moving Average (EWMA) method to smooth the errors and finally apply the intelligent detector with a dynamic threshold. This method is followed by an anomaly pruning procedure that basically removes some non-prominent anomalies if a new, more obvious anomaly is detected.

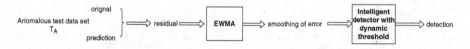

Fig. 9. The error detection using the dynamic thresholding.

4.4 Evaluation

The small errors are harder to detect, and it is essential to evaluate how the error detection capabilities depend on the error magnitude. As was mentioned, in our fault injection experiments, we vary the error magnitude from 0.1 to 1 with step 0.1. For each magnitude value, we have computed two precision and recall. The results are summarized in 12 plots in the next section. The precision and recall are the most critical metrics in anomaly detection. They are calculated using the estimated number of True Positives (TP), True Negatives (TN), and False Positives (FP) with the following equations:

$$precision = \frac{TP}{TP + TN} \tag{1}$$

$$recall = \frac{TP}{TP + FP} \tag{2}$$

Where TP is the number of injected errors that were detected, TN is the number of injected errors that were not detected, and FP is the number of false alarms.

5   Results of the Experiments

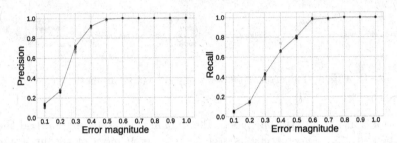

Fig. 10. The error detection performance. Robot2 Sensor1. Gaussian distribution method.

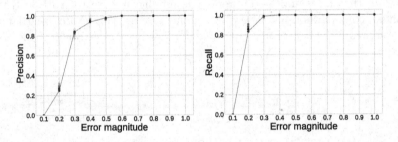

Fig. 11. The error detection performance. Robot2 Sensor1. Dynamic threshold method.

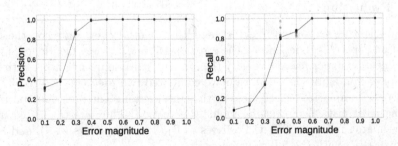

Fig. 12. The error detection performance. Robot2 Sensor2. Gaussian distribution method.

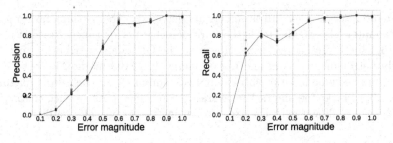

Fig. 13. The error detection performance. Robot2 Sensor2. Dynamic threshold method.

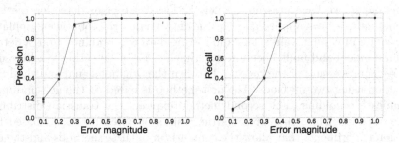

Fig. 14. The error detection performance. Robot2 Sensor3. Gaussian distribution method.

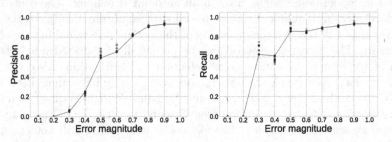

Fig. 15. The error detection performance. Robot2 Sensor3. Dynamic threshold method.

The results of our experiments are summarized in 12 plots shown in Fig. 10, 11, 12, 13, 14 and 15. We tested the introduced method on three sensor signals of the reference Simulink model. The exemplar shapes of the signals are shown in Fig. 4. For each signal, we have computed the dependencies of the precision (left) and recall (right) metrics on the error magnitude using the two discussed error detection methods. The plots show the expected increase of both metrics with the increase of the error magnitude. Each plot can be divided into three intervals from left to right: (i) the error magnitude is too small, and the error detector performance is negligibly low, (ii) the middle interval where the performance dynamically increases with the increase of the error magnitude, and (iii) the right-hand interval where all the errors are detected correctly. The shorter are the first two intervals - the better is the error detector performance. In general, both detectors show similar performs. However, the Gaussian distribution method is slightly better in precision, and the dynamic threshold method is better in the recall. As mentioned, we performed 100 exterminates for each error magnitude value. The black dot shows the average value of a performance metric. The convergence is shown with the grey dots using the gray-scale gradient.

6   Conclusion

In this paper, we have presented a new LSTM-based error detection methods. The method has been applied for a system of two industrial robotic manipulators. The required training, validation, and testing data was obtained from a detailed Simulink model and fault injection experiments. Error detection is achieved via intelligent processing of the residual between the original signal and the LSTM prediction using two methods. The first method is based on the non-parametric dynamic thresholding. The second method exploits the Gaussian distribution of the residual. The paper presents the results of extensive model-based fault injection experiments that allow the comparison of these methods and the evaluation of the error detection performance for varying error magnitude. The paper demonstrates that such LSTM based error detection method can be created and applied in model-based engineering in an automated manner. The control system developed in Simulink can be delivered with an automatically created error detector that will observe the operation of the system and signal in case of critical errors. The discussed method can be potentially integrated into a Digital Twin of the system for online error detection and mitigation. Also, the quality of the data used for the LSTM training is extremely important. Potentially, the formal methods (e.g., integrated into Simulink Design Verifier) could help to trigger critical system execution scenarios and feed the LSTM not only with common system execution data but also with unusual but still not anomalous borderline scenarios.

References

1. Ahmad, S., Lavin, A., Purdy, S., Agha, Z.: Unsupervised real-time anomaly detection for streaming data. Neurocomputing (2017). https://doi.org/10.1016/j.neucom.2017.04.070
2. Buda, T.S., Caglayan, B., Assem, H.: DeepAD: a generic framework based on deep learning for time series anomaly detection. In: Phung, D., Tseng, V.S., Webb, G.I., Ho, B., Ganji, M., Rashidi, L. (eds.) PAKDD 2018. LNCS (LNAI), vol. 10937, pp. 577–588. Springer, Cham (2018). https://doi.org/10.1007/978-3-319-93034-3_46
3. Chalapathy, R., Chawla, S.: Deep learning for anomaly detection: a survey (2019)
4. Chandola, V., Banerjee, A., Kumar, V.: Anomaly detection: a survey. ACM Comput. Surv. (CSUR) **41**(3), 15 (2009)

5. Chauhan, S., Vig, L.: Anomaly detection in ECG time signals via deep long short-term memory networks. In: 2015 IEEE International Conference on Data Science and Advanced Analytics (DSAA), pp. 1–7. IEEE (2015)
6. Clark, J., Liu, Z., Japkowicz, N.: Adaptive threshold for outlier detection on data streams. In: 2018 IEEE 5th International Conference on Data Science and Advanced Analytics (DSAA), pp. 41–49. IEEE (2018)
7. Ding, K., Ding, S., Morozov, A., Fabarisov, T., Janschek, K.: On-line error detection and mitigation for time-series data of cyber-physical systems using deep learning based methods. In: 2019 15th European Dependable Computing Conference (EDCC), pp. 7–14. IEEE (2019)
8. Ergen, T., Mirza, A.H., Kozat, S.S.: Unsupervised and semi-supervised anomaly detection with LSTM neural networks. arXiv preprint arXiv:1710.09207 (2017)
9. Fabarisov, T.: Fault injection block (2020). https://github.com/Flatag/FIBlock/
10. MATLAB and Simulink files for modeling and simulation of ROBOTIS OpenManipulator. https://github.com/mathworks-robotics/designing-robot-manipulator-algorithms. Accessed 20 May 2020
11. Hochreiter, S., Schmidhuber, J.: Long short-term memory. Neural Comput. $9(8)$, 1735–1780 (1997)
12. Hundman, K., Constantinou, V., Laporte, C., Colwell, I., Soderstrom, T.: Detecting spacecraft anomalies using LSTMs and nonparametric dynamic thresholding. In: Proceedings of the 24th ACM SIGKDD International Conference on Knowledge Discovery & Data Mining, pp. 387–395 (2018)
13. Lindemann, B., Jazdi, N., Weyrich, M.: Anomaly detection for quality control based on sequence-to-sequence LSTM networks. AT-Automatisierungstechnik $67(12)$, 1058–1068 (2019)
14. Lindemann, B., Fesenmayr, F., Jazdi, N., Weyrich, M.: Anomaly detection in discrete manufacturing using self-learning approaches. Proc. CIRP 79, 313–318 (2019)
15. Malhotra, P., Ramakrishnan, A., Anand, G., Vig, L., Agarwal, P., Shroff, G.: LSTM-based encoder-decoder for multi-sensor anomaly detection. arXiv preprint arXiv:1607.00148 (2016)
16. Malhotra, P., Vig, L., Shroff, G., Agarwal, P.: Long short term memory networks for anomaly detection in time series. In: Proceedings, p. 89. Presses universitaires de Louvain (2015)
17. Designing Robot Manipulator Algorithms. https://ww2.mathworks.cn/matlab central/fileexchange/65316-designing-robot-manipulator-algorithms. Accessed 20 May 2020
18. Park, D., Hoshi, Y., Kemp, C.C.: A multimodal anomaly detector for robot-assisted feeding using an LSTM-based variational autoencoder. IEEE Robot. Autom. Lett. $3(3)$, 1544–1551 (2018)
19. Park, D., Kim, S., An, Y., Jung, J.Y.: LiReD: a light-weight real-time fault detection system for edge computing using LSTM recurrent neural networks. Sensors 18, 2110 (2018). https://doi.org/10.3390/s18072110
20. Schervish, M.: P values: What they are and what they are not. Am. Stat. 50, 203–206 (1996). https://doi.org/10.1080/00031305.1996.10474380
21. Shipmon, D.T., Gurevitch, J.M., Piselli, P.M., Edwards, S.T.: Time series anomaly detection; detection of anomalous drops with limited features and sparse examples in noisy highly periodic data. arXiv preprint arXiv:1708.03665 (2017)
22. Singh, A.: Anomaly detection for temporal data using long short-term memory (LSTM) (2017)

23. Wang, K., Stolfo, S.J.: Anomalous payload-based network intrusion detection. In: Jonsson, E., Valdes, A., Almgren, M. (eds.) RAID 2004. LNCS, vol. 3224, pp. 203–222. Springer, Heidelberg (2004). https://doi.org/10.1007/978-3-540-30143-1_11
24. Zhu, L., Laptev, N.: Deep and confident prediction for time series at Uber. In: 2017 IEEE International Conference on Data Mining Workshops (ICDMW), pp. 103–110. IEEE (2017)
25. Zohrevand, Z., Glässer, U.: Should i raise the red flag? A comprehensive survey of anomaly scoring methods toward mitigating false alarms. arXiv preprint arXiv:1904.06646 (2019)

U-Map: A Reference Map for Safe Handling of Runtime Uncertainties

Nishanth Laxman[1]([⊠]), Chee Hung Koo[2], and Peter Liggesmeyer[1]

[1] Software Engineering: Dependability, Technische Universität Kaiserslautern, Kaiserslautern, Germany
{nishanth.laxman,liggesmeyer}@cs.uni-kl.de
[2] Corporate Sector Research and Advanced Engineering, Robert Bosch GmbH, Renningen, Germany
cheehung.koo@bosch.com

Abstract. "Uncertainty is certain" – a well-stablished fact that challenges design and engineering of dynamic systems. Cyber Physical Systems (CPSs) must function and perform tasks safely in real world contexts that might not be engineered specifically for them. These dynamic contexts are often accompanied by the pervasive presence of uncertainty. The dynamic nature of such systems as well as their ever-growing complexity further complicate safety assurance and require a paradigm shift towards more effective runtime safety assurance techniques. Many of the present runtime safety assurance techniques consider certain dynamic aspects of the system and its context, but not the uncertainty aspects completely. This paper presents results from an ongoing research to effectively handle runtime uncertainties in a model-based approach to assure system safety. In this paper, we propose a reference map called Uncertainty Map (U-Map) that can be used during system design to handle runtime uncertainties and apply it to a case study. The U-Map consists of an exhaustive set of possible uncertainties that are mapped to sets of potentially resulting hazards as well as possible runtime mitigation measures. It is intended to facilitate the identification of uncertainty-induced hazards during early design and contribute to the safe handling of runtime uncertainties.

Keywords: Safety · Runtime uncertainty · Uncertainty handling · Cyber physical systems · Hazard analysis · MBSA · Bayesian networks

1 Introduction

Embedded systems of today have evolved through time and are becoming more complex, dynamic, adaptive, well integrated into our daily life and supposedly

The work leading to this paper was partially funded by the German Federal Ministry of Education and Research under grant number 01IS16043 Collaborative Embedded Systems (CrESt).

© Springer Nature Switzerland AG 2020
M. Zeller and K. Höfig (Eds.): IMBSA 2020, LNCS 12297, pp. 227–241, 2020.
https://doi.org/10.1007/978-3-030-58920-2_15

smart. These dynamic intelligent systems are increasingly appealing for domains like manufacturing and production, healthcare, automobiles, energy, agriculture and avionics, most of which are safety-critical in nature. Traditional systems have a static relation to their surrounding environment and are engineered based on the computational myth that their operational context is predictable and fully specifiable. Modern-day embedded systems are composed of an increasing number of parts, abstraction layers and frameworks which are developed independently and might result in scenarios which are not completely understood or even fully specified a priori [11]. These embedded systems are envisioned to dynamically interact and collaborate with each other to achieve a common goal and are commonly called Cyber Physical System (CPS), Collaborative Embedded System (CES), System of System (SOS) or Multi Agent System (MAS). A CPS constitutes the system under consideration along with its environment (context) that is necessary for its functioning. This paper is written in the context of CPS.

Uncertainty in the context of systems engineering and development has gained increasing importance in recent years. Through rapid changes in system types and system boundaries, the associated uncertainty remains inevitable due to the fact that the physical world is inherently uncertain. *Uncertainty* as a term is very broadly used and is researched upon in domains like economics [23], robotics [29], artificial intelligence [18] and primarily in systems engineering [8,28]. In the domain of systems engineering alone, there are varied definitions and understandings of the term *uncertainty*. One of the most suitable definitions for this paper is provided by Ramirez et al. [27], and they describe uncertainty as "*a system state of incomplete or inconsistent knowledge such that it is not possible for the system to know which of two or more alternative states/configurations/values is true*". According to the authors, uncertainty can be introduced into the system at any point in time during its development. These uncertainties can propagate through different stages of development and manifest themselves at runtime (i.e. during system's operation) if left unresolved [27]. At runtime, uncertainty can lead to component failures because of ambiguity, imprecision or inconsistency in information exchanges or due to uncertain contexts, further resulting in unforeseen behavior of the system. These uncertainties at runtime will be the prime focus of this research.

Uncertainty is often confused for the variability of the system and its context, because of the obscure differences between them. The differentiation between uncertainty and system variability is vital for the system development as well as safety assurance. Anderson and Hattis [1] provide some perception on how to differentiate uncertainty and variability in general. Koopman et al. [22] justifies embracing both uncertainty and variability together in real world scenarios. Additionally, Hoffman and Hammonds [15] provide some insights into the association between uncertainty and variability and the need to distinguish them. In reality, this differentiation is very subjective to the use case and human expertise involved in modeling sophisticated CPS. The presented approach in this paper is developed by considering the system variability as well, thus providing flexibility in adapting it to suit different use cases.

Traditional safety assurance techniques presume that the complete set of system specifications and configurations are available during system design. Such presumptions can no longer be applied to the development of CPS due to its unpredictability at runtime. This scenario demands development of different runtime safety assurance techniques. Most of the existing techniques do consider dynamic aspects of the system and its variability, but not uncertainties (runtime) explicitly. The runtime uncertainties, both the epistemic and the aleatory form [26], might put the system into a hazard state which in turn might result in an accident/harm. Early possible detection of such hazards can ensure appropriate measures being taken to avoid catastrophic events. The research on handling uncertainties is branched and primarily based on mitigation of specific categories of uncertainty (explained in Sect. 2). This paper presents a novel method based on the model-based approach, which can be used to consider relevant uncertainties and handle them together, encompassing different mitigation strategies, specific to the uncertainties. To facilitate this, a reference map (framework) called the Uncertainty Map (U-Map) is introduced which encapsulates all relevant uncertainties, early detection of uncertainty-induced safety concerns at the design stage and corresponding mitigation measures. The U-Map in turn can be used at runtime to monitor uncertainty manifestations and handle them accordingly based on its defined mitigation measures.

The presented approach in this paper is used to handle uncertainties from the view point of safety assurance and is structured as follows. Sect. 2 briefly summarizes relevant works from the literature. In Sect. 3, the U-Map as a reference map is introduced along with the methodology to develop it. The application of the U-Map is demonstrated with the help of a use case in Sect. 4. Section 5 concludes this paper and gives an overview of future works.

2 Related Work

In the following, an overview of different runtime uncertainty classifications is given, followed by state-of-the-art techniques for handling uncertainties. Since many of these techniques do not handle the uncertainties from a safety assurance perspective, an overview of various relevant runtime safety assurance techniques are also provided.

2.1 Runtime Uncertainty Classification

There is a multitude of research conducted in the field of uncertainty to identify and classify different possible uncertainties. These classifications lead to further research pathways to identify uncertainties with greater granularity and more specific to the use cases. These classifications are able to provide insights for our uncertainty handling approach to deal with aspects that might be neglected by the existing standards today. An extensive and well-defined classification promises an enhanced safety assurance.

An early inception of uncertainty classification that targets systems engineering was done by Walker et al. [33], where uncertainties are classified based on three dimensions: *location* of manifestation of uncertainty, *level* of uncertainty (variation in a spectrum between total unawareness and deterministic knowledge) and *nature* of uncertainty (whether the uncertainty is due to inherent randomness or associated with imperfect knowledge).

Ramirez et al. [27] provide a taxonomy with a well elicited list of uncertainties and have classified the sources of uncertainty based on the different stages of system development. According to the authors, runtime uncertainty predominantly occurs due to the interaction between systems and their contexts. For instance, runtime uncertainties caused by sensor failures and unpredictable context might lead to inaccuracy, ambiguity or inconsistency, in which incomplete information available to the system might result in incorrectly interpreted events. Apart from the taxonomy, the authors also provide information regarding mitigation techniques to solve certain specific uncertainties.

The research on uncertainties for Self Adaptive System (SAS) that possess self-adaptation capabilities recognizes further new challenges and paves way for a separate branch of research [7]. With the focus on SAS, Perez-Palacin and Mirandola [26] present a taxonomy with more granular definitions based on the three similar categories provided by [33]. The authors characterize the uncertainty to be either epistemic or aleatory, based on its nature. An epistemic uncertainty is the result of the imperfection in the knowledge acquired. Possible reasons that cause epistemic uncertainty can be, a lack of information that would be required to create a reliable knowledge base, inaccurate measurements or models due to the negligence of certain aspects of context, or imperfection in processing the information. An aleatory uncertainty is the result of the inherent randomness of the system behavior and its operating context. The proposed approach in this paper takes both epistemic and aleatory uncertainty into account.

An extensive and sophisticated classification for sources of uncertainty in the context of SAS is also provided by Mahdavi-Hezavehi et al. [24]. Cámara et al. [5] further extend the classification of [24] by combining it with the classification provided by [27]. Both these studies, [24] and [5], classify the uncertainties in five dimensions: *location* where the uncertainty emerges, different *sources* of uncertainty, *nature* of uncertainty, *level/spectrum* as to on what scale the uncertainty is specified in (statistical or scenario based) and *emerging time* as to in which stage of system development, the uncertainty will emerge (manifest). These classifications are the most comprehensive ones available in the literature, which helps to identify a myriad of uncertainty possibilities and scenarios.

Hildebrandt et al. [14] also provide an uncertainty classification for epistemic uncertainties that deals with runtime information exchange between systems. The authors classify the communication-induced epistemic uncertainties into four type-level and four instance-level uncertainties based on a simplified knowledge modeling procedure using the ontology based approach [32]. These classification schemes serve as a checklist to conduct a systematic analysis on potential uncertainties.

2.2 Uncertainty Handling Techniques

Brun et al. [4] explain how uncertainty can be handled during the development of SAS with the help of feedback loops. The Monitor-Analyze-Plan-Execute-Knowledge (MAPE-K) feedback loops introduced by Kephart and Chess [19] take prime importance in their work. The MAPE-K feedback loops are envisioned to be one of the most prominent reference control models for autonomous systems. Runtime models are used to represent a system and its surrounding, are built for specific purposes and are expected to provide an acceptable level of accuracy and precision [3]. Giese et al. [13] investigate as to how runtime models help cope with uncertainty. They propose an extension to the existing MAPE-K feedback loop by combining them with the runtime models to handle uncertainty. Garlan et al. [12] propose a so-called Rainbow approach, using an architecture-based self-adaptation technique with reusable infrastructure and software architectures to support self-adaptation of software systems. This approach is also primarily based on the MAPE-K feedback loops. The proposed U-Map in this paper can also be integrated into the MAPE-K feedback loop for the runtime aspects of uncertainty handling.

Esfahani et al. [10] introduce a quantitative approach called POISED to determine the consequences of uncertainty. This approach aids in making adaptation strategies that will result in the best possible behavior considering the specific use case. Elkhodary et al. [9] propose FUSION, an approach based on probability theory that uses machine learning capabilities, and includes feature orientation and dynamic optimization to tune the adaptation behavior of the system in presence of uncertainty. Cámara et al. [6] contribute a formal framework to reason about the human participation in self-adaptation, particularly during its execution stage. Their work illustrates how explicit modeling of humans as participants (effectors) can provide a better insight into the involvement of humans for adaptation.

2.3 Runtime Safety Assurance Techniques

One of the well-known concepts to deal with runtime safety is proposed by Schneider et al. [30] that applies Conditional Safety Certificates (ConSerts) to certify open adaptive systems at runtime. ConSerts evaluate runtime evidences/preconditions to provide the necessary guarantees for safe system collaborations. Other relevant approaches for runtime safety analysis in the automotive domain are proposed by Östberg and Bengtsson [25] and by Kabir et al. [17] that focus mainly on cooperative automotive systems. To enable a better dependability analysis and assurance throughout the lifetime of a system, a concept using Digital Dependability Identities (DDIs) is also proposed by Schneider et al. [31] that utilize digital artifacts to describe dependability-related information. In the context of reconfigurable production systems, Koo et al. [21] propose a method using analysis modules called SAM-RT to allow runtime analysis and monitoring of safety aspects. These runtime safety assurance techniques can be integrated with the U-Map proposed in this paper.

3   The Uncertainty Map (U-Map)

The Uncertainty Map (U-Map) is a reference map, which acts as a knowledge base and also as guidelines for handling uncertainties at runtime. The U-Map consists of well identified possible list of uncertainties, mapped explicitly to different possible hazards which in turn are appropriately mapped to their corresponding mitigation measures.

Saffiotti [29] summarizes three attitudes towards problems involving uncertainty:

1. Removing the uncertainty: by using better hardware, sophisticated and high precision sensors and carefully engineering every aspect of the system and its environment.
2. Tolerating the uncertainty: by accepting the presence of uncertainty and using robust techniques to operate in wide range of situations and to recover from them.
3. Reasoning about the uncertainty: by explicit representation and manipulation of uncertain information and reasoning about its effects.

The first attitude involves high cost and does not cater to all runtime uncertainties, specifically not to the aleatory form of uncertainty. This attitude is more suitable for simple systems where all possible interactions can be modeled. As the CPS of our concern are highly complex and safety critical, the presented approach is a combination of both second and third attitudes to handle uncertainty, taking the tolerating attitude and enriching it by reasoning about the uncertainty.

The development of U-Map is done during system design and implemented during system integration. Here we introduce a three-fold mitigation strategy to yield its flexibility and applicability for wide range of use cases. The mitigation measures are split into three steps, undertaken either sequentially or independently. The three steps of mitigation measures are:

* Rectification measure
* Degradation measure
* Additional protective measure

Rectification measure is the step taken as an attempt to eliminate some uncertainty during the integration of systems at runtime. There is some quotient of possibility associated with this step, and the steps taken are highly use case specific. It is already established in previous sections that eliminating uncertainty completely is not possible, however in this step uncertainty with respect to missing information and ambiguous information during information exchange at runtime is reduced (sometimes eliminated). The uncertainties that can be mitigated through rectification measure are generally associated with information exchange. Degradation measure refers to change in the functionality or configuration of the system to prevent hazardous event and ensure safety. This step involves runtime adaptation through reconfiguration. Provision for additional protective measures is available when a critical state is reached and hazards cannot be prevented through rectification or degradation. These measures help reduce the severity of the accident which is most likely to occur. The mitigation steps taken are highly dependent on the type of uncertainty and level of uncertainty being considered. Few uncertainties can be completely eliminated during rectification, few might still lead to certain hazards after rectification and hence have to be mitigated through degradation measures or additional protective measures or both. Few other uncertainties might have to be mitigated independently and this very flexibility is offered by U-Map. Figure 1 shows the visualization of U-Map.

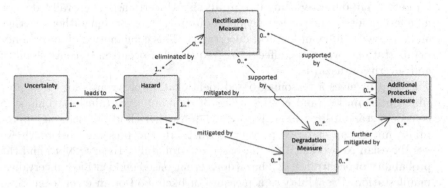

Fig. 1. The Uncertainty Map (U-Map)

In the following sections, we will focus on how the U-Map can be developed, its design and runtime aspects, as well as an exemplary case study to demonstrate its application.

3.1 Methodology to Develop the U-Map at design time

The development of U-Map is done in parallel to the system design after the initial scope of the system is defined. Once developed, the U-Map is implemented by providing suitable channels and interfaces for monitoring of the system and its context, and for execution of mitigation measures. The following are the important steps involved in creation of U-Map:

1. **Uncertainty identification**: This is a crucial and important step for runtime uncertainty handling and it is highly use case specific. This is done during development of CPS, so that appropriate channels are available at runtime for smooth integration of systems.

   This step involves listing out all possible runtime uncertainties based on the scope of the use case. To facilitate this step we make use of the uncertainty classifications explained in Sect. 2.1 from the research community, to look into the aspects of system interactions and behaviors that are generally not considered in the system development. The most sophisticated and extensive classification by [5] is used in our approach to list out all relevant uncertainties that might manifest. Additionally, to identify uncertainties specifically with respect to the information exchange at runtime, classification by [14] is used. Both these classifications serve as a check list to identify possible uncertainties.

First the relevant categories from the classification are identified, following which individual instances of possible uncertainty manifestations are listed for every category specific to the use case. They are further iterated with granular specifications. These granular specifications serve as the parameters for runtime monitoring.

2. **Uncertainty-oriented hazard analysis**: Uncertainties generally do not manifest in a sequence or independently from each other, but rather together and often with different levels of uncertainty. This combination of uncertainty manifestations over time, affects the frequency of occurrence, controllability and severity of hazards.

   This step involves a reasoning-based identification of hazards for every possible uncertainties (and combinations of different uncertainties). This step considers standardized hazards to alleviate further efforts in defining appropriate mitigation steps to prevent hazards. In the presented approach we use Bayesian Networks (BNs) [2], based on probability theory [20] to find the probability of occurrence of a hazardous event based on identified uncertainty manifestation. Probability is a measure of likelihood of an event occurring, and is usually quantified as a number in interval [0, 1], where 0 represents impossibility and 1 represents certainty [20]. Through this approach we can see how probable a hazardous event will occur if the identified uncertainty manifests at runtime. BNs use Directed Acyclic Graphs (DAG) [2] for graphical representation of probabilistic models. In this paper, we use this as a representative method, which will be further explained in the context of a specific use case. However, detailed probabilistic modeling based on BNs is out of the scope for this paper.

3. **Mitigation planning**: This step involves defining appropriate counter measures to prevent and mitigate hazards, which requires a certain amount of planning along with reasoning. This mitigation planning involves checking whether it is feasible to reduce the uncertainty through rectification at runtime, and to ensure that corresponding channels and interfaces are available to do it. As explained in previous section, some of the uncertainties that can be rectified might still raise the question on whether the associated hazard can be eliminated completely. As some cases of uncertainty manifestations cannot be rectified completely through system design, they have to be mitigated through degradation measure, additional protective measure or the combination of both these measures at runtime. Here, we consider the mitigation steps recommended by existing standards and characterize them based on the three-fold mitigation technique, as defined in our approach.

4. **Consolidation of U-Map**: This step involves physical creation of the U-Map by combining the individual outputs from all the previous steps. In this step, all the identified uncertainties and their combinations are mapped to

corresponding hazards, which in turn to their mitigation steps to create a complete reference map architecture to handle uncertainties at runtime.

3.2   Runtime Aspects of the U-Map

The U-Map can be either integrated into the MAPE-K feedback loop architecture as the knowledge base and used as a standalone method to handle uncertainty, or be included into the existing runtime safety analysis techniques presented in Sect. 2.3. Alternatively, they can also be integrated into other general system architectures that have the capability of runtime monitoring and execution of mitigation measures during operation. At runtime, system and its context has to be continuously monitored for uncertainty manifestations. The uncertainty manifestations are then analysed based on the available information in U-Map to identify possible hazards and to execute corresponding mitigation measures to ensure safety. Depending on the use case, the runtime uncertainty analysis can be done when the system is in operation or during the planned downtime for reconfiguration. For both these scenarios, rectification measures can be defined accordingly. After the successful rectification, the likelihood of a particular hazardous event is expected to be reduced. Otherwise, other measures as described in U-Map will be used to handle the residual uncertainty during operation. The detailed explanation for the runtime uncertainty handling using U-Map will be provided in future publications.

4   Case Study

The application of the presented concept will be demonstrated using a use case based on an adaptable production scenario. Current trends in the production domain are moving towards the usage of automated and mobilized industrial robots. A Movable Robot (MR) is usually installed on a movable platform (e.g. Automated Guided Vehicle (AGV)) to guarantee its maximum production flexibility. It can be envisaged that such MR can be integrated instantaneously into a new production environment to perform a completely new production task. Through the existing infrastructure for Machine-to-machine (M2M) communication and process orchestration, a newly integrated MR receives concrete production instructions from the Orchestration Unit (OU), identifies actual configuration in the environment and performs the production tasks.

As shown in Fig. 2, a MR is integrated into a new Production Environment (PE) to perform a Production Goal (PG). PG is used as an umbrella term to explain all interactions of the MR with the rest of the production system. M2M communication and the task allocation can be made possible, thanks to the OU. We also consider Human Task Factor (HT) for the overall production context. The integration and setup of a new MR in the PE is done as follows:

1. MR communicates with the OU to provide information w.r.t its services, available degradation modes, runtime localization and its hazard zones.

2. OU considers the overall production process and assign tasks to MR, which includes working coordinates of the PG along with the motion planning.
3. MR might provide details regarding inherent safety devices (e.g. safety laser scanners) to monitor the surrounding.

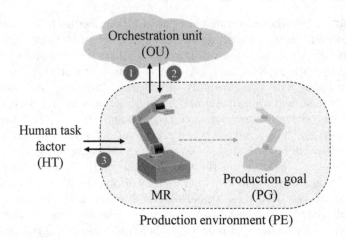

Fig. 2. The industrial scenario involving the integration of a Movable Robot (MR) into a new Production Environment (PE)

As the concrete MR to be integrated is usually unknown at design time, different uncertain situations might manifest during runtime integration which will lead to the emergence of safety concerns. In this paper, to ease the understanding we consider only few uncertainties from the perspective of one newly introduced MR. The first step involves identifying the relevant possible uncertainties (**UnC**) by using the classification from research community as a check list, described in Sect. 2.1. The following uncertainties were derived:

- **UnC1**: Unintended entering of human into the hazard zone (Aleatory type).
- **UnC2**: Mismatch in the hazard zone description defined by MR and OU because of different ontologies used for their development. (Epistemic type).
- **UnC3**: Unavailable or failure of safety devices.

These identified uncertainties, can be traced back to various root causes considering the MR's interactions with the environment. Especially in terms of data communication with the OU, a high amount of uncertainties might manifest during runtime integration. For the identified uncertainties, following possible hazards (**H**), based on the safety standard ISO 12100:2010 [16] are considered:

- **H1**: Impact of moving robot arm with the human.
- **H2**: New crushing point due to the formation of new hazard zone after integration of MR.
- **H3**: Shearing, cutting or damage to the work piece.
- **H4**: Trapping of human in the hazard zone.

The probability of occurrence of the hazards based on uncertainty manifestation probabilities is modeled using BNs as shown in Fig. 3 (The probability values for manifestation of uncertainties are only representative. In actual practice, they are retrieved based on frequentistic or subjectivistic methods). Here, the uncertainty **UnC1** manifests with a frequency of low (1–5 times per hour), med (5–10 times per hour) or high (10–15 times per hour) based on number of times there is unintended entering of human into the hazard zone. **UnC2** is based on whether there is a mismatch in the hazard zone definitions between MR and OU depending on respective ontology during integration. **UnC3** shows whether a particular inherent safety device is available or not. Initially, we can consider that the availability of safety device is high when the MR is being integrated, but it might be unavailable at runtime due to potential failure. In our BN, we have also identified the likelihood of the hazard resulting in an accident (instantaneously) or a delayed accident (after a certain time) or no accident and mapped individual probabilities of uncertainty manifestation to them.

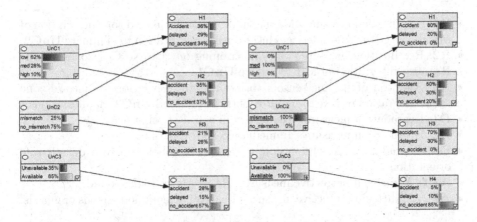

Fig. 3. Bayesian network model showing probability of occurrence of identified hazards based on probability of uncertainty manifestation

Fig. 4. Bayesian network model with evidence of uncertainty manifestation at runtime

A possible scenario is considered: a "med" frequency (5–10 times per hour) of unintended entering of human into hazard zone (**UnC1**) detected by the sensors, a mismatch in hazard zone definitions (**UnC2**), and availability of the inherent safety device. With these evidences, changes in the probability of occurrence of the identified hazards can be seen in the Fig. 4. Once the probability of occurrence of different hazards is known based on these BNs, the necessary mitigation measures can be defined. The following mitigation measures are identified:

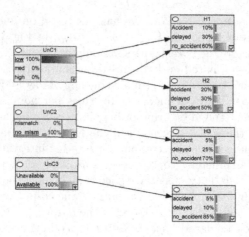

Fig. 5. Bayesian network model after rectification (R1, R2 and R3)

- **R1**: Rectification measure - Manual addition of the hazard zone description of MR to the OU by the safety engineer during certification to eliminate **UnC2**.
- **R2**: Rectification measure - Specific training on "Go/No Go" zones for the HT after integration of MR to reduce **UnC1**.
- **R3**: Addition of specific sensors to monitor the newly formed hazard zone after integration of MR to monitor both **UnC1** and **UnC2** manifestations.
- **D1**: Degradation measure - Reduction in speed of robot arm.
- **D2**: Degradation measure - Immediate STOP function.
- **D3**: Degradation measure - Slow retraction of robot arm to a default safe orientation.
- **AP1**: Additional protective measure - Raise Alarm (light/sound).
- **AP2**: Additional protective measure - Usage of attenuation screens or guards.

The rectification measures (**R1**, **R2** and **R3**) were appropriately undertaken, thereby completely eliminating **UnC2**, and reducing the probability of manifestation of **UnC1**. Corresponding degradation measures and additional protective measures (because of 35% probability of unavailability of inherent safety devices for **UnC3**) were also installed. It can be noted that the probability of occurrence of hazards (predominantly accidents) has greatly reduced, as shown in Fig. 5.

The complete visualisation of the resulting U-Map for the use case is shown in Fig. 6. It can be noticed that even after rectification, some uncertainty regarding randomness of human behavior will be present and can be mitigated by additional protective measures. For some hazards (**H1** and **H2**), both rectification and degradation measures are to be undertaken and one particular hazard (**H4**) can be mitigated only by additional protective measure.

usecase.png

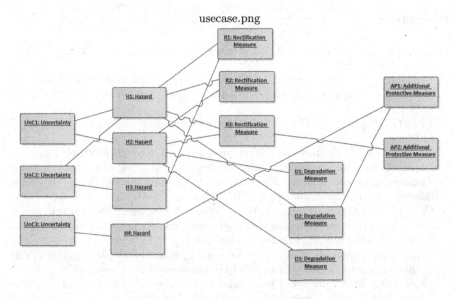

Fig. 6. U-Map for the use case

5 Conclusion and Future Work

Uncertainty pertaining to CPS is one constant aspect that cannot be completely eliminated. These uncertainties constantly pose safety-related issues and make it very crucial for safety critical systems. Ideally, through the operating life of the system, the level of uncertainty should slowly decrease over time, as different decisions are undertaken at runtime and likewise more information is being available to the system. However, this might be the exact opposite in reality. Therefore it is very important and necessary to address this problem by defining strategies to safely handle the uncertainties at runtime.

The proposed U-Map in this paper contributes well and serves as a reference map to handle runtime uncertainties in a highly flexible and scalable manner to suit different use cases. It can be used as a reference document in use cases where manual approach with safety engineers is used for safety assurance. In automated systems, it can be used as a knowledge base in MAPE-K feedback loops to analyse the uncertainty and execute identified mitigation steps.

Currently, the information on uncertainty sources and classifications is mainly based on existing literature, which might be incomplete for the proposed U-Map. A separate safety relevant taxonomy for runtime uncertainties should be investigated into and created in the future. Other future works involve the creation of U-Map for other domains, consideration of the temporal aspects of uncertainty manifestations while modeling BNs, defining monitor specifications for runtime monitoring of systems while considering scenario analysis and the identification of appropriate means to integrate the U-Map into the safety life cycle. The possibility of automating the creation of U-Map, also represents one of the interesting and challenging research directions in the future.

References

1. Anderson, E.L., Hattis, D.: A. uncertainty and variability. Risk Analysis **19**(1), 47–49 (1999)
2. Ben-Gal, I.: Bayesian networks. In: Encyclopedia of Statistics in Quality and Reliability, vol. 1. Springer, Dordrecht (2008). https://doi.org/10.1007/978-1-4020-6754-9_1624
3. Blair, G., Bencomo, N., France, R.B.: Models@ run. time. Computer **42**(10), 22–27 (2009)
4. Brun, Y., et al.: Engineering self-adaptive systems through feedback loops. In: Cheng, B.H.C., de Lemos, R., Giese, H., Inverardi, P., Magee, J. (eds.) Software Engineering for Self-Adaptive Systems. LNCS, vol. 5525, pp. 48–70. Springer, Heidelberg (2009). https://doi.org/10.1007/978-3-642-02161-9_3
5. Cámara, J., Garlan, D., Kang, W.G., Peng, W., Schmerl, B.: Uncertainty in self-adaptive systems: Categories, management, and perspectives. Carnegie-Mellon Univ Pittsburg PA United States, Technical report (2017)
6. Cámara, J., Moreno, G., Garlan, D.: Reasoning about human participation in self-adaptive systems. In: 2015 IEEE/ACM 10th International Symposium on Software Engineering for Adaptive and Self-Managing Systems, pp. 146–156. IEEE (2015)
7. Cheng, B.H.C., et al.: Software engineering for self-adaptive systems: a research roadmap. In: Cheng, B.H.C., de Lemos, R., Giese, H., Inverardi, P., Magee, J. (eds.) Software Engineering for Self-Adaptive Systems. LNCS, vol. 5525, pp. 1–26. Springer, Heidelberg (2009). https://doi.org/10.1007/978-3-642-02161-9_1
8. Cheng, S.W., Garlan, D.: Handling uncertainty in autonomic systems. In: International Workshop on Living with Uncertainty (2007)
9. Elkhodary, A., Esfahani, N., Malek, S.: Fusion: a framework for engineering self-tuning self-adaptive software systems. In: Proceedings of the Eighteenth ACM SIGSOFT International Symposium on Foundations of Software Engineering, pp. 7–16 (2010)
10. Esfahani, N., Kouroshfar, E., Malek, S.: Taming uncertainty in self-adaptive software. In: Proceedings of the 19th ACM SIGSOFT Symposium and the 13th European Conference on Foundations of Software Engineering, pp. 234–244 (2011)
11. Garlan, D.: Software engineering in an uncertain world. In: Proceedings of the FSE/SDP Workshop on Future of Software Engineering Research, pp. 125–128 (2010)
12. Garlan, D., Cheng, S.W., Huang, A.C., Schmerl, B., Steenkiste, P.: Rainbow: architecture-based self-adaptation with reusable infrastructure. Computer **37**(10), 46–54 (2004)
13. Giese, H., et al.: Living with uncertainty in the age of runtime models. In: Bencomo, N., France, R., Cheng, B.H.C., Aßmann, U. (eds.) Models@run.time. LNCS, vol. 8378, pp. 47–100. Springer, Cham (2014). https://doi.org/10.1007/978-3-319-08915-7_3
14. Hildebrandt, C., Bandyszak, T., Petrovska, A., Laxman, N., Cioroaica, E., Törsleff, S.: EURECA: epistemic uncertainty classification scheme for runtime information exchange in collaborative system groups. SICS Software-Intens. Cyber-Phys. Syst. **34**(4), 177–190 (2019)
15. Hoffman, F.O., Hammonds, J.S.: Propagation of uncertainty in risk assessments: the need to distinguish between uncertainty due to lack of knowledge and uncertainty due to variability. Risk Anal. **14**(5), 707–712 (1994)

16. International Organization for Standardization (ISO): ISO 12100: Safety of machinery-General principles for design-Risk assessment and risk reduction (2010)
17. Kabir, S., et al.: A runtime safety analysis concept for open adaptive systems. In: Papadopoulos, Y., Aslansefat, K., Katsaros, P., Bozzano, M. (eds.) IMBSA 2019. LNCS, vol. 11842, pp. 332–346. Springer, Cham (2019). https://doi.org/10.1007/978-3-030-32872-6_22
18. Kanal, L.N., Lemmer, J.F.: Uncertainty in Artificial Intelligence. Elsevier, Amsterdam (2014)
19. Kephart, J.O., Chess, D.M.: The vision of autonomic computing. Computer **36**(1), 41–50 (2003)
20. Kolmogorov, A.N., Bharucha-Reid, A.T.: Foundations of the Theory of Probability: Second, English edn. Courier Dover Publications, Mineola (2018)
21. Koo, C.H., Laxman, N., Möhrle, F.: Runtime safety analysis for reconfigurable production systems. In: The 30th European Safety and Reliability Conference (ESREL). Research Publishing, Singapore (2020, in press)
22. Koopman, P., Osyk, B., Weast, J.: Autonomous vehicles meet the physical world: RSS, variability, uncertainty, and proving safety. In: Romanovsky, A., Troubitsyna, E., Bitsch, F. (eds.) SAFECOMP 2019. LNCS, vol. 11698, pp. 245–253. Springer, Cham (2019). https://doi.org/10.1007/978-3-030-26601-1_17
23. Laffont, J.J.: Economie de l'incertain et de l'information. MIT Press, Cambridge (1989)
24. Mahdavi-Hezavehi, S., Avgeriou, P., Weyns, D.: A classification framework of uncertainty in architecture-based self-adaptive systems with multiple quality requirements. In: Managing Trade-Offs in Adaptable Software Architectures, pp. 45–77. Elsevier (2017)
25. Östberg, K., Bengtsson, M.: Run time safety analysis for automotive systems in an open and adaptive environment (2013)
26. Perez-Palacin, D., Mirandola, R.: Uncertainties in the modeling of self-adaptive systems: a taxonomy and an example of availability evaluation. In: Proceedings of the 5th ACM/SPEC International Conference on Performance Engineering, pp. 3–14 (2014)
27. Ramirez, A.J., Jensen, A.C., Cheng, B.H.: A taxonomy of uncertainty for dynamically adaptive systems. In: 2012 7th International Symposium on Software Engineering for Adaptive and Self-Managing Systems, pp. 99–108. IEEE (2012)
28. Rowe, W.D.: Understanding uncertainty. Risk Anal. **14**(5), 743–750 (1994)
29. Saffiotti, A.: Handling uncertainty in control of autonomous robots. In: Hunter, A., Parsons, S. (eds.) Applications of Uncertainty Formalisms. LNCS (LNAI), vol. 1455, pp. 198–224. Springer, Heidelberg (1998). https://doi.org/10.1007/3-540-49426-X_10
30. Schneider, D., Becker, M., Trapp, M.: Approaching runtime trust assurance in open adaptive systems. In: Proceedings of the 6th International Symposium on Software Engineering for Adaptive and Self-Managing Systems, pp. 196–201. Association for Computing Machinery, New York (2011)
31. Schneider, D., Trapp, M., Papadopoulos, Y., Armengaud, E., Zeller, M., Höfig, K.: WAP: digital dependability identities. In: 2015 IEEE 26th International Symposium on Software Reliability Engineering (ISSRE), pp. 324–329. IEEE (2015)
32. Staab, S., Studer, R.: Handbook on Ontologies. Springer, Heidelberg (2010). https://doi.org/10.1007/978-3-540-92673-3
33. Walker, W.E., et al.: Defining uncertainty: a conceptual basis for uncertainty management in model-based decision support. Integrat. Assess. **4**(1), 5–17 (2003)

Tool Demos

Lowering Barriers for Applying Model-based FMEA – Results of the qSafe Project

Florian Grigoleit[1(✉)], Marcus Heine[2], Julian Rhein[1], Peter Struss[1], and Jana K. v. Wedel[3]

[1] Technische Universität München, 85748 Garching, Germany
{florian.grigoleit,julian.rhein,struss}@tum.de
[2] EnCo Software GmbH, 81241 Munich, Germany
m.heine@enco-software.com
[3] INVENSITY GmbH, 80802 Munich, Germany
jana.wedel@invensity.com

Keywords: Functional safety analysis · FMEA · Model-based reasoning · Qualitative modeling · Deviation models

Theories and solutions for automating failure-modes-and-effects analysis (FMEA) using model-based systems technology from Artificial Intelligence have been developed several decades ago[1], but failed to achieve a breakthrough towards industrial practice. Major barriers hampering the application of the technology are a) the difficulties and costs involved in obtaining appropriate models, in particular, models tailored to specific systems and objectives of the analysis, which causes b) the necessity of producing and handling multiple, rather than unique, component models, c) the need for providing formalized representations of effects and scenarios, and d) a seamless integration into the human work process.

We created the qSafe,[2] project [1] to overcome these obstacles and to take a major step towards producing tools that can provide model-based support for FMEA. It joined the expertise of two companies and two research groups: EnCo Software GmbH as a tool provider, INVENSITY GmbH, a technology consultancy company, the Flight System Dynamics chair at the Technical University of Munich (TUM), and the Model-based systems and Qualitative Modeling group of TUM.

qSafe created tools that help overcoming the abovementioned problems. The heart of the qSafe architecture is an answer to problem b), SMM (System for Multiple Modeling), which allows to specify a domain or application-specific ontology for modeling system behavior in terms of types of components, terminals (for connecting components), relevant quantities, and their considered aspects (e.g. magnitude, derivative, deviation). It builds on the insight that reasoning about the behavior of systems in multiple tasks and scenarios requires choices among the alternatives spanned by the ontology. SMM allows connecting this abstract representation to

---

[1] Grigoleit F. et al.: The qSafe Project – Developing a Tool for Current Practice in Functional Safety Analysis. 28th Int. Workshop on Principle of Diagnosis, 2017.

[2] The project was funded by the German Federal Ministry of Economics and Technology under the ZIM program (ZF4086001BZ5).

© Springer Nature Switzerland AG 2020
M. Zeller and K. Höfig (Eds.): IMBSA 2020, LNCS 12297, pp. 245–247, 2020.
https://doi.org/10.1007/978-3-030-58920-2

various implementations of the systems behavior, e.g. in numeric models or finite constraint models, by offering abstract interfaces to different classes of such modeling systems.

Regarding problem a), models tailored to specific systems, requirements, scenarios, effects, and purposes should be generated, rather than handcrafted. Based on the assumption, that often numerical models of components or subsystems (e.g. in Matlab, Modelica, etc.), which have been developed for design and validation purposes, are available, the Automated Model Transformation (AMT) module offers the automated abstraction of such numerical models into case-specific qualitative models. This was realized with an abstraction operator that executes models in Matlab/Simulink and, from the results, generates a model in terms of finite constraints.

The Requirements Formalization Module (RFM) provides support for transforming informally written requirements into a formal representation in order to overcome problem c). The user selects the level on which to specify requirements (e.g. ECU level, interaction with the environment) and optionally the topic of the requirement (e.g. calculation of an output, dependencies between variables). Based on this selection, a set of requirement templates is provided, covering conditions, main effect, and additional effects. Those templates can be combined by the user to create an overall template that fits the requirement to be written. The requirement templates are linked to the ontology in SMM. This allows for offering a choice of suitable concepts to be filled in and, more importantly, for a mapping of aspects mentioned in requirements to system components, their variables, and ranges of values of respective models available within SMM, which are themselves also linked to the ontology. RFM uses this information to create a formalized requirements and information regarding the system architecture, which can be exported in XML format for use in later engineering activities, e.g. performing a FMEA in qSafe, and to facilitate reuse in later projects.

The Interactive Functional Safety Analysis (IFS) module covers problem d) by providing various means to the functional safety engineer to creation, navigate and visualize hierarchical system models, including safety-relevant properties (e.g. component failure modes and effects). FMEA tables and fault trees are created based on formalized safety requirements, which can be imported from the RFM module or defined manually. The qualitative representation of the system model is composed before the analysis from the individual component models generated by the AMT operator. The results can be edited by the analyst (e.g. by hiding results that overestimate the order of magnitude of an effect). To avoid the burden of applying the same revisions to the next iteration of the analysis (for example, after modifications to the system architecture), they can be stored and re-applied based on specified conditions. Furthermore, the IFS module allows to trace the results of the automatic analysis by the calculation of fault propagation paths from the qualitative behavior models, which can be visualized on the model graph.

As a benchmark, the qSafe solution was applied to an example given in the ARP 4761 standard[3], an aircraft wheel brake system, and the voltage monitoring function of

---

[3] SAE: ARP4761: Guidelines and Methods for Conducting the Safety Assessment Process on Civil Airborne Systems and Equipment, SAE International, 1996.

the power supply subsystem of the braking system control unit. More than just reproducing the FMEA result provided in the standard, the automatically generated FMEA table revealed an error contained in the standard document.

Generative Engineering for Safety-Critical System Design

Amr Hany Saleh[✉], Jonathan Menu, Johan Vanhuyse, and Mike Nicolai

Siemens Industry Software NV, Interleuvenlaan 68, 3001 Leuven, Belgium
{amr.saleh,jonathan.menu,johan.vanhuyse,mike.nicolai}@siemens.com

Abstract. We present our software for generative engineering, in which the work-flow can be divided into three main procedures: capture, explore and discover. The first is for capturing user's knowledge in designing a safety-critical system requirements. Then, it explores all possible design architectures. Besides, by connecting component fault trees to different system components in the capture procedure, we can automate the process of fault tree analysis for the resulting designs. The discover procedure compares the resulting fault-tree analysis for each design.

Keywords: Generative engineering · Component fault trees

Generative engineering, a generalization of generative design [2], provides a methodology for exploring different systems' architectures in the conceptual design phase. The process starts by capturing the system's requirements in a meta-model. A system designer enters the components required to build the system and interface these components with ports that represent the communication between them.

After creating the formal model, we utilize our solvers to explore the topological design space to discover architectures that comply with the given meta-model. We also verify that the found architectures are the only ones that comply with the given meta-model. The explored designs can be automatically exported to different simulation or evaluation tools to be tested for different performance indicators. This benefits the designer to select the best architecture that fits their needs.

We provide an application that enables the generative engineering technology. The application is web-based and includes the domain-specific language (DSL) for capturing the designer's knowledge. It can also connect and auto-export discovered architectures to various simulation and evaluation tools such as Simcenter Amesim and Fault-tree analysis tools.

In this demonstration, we investigate several architectures for an all-electric multicopter. The focus is on the electrical propulsion unit: the combined electrical power distribution and propulsion subsystem for such a vehicle. We use our application enabling generative engineering to explore different architectures. Besides, the support for component fault trees [1] reusable reliability models

© Springer Nature Switzerland AG 2020
M. Zeller and K. Höfig (Eds.): IMBSA 2020, LNCS 12297, pp. 248–249, 2020.
https://doi.org/10.1007/978-3-030-58920-2

that represent the failure behavior of the components, enables the straightforward evaluation of architectures with respect to safety criteria.

Figure 1a shows the system hierarchical view , which is synthesized based on the designer's DSL model. The green ports describe the electrical connections between different components. The red ports represent the torque, and blue ports represent connections to the switches. The top right numbers in each component block show the possible instances of this component that can exist in an architecture. Figure 1b shows an example of a generate architecture.

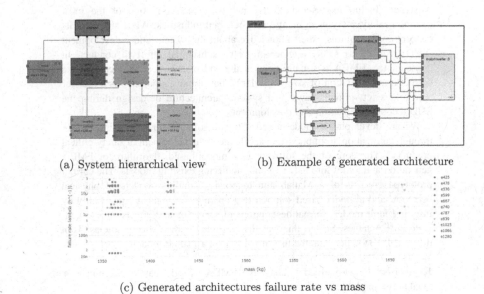

(a) System hierarchical view   (b) Example of generated architecture

(c) Generated architectures failure rate vs mass

Fig. 1: High-level system description, example architecture, and safety evaluation.

Each component is connected to a component fault tree. The architectures are then automatically exported to the corresponding component fault trees. Then, we can automatically run the fault-tree analysis of each architecture. Figure 1c compares the architectures' failure rate with respect to their mass. Each point on this graph represents one architecture.

References

1. Kaiser, B., et al.: Advances in component fault trees. In: Proceedings of the 28th European Safety and Reliability Conference (ESREL) (2018)
2. McCormack, J., Dorin, A., Innocent, T., et al.: Generative design: a paradigm for design research. In: Proceedings of Futureground, Design Research Society, Melbourne (2004)

Paitron – a Tool for Automated FMEA

Arnold Bitner, Florian Grigoleit$^{(\boxtimes)}$, and Iliya Valchev

Technische Universität München, Garching b., 85748 Munich, Germany
{a.bitner,florian.grigoleit,iliya.valchev}@tum.de

Abstract. Failure-modes-and-effects analysis (FMEA) is one of the most common safety analyses in many safety-relevant industries. While simple in its conception, it requires expert knowledge about the system under development (SUD) as well as safety engineering, plus substantial effort to conduct. In consequence, FMEA is usually done at the end of a project to document the correct implementation of safety standards, but not so commonly as a tool for detecting safety-critical flaws in a systems architecture or design during the SUD's conceptualization and development.

We are developing a model-based software solution for supporting FMEA through automation, to improve and accelerate the development of safety-critical products[1]. The core of the software is a model-based algorithm for FMEA generation and a tool for analyzing and modifying existing models. The current prototype consists of a Matlab app to obtain Simulink models of physical behavior, and a model-based solution to prepare it for analysis, specifically by inserting fault modes, formal descriptions of scenarios and effects, and to generate FMEA tables. So far, this was demonstrated with two case studies. Tool demo at IMBSA presents the use of paitron on a matlab model.

Keywords: Functional safety analysis · FMEA · Model-based reasoning · Qualitative modeling

1 Modelwise *Paitron*

The Model-based Systems and Qualitative Reasoning group[2] of the Technical University of Munich has conducted significant research on model-based safety analysis, [1]. Supported by the EXIST transfer of research program, which aims at turning promising technologies into businesses, we are developing a model-based solution – paitron - for supporting safety analyses and later safety engineering in general. Now, after the first half of the project, we have created and evaluated a first prototype of *paitron* for automated FMEA.

The idea behind *paitron* is to combine model-based techniques for analyzing and existing models, directed and undirected (equation-based), transforming them into finite constraint behavior descriptions, enriching them with formal descriptions (in

---

[1] The project is funded by the German Federal Ministry of Economics and Technology under the EXIST Transfer of Research program (Ref. 03EFMBY194).

[2] www.mqm.in.tum.de.

© Springer Nature Switzerland AG 2020
M. Zeller and K. Höfig (Eds.): IMBSA 2020, LNCS 12297, pp. 250–251, 2020.
https://doi.org/10.1007/978-3-030-58920-2

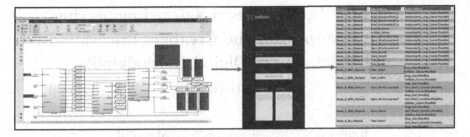

Fig. 1. Model flow of *paitron*.

form of finite-domain constraints over system variables) of scenarios and effects, and conducted the FMEA on the resulting constraint network, see Fig. 1.

The current prototype consists of a qualitative abstraction for creating finite constraint behavior descriptions from Simulink models and the FMEA algorithm. The algorithm exploits SAT solving with SunnyCP[3]. Fault models of system components can either be created in Matlab or be automatically injected into Matlab models.

To evaluate *paitron*, we conducted two preliminary case studies. The first one aimed at reproducing the results from a project on safety analysis of a simplified landing gear system [2]. In [2], the landing gear was modeled, simulated in Matlab/Simulink, and extracted using a qualitative abstractor operator and an FMEA algorithm. *paitron* was able to generate identical FMEA tables. In the second case study, we created a Simulink model of an Arexx Robot Arm V3 and conducted an FMEA for an application scenario [3]. *paitron* generated a FMEA table matching one created manually.

After the case studies, the next steps include – apart from further proof of concept projects – the implementation of GUIs for scenario and effect formalization and model editing, an interface to Modelica, as well as the development of an abstraction operator for generating deviation models from (un-)directed models. For 2021, a certification for Tool Confidence Level 3 (ISO 26262) is planned.

References

1. Struss, P.: Model-based analysis of embedded systems: placing it upon its feet instead of on its head – an outsider's view. In: 8th International Conference Software Engineering and Applications, Reykjavik (2013)
2. Alessandro, F.: Model-based failure-modes-and-effects analysis and its application to aircraft subsystems. Dissertationen zur Künstlichen Intelligenz DISKI 326, AKA Verlag (2009)
3. Stark, M.: Qualitative modeling of an embedded system as basis for functional safety analysis. Bachelor's Thesis in Computer Science, Technical University Munich (2020)

---

[3] https://github.com/CP-Unibo/sunny-cp.

An Eclipse Epsilon-Based Safety Engineering Tool Framework for the Creation, Integration and Validation of Digital Dependability Identities

Jan Reich[1]([⊠]), Ioannis Sorokos[1], and Marc Zeller[2]

[1] Fraunhofer IESE, Kaiserslautern, Germany
{jan.reich,ioannis.sorokos}@iese.fraunhofer.de
[2] Siemens AG, Munich, Germany
marc.zeller@siemens.com

Abstract. Creating and maintaining a safety case with all its supporting modeling artifacts such as architecture, failure logic or safety requirements is a tedious task, particularly when multi-tier supply chains must be bridged, and different safety engineering tools are used. *Digital Dependability Identities (DDI)* are model-based abstractions of the safety properties of a component, system or system of systems. DDIs conform to the *Open Dependability Exchange* (ODE) Metamodel, which formally integrates the OMGs Structured Assurance Case Metamodel (SACM) with evidence metamodels capturing the essence and relation between mentioned safety aspects. In this tool demonstration, we present a safety engineering tool framework that a) enables the creation, integration and validation of DDIs from different tools, b) supports automation for DDI analysis and c) facilitates common multi-tier supply chain problems such as intellectual property hiding or semi-automated integration safety analysis. The tool framework, developed in the H2020 DEIS Project, technically uses the Eclipse Modeling Framework to express metamodels and leverages from Eclipse Epsilon for model manipulation, transformation, and analysis.

Keywords: Tool automation · Safety case integration · Safety case tool · Multi-tier safety engineering · Safety tool adapter

1 Introduction

The **D**ependability **E**ngineering **I**nnovation for Cyber-Physical **S**ystems (DEIS) H2020 research project set out to address multiple challenges associated with the development of open and adaptive Cyber-Physical Systems (CPS). Specifically, these systems typically feature enhanced degrees of variability, both in their composition, the interrelationship between their constituent subsystems, as well as the external systems with which they interact during operation. The tool support DEIS developed is based around the Digital Dependability Identity (DDI) concept. A DDI represents an SACM-based assurance case that is formally integrated with safety aspect models supporting the safety argumentation. This short paper addresses the DEIS tool support for (semi-)

© Springer Nature Switzerland AG 2020
M. Zeller and K. Höfig (Eds.): IMBSA 2020, LNCS 12297, pp. 252–253, 2020.
https://doi.org/10.1007/978-3-030-58920-2

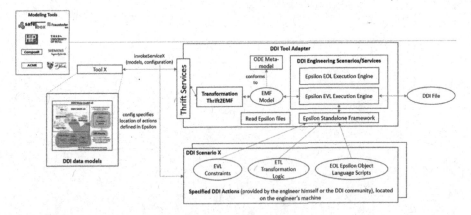

Fig. 1. Architecture of the DEIS tool adapter and its usage from external tools

automated creation, integration and validation of DDIs in multi-tier engineering scenarios. Further information can be found via the DEIS website[1].

2 DDI-Based Tool Support for CPS Development

A major technical challenge for the development of CPS involving multiple organizations is the heterogeneous toolset being used for safety engineering. To enable seamless integration of safety engineering tools, DDIs focus on modularization, interface formalization and the formal integration of different safety aspects into the safety argument. DEIS identified generic middleware technology to support user stories around the generation of DDIs from models in various tools, their integration with each other and the automated analysis of the integrated assurance case.

To facilitate the usage of the DDI framework, users can use our generic tool adapter (**Fig. 1**), based on Apache Thrift[2], which provides external tools a service interface for the execution of DDI operations (creation, manipulation, analysis) from various programming languages (e.g. C++, C#, or Java). The framework further supports custom DDI script definition and execution using the Epsilon language family[3], supporting generic model manipulation. Notable features include the usage of external analysis tools (abstract service invocation and results conversion into DDIs), semi-automated integration of subsystems and hiding of Intellectual Property (IP) during DDI export. The tool framework's software components are publicly available in the DEIS repository[4]. We will provide a short, live demonstration[5] of our tools' capabilities during IMBSA 2020.

---

[1] http://www.deis-project.eu/

[2] https://thrift.apache.org/

[3] https://www.eclipse.org/epsilon/

[4] https://github.com/DEIS-Project-EU/

[5] Video of DEIS Toolset Demonstration: https://youtu.be/dlcUkhwhinw

Author Index

Printed in the United States
By Bookmasters